KNOW ENGLISH

second edition

THOM SUNEGA
George Brown College

PRENTICE HALL CANADA INC.
SCARBOROUGH, ONTARIO

Canadian Cataloguing in Publication Data

Sunega, Thom, 1949– .
Know more English

2nd ed.
ISBN: 0-13-102757-3

1. English language – Composition and exercises.
2. English language – Grammar. I. Title

PE1408.S8 1995 428.2 C94-931340-8

Prentice-Hall, Inc., Englewood Cliffs, New Jersey
Prentice-Hall International (UK) Limited, London
Prentice-Hall of Australia, Pty. Limited, Sydney
Prentice-Hall Hispanoamericana, S.A., Mexico City
Prentice-Hall of India Private Limited, New Delhi
Prentice-Hall of Japan, Inc., Tokyo
Simon & Schuster Asia Private Limited, Singapore
Editora Prentice-Hall do Brasil, Ltda., Rio de Janeiro

ISBN: 0-13-102757-3

Acquisitions Editor: Michael Bickerstaff
Production Editor: Kelly Dickson
Copy Editor: Rodney Rawlings
Production Coordinator: Sharon Houston
Cover Design: Olena Serbyn
Page Layout: Steve Lewis
Photos: Thom Sunega
Artwork: Mike Robbyns

1 2 3 4 5 RRD 99 98 97 96 95

Printed and bound in the USA

To My Three Loves,
Barbara, Stephanie, and Jennifer

CONTENTS

PREFACE

Know More English, Second Edition, remains both a reference guide and a refresher text for all students who wish to upgrade their English skills in preparation for employment, post-secondary studies, or vocational training.

In this edition several changes and additions have been made to maintain the book's philosophy of enabling students to *know* more English by covering *more* details of *English* grammar and usage. Foremost is the increase in the number of exercises by more than 100%. In addition, all sentences have been completely rewritten.

New Items have been introduced, and information in the original Units has been expanded. Some Units have been reorganized and rewritten.

The focus continues to be on improving communication skills. Through an understanding of the fundamentals of composition, punctuation, sentence structure, and spelling, learners should master the English usage skills necessary to attain their immediate and lifelong goals. For those who lack a basic knowledge of the language or who need to refresh their skills, three Addenda on the parts of speech are included.

As in the first edition, all material is presented in a simple, self-teaching manner suitable for both continuous-intake and semestered classes. The Units and Items are self-contained lessons, complete with examples and exercises.

Additional exercises and tests with answers are available in the *Instructor's Manual.*

How to Use This Book

Know More English, Second Edition, is easy to use.

All Units begin with a Pre-Test, whose answers immediately follow. When you begin a Unit, first complete the Pre-Test; then check your answers. This will help you assess your starting knowledge of the material in the Unit. Of course, you are the best judge of how much work you need to do, but if you are unsure consult your instructor.

If you have made errors in the Pre-Test, turn to the appropriate Item(s) in the Unit, and carefully read the information, study the examples, and complete all the Exercises. As you complete each Exercise, check your answers against the Answer Key which is located at the back of the book.

At the end of each Unit there is a Post-Test to measure how well you have grasped the material you have studied. If you feel the need for more practice, your instructor can provide you with additional exercises from the *Instructor's Manual* that is available for this book.

ACKNOWLEDGEMENTS

To Marjorie Munroe, Senior Acquisitions Editor, for encouraging a second edition, as well as Kelly Dickson, Linda Gorman, and Michael Bickerstaff of Prentice Hall for their dedication and support, my sincere thanks.

I am also grateful to the many instructors and students for their insightful observations to improve this second edition.

To my colleagues from the Communications Working Group of the Adult Preparatory Programs Articulation and Standards Project for sustaining the value of excellence in communications: Sue Adams, Sheridan College; Mary Margaret Branscombe, Fanshaw College; Allison Chiappetta, Niagara College; Bill Dickey, Loyalist College; Marlene Ferguson, Sault College; Gloria Joanesse-Romaniuk, Northern College; G. Dale Lovering, Georgian College; Marion McNall, Humber College; and Jean Timbury, Algonquin College.

A special thanks to my wife Barbara for her generous reading and re-reading of the manuscript.

U • N • I • T 1

SPELLING AND USAGE IMPROVEMENT

Poor spelling and incorrect usage reduce the effectiveness of your writing. When you write, it is always a good practice to use a dictionary. Never assume a doubtful word is spelled a certain way; there are exceptions to many spelling rules. When in doubt, check it out!

In Unit 1 you will learn a number of spelling and usage guidelines. Complete the following sections step by step. Read the examples, and do as many exercises as you or your teacher feels is necessary.

UNIT • 1 • PRE-TEST

This Pre-Test will help you determine your initial knowledge of the material covered in Unit 1. The answers immediately follow.

I. Form the plurals of the following words.

1. dinner ____________________

2. half ____________________

3. joy ____________________

4. stereo ____________________

5. mercy ____________________

6. crisis ____________________

7. mouse ____________________

8. brother-in-law ____________________

9. play ____________________
10. wash ____________________

II. Insert *ie* or *ei* to complete the correct spelling of the following words.

1. bel__ve
2. rel__f
3. s__ze
4. l__sure
5. conc__ve

III. Correctly join the suffixes to the following words.

1. achieve + ing ____________________
2. lovely + ness ____________________
3. sincere + ty ____________________
4. argue + ment ____________________
5. due + ly ____________________
6. level + ed ____________________
7. commit + ing ____________________
8. video + ing ____________________
9. book + ed ____________________
10. copy + ed ____________________

IV. Place *a, an,* or *the* in the blanks in the following sentences.

1. What is ____ name of your doctor?
2. This will be ____ open-book test.
3. A thesaurus can be ____ useful book.
4. I know that Fred is ____ honest person.
5. Your new baby is ____ beauty.

V. Use apostrophes where required in the following sentences.

1. I cant wait to read Davids short story.
2. Glenn and Melissas dog is a fox terrier.
3. All the doctors offices are being painted.
4. Last nights movie was really scary.
5. Is this recipe hers or her sister-in-laws?

VI. Use capitals in the following sentences where required.

1. how long has ottawa been the capital of canada?
2. this danish pastry came from the scandinavian pastry shop.
3. what did uncle joe say you should do with your burmese cat?
4. read the novel *capricornia* by xavier herbert; it's great.
5. by autumn the space probe should reach the planet neptune.

ANSWERS • TO • UNIT • 1 • PRE-TEST

I. Form the plurals of the following words.

1. dinner	dinners
2. half	halves
3. joy	joys
4. stereo	stereos
5. mercy	mercies
6. crisis	crises
7. mouse	mice
8. brother-in-law	brothers-in-law
9. play	plays
10. wash	washes

II. Insert *ie* or *ei* to complete the correct spelling of the following words.

1. believe
2. relief
3. sieze
4. leisure
5. conceive

III. Correctly join the suffixes to the following words.

1. achieve + ing	achieving
2. lovely + ness	loveliness
3. sincere + ity	sincerity
4. argue + ment	argument
5. due + ly	duly

6. level + ed — leveled
7. commit + ing — committing
8. video + ing — videoing
9. book + ed — booked
10. copy + ed — copied

IV. Place *a, an,* or *the* in the blanks in the following sentences.

1. What is _the_ name of your doctor?
2. This will be _an_ open-book test.
3. A thesaurus can be _a_ useful book.
4. I know that Fred is _an_ honest person.
5. Your new baby is _a_ beauty.

V. Use apostrophes where required in the following sentences.

1. I can't wait to read David's short story.
2. Glenn and Melissa's dog is a fox terrier.
3. All the doctors' offices are being painted.
4. Last night's movie was really scary.
5. Is this recipe hers or her sister-in-law's?

VI. Use capitals in the following sentences where required.

1. How long has Ottawa been the capital of Canada?
2. This Danish pastry came from the Scandinavian pastry shop.
3. What did Uncle Joe say you should do with your Burmese cat?
4. Read the novel *Capricornia* by Xavier Herbert; it's great.
5. By autumn the space probe should reach the planet Neptune.

Item I: Quick and Easy Spelling Rules

1. Rules for Forming the Plural of Most Words

a. For most nouns, add *s* to form the plural.

EXAMPLES:

singular	*plural*
collar	collars

light	lights
winner	winners

b. For words that end in *ch*, *ss*, *sh*, and *x*, add *es* to form the plural.

EXAMPLES:

singular	*plural*
prefix	prefixes
search	searches
stress	stresses

c. For most words that end in *f* or *fe*, change the *f* to *v* and add *s* or *es* to form the plural; for the others, simply add *s*.

EXAMPLES:

singular	*plural*
half	halves
loaf	loaves
wife	wives
cliff	cliffs
grief	griefs
safe	safes

d. For words that end in *y* preceded by a vowel (*a*, *e*, *i*, *o*, *u*), add *s* to form the plural.

EXAMPLES:

singular	*plural*
joy	joys
survey	surveys
valley	valleys

e. For words that end in *y* preceded by a consonant, change the *y* to *i* and add *es*.

EXAMPLES:

singular	*plural*
flurry	flurries
possibility	possibilities
study	studies

f. For most words that end in *o* preceded by a consonant, add *es*. However, remember that there are some exceptions to this rule.

EXAMPLES:

singular	*plural*
hero	heroes
potato	potatoes
zero	zeroes
burro	burros
silo	silos
tornado	tornados OR tornadoes

g. To form the plurals of musical terms that end in *o*, add *s*.

EXAMPLES:

singular	*plural*
contralto	contraltos
solo	solos
stereo	stereos

h. To form the plurals of compound words, add *s* to the most important part.

EXAMPLES:

singular	*plural*
father-in-law	fathers-in-law
second cousin	second cousins
passerby	passersby

i. Some words have irregular plural forms which should be memorized.

EXAMPLES:

singular	*plural*
louse	lice
tooth	teeth
woman	women

j. Some words have the same form in the singular and the plural.

EXAMPLES:

singular	*plural*
one caribou	two caribou
one grouse	three grouse
one moose	four moose

k. Many foreign words used in English, particularly Greek and Latin words, keep their original plural forms. However, the more commonly used words tend to adopt the English rules for forming the plural. Always consult your dictionary to be sure.

EXAMPLES:

singular	*plural*
alumnus	alumni
basis	bases
crisis	crises
datum	data
larva	larvae
apparatus	apparatus OR apparatuses
curriculum	curricula OR curriculums
formula	formulae OR formulas
octopus	octopi OR octopuses

EXERCISE • 1

Form the plurals of the following nouns.

EXAMPLE:

tax <u>taxes</u>

1. delay ____________________
2. fax ____________________
3. wash ____________________
4. foot ____________________
5. ability ____________________
6. hypothesis ____________________
7. daughter-in-law ____________________

8. innuendo ____________________
9. suffix ____________________
10. sheaf ____________________

EXERCISE • 2

Follow the instructions for Exercise 1.

1. swish ____________________
2. waltz ____________________
3. mulatto ____________________
4. fizz ____________________
5. thesis ____________________
6. stitch ____________________
7. piccolo ____________________
8. prime minister ____________________
9. embargo ____________________
10. mouse ____________________

EXERCISE • 3

Follow the instructions for Exercise 2.

1. brief ____________________
2. entity ____________________
3. baby ____________________
4. stretch ____________________
5. halo ____________________
6. phenomenon ____________________
7. lily of the valley ____________________
8. tomato ____________________
9. deer ____________________
10. leaf ____________________

EXERCISE • 4

Form the plurals of the words in parentheses to complete the following sentences.

EXAMPLE:

Wash the (paintbrush) paintbrushes when you are finished.

1. Cut all the muffins into (half) __________ .
2. The (necessity) __________ of life are different for all of us.
3. There are not many happy (turkey) __________ on Thanksgiving Day.
4. The (soprano) __________ in the church choir are excellent.
5. Why does Fred have three (mother-in-law) __________ ?
6. Rice, corn, and wheat contain (starch) __________ .
7. Did you see the (wolf) __________ at the county fair?
8. The realty agent wanted to know which (studio) __________ we liked best.
9. The (moose) __________ we saw in the marsh were enormous.
10. "Good news!" exclaimed Jia. "English (class) __________ are canceled for the rest of the week."

EXERCISE • 5

Write sentences using the following words in their plural form.

EXAMPLE:

knife

The *knives* came as a bonus when I bought the compact discs.

1. thief
2. ditch
3. torch
4. calf
5. worry
6. lady
7. passerby
8. ferry
9. dress
10. mosquito

2. The *ie/ei* Rule

Always use *i* before *e* except after *c*, or when *e* and *i* together sound like the "long *a*" as in *veil* or *eight*.

EXAMPLES:

*usually **i** before **e***	*except after **c***	*or when long **a** sound*
achieve	ceiling	eight
believe	conceive	neighbour
brief	deceive	their
chief	perceive	sleigh
relieve	receipt	weigh
wield	receive	veil

Remember, however, that — like many spelling rules — this one has exceptions. The following examples do not follow the *ie/ei* rule.

EXAMPLES:

e** before **i	*after **c***
caffeine	ancient
either	efficient
foreign	glacier
leisure	
seize	
neither	
weird	
Fahrenheit	

EXERCISE • 6

Use *ie* or *ei* to complete the correct spelling of the following words.

EXAMPLE:

p__ce   piece

1. cod__ne
2. s__ve
3. ach__ve
4. forf__t
5. rec__ve
6. v__l
7. fr__nd
8. s__ge
9. n__ther
10. rel__f

EXERCISE • 7

Follow the instructions for Exercise 6.

1. s__ze
2. c__ling
3. bel__ve
4. conc__ve
5. Fahrenh__t
6. sl__gh
7. conc__t
8. w__gh
9. h__r
10. spec__s

EXERCISE • 8

Complete the following *ie/ei* words, and write sentences using them.

EXAMPLE:

n__ther

Neither of the students likes this exercise.

1. b__ge
2. w__rd
3. glac__r
4. p__r
5. h__nous
6. th__r
7. l__sure
8. br__f
9. bel__ve
10. __ther

EXERCISE • 9

Follow the instructions for Exercise 8.

1. hyg__ne
2. fr__ght
3. ch__f
4. br__fly
5. v__ns
6. y__ld
7. dec__ve
8. f__rce
9. n__gh
10. retr__ve

EXERCISE • 10

Follow the instructions for Exercise 9.

1. anc__nt
2. perc__ve
3. rel__ve
4. v__l
5. s__ze
6. __ght
7. caff__ne
8. h__ght

9. sl__ght of hand
10. conc__ve

3. The "Silent *e*" Rule

For words that end in a "silent *e*" (an *e* that is not pronounced), drop the *e* before adding a suffix that begins with a vowel (*a, e, i, o, u*). (A **suffix** is an ending added to a word to change its meaning as in the following examples.)

EXAMPLES:

believe + able	-	believable
hose + ing	-	hosing
desire + ous	-	desirous
resemble + ance	-	resemblance
sensitive + ity	-	sensitivity
cure + able	-	curable

However, if the suffix begins with a consonant, retain the silent *e*.

EXAMPLES:

encourage + ment	-	encouragement
hate + ful	-	hateful
nice + ly	-	nicely

name + less - nameless
sincere + ly - sincerely

Note the following exceptions to the "silent *e*" rule.

EXAMPLES:

canoe + ing - canoeing
dye + ing - dyeing
mile + age - mileage

argue + ment - argument
true + ly - truly

In addition, there are exceptions to the "silent *e*" rule for words that end in *ce* or *ge*. These words retain the final *e* before a suffix that begins with *a* or *o*.

EXAMPLES:

change + able - changeable
notice + able - noticeable
outrage + ous - outrageous

Words that end with two *e*'s also retain the final *e* before adding a suffix that begins with a vowel.

EXAMPLES:

agree + ing - agreeing
flee + ing - fleeing

EXERCISE • 11

Combine the following words with the endings indicated.

EXAMPLE:

care + ful careful

1. care + ing ____________________
2. hope + ful ____________________
3. devote + ion ____________________
4. engage + ment ____________________
5. discourage + ing ____________________
6. key + ing ____________________
7. notice + able ____________________

8. budget + ing ____________________
9. estimate + ion ____________________
10. ice + ing ____________________

EXERCISE ♦ 12

Follow the instructions for Exercise 11.

1. pollute + ing ____________________
2. feminine + ity ____________________
3. sedate + ly ____________________
4. glue + ing ____________________
5. sensuous + ly ____________________
6. perforate + ion ____________________
7. involve + ment ____________________
8. reduce + ion ____________________
9. marriage + able ____________________
10. ski + ing ____________________

EXERCISE ♦ 13

Combine the words with the endings indicated in the following sentences.

EXAMPLE:

The temperature can be very (change + able) <u>changeable</u> this time of year.

1. Phuong and David have a very (harmony + ous) ________________ relationship.
2. Why is Peter always (snore + ing) ________________ in English class?
3. The spring (festive + al) ________________ will soon be here.
4. How long have Alphonso and Maria been (manufacture + ing) ________________ ceramic door knobs?
5. The (evaporate + ion) ________________ of last night's rain was quick after the sun came out.
6. The salesperson was (pressure + ing) ________________ Trinh to buy a new car.
7. It is not (advise + able) ________________ to be rude to your teachers.
8. Doug Gilmour of the Toronto Maple Leafs displayed no (hesitate + ion) when he fired the puck at the goalie.
9. The thief's steps were (trace + able) ________________ in the fresh snow.
10. Tonight we're (dine + ing) ________________ at Frank and Pam's house.

EXERCISE • 14

Combine the following words with the endings indicated, and use them in sentences.

EXAMPLE:

whistle + ing
Why is Wendell always *whistling* the same song?

1. deceive + ing
2. astute + ness
3. stare + ing
4. retrieve + able
5. malice + ious
6. adore + able
7. confuse + ing
8. manage + able
9. whine + ing
10. embrace + able

EXERCISE • 15

Follow the instructions for Exercise 14.

1. insure + able
2. virtue + ous
3. retire + ment
4. definite + ly
5. solve + able
6. entice + ing
7. advantage + ous
8. see + ing
9. dispose + able
10. style + ize

4. The Final *y* Rule

For words that end in *y*, change the *y* to *i* before an ending. If the ending begins with *i*, retain the *y*.

EXAMPLES:

mighty + ly	-	mightily
lazy + er	-	lazier
ply + able	-	pliable
gratify + ing	-	gratifying
hurry + ing	-	hurrying
study + ing	-	studying

EXERCISE ♦ 16

Combine the following words with the endings indicated.

EXAMPLE:

steady + ness   steadiness

1. salty + er ____________________
2. imply + ing ____________________
3. fancy + est ____________________
4. play + able ____________________
5. windy + er ____________________
6. fortify + ing ____________________
7. hairy + er ____________________
8. dry + ing ____________________
9. moody + ness ____________________
10. employ + able ____________________

EXERCISE ♦ 17

Follow the instructions for Exercise 16.

1. creamy + er ____________________
2. verify + ing ____________________
3. angry + est ____________________
4. scary + er ____________________
5. noisy + ly ____________________
6. sunny + er ____________________
7. hardy + ness ____________________
8. qualify + ing ____________________

9. fancy + ful ____________
10. merry + ment ____________

EXERCISE ◆ 18

Follow the instructions for Exercise 17.

1. healthy + er ____________
2. satisfy + ing ____________
3. lively + hood ____________
4. rusty + est ____________
5. haughty + er ____________
6. worry + some ____________
7. sandy + er ____________
8. ready + ness ____________
9. friendly + er ____________
10. paunchy + ness ____________

EXERCISE ◆ 19

Combine the following words with the endings indicated, and use them in sentences.

EXAMPLE:

ratify + ing

The General Motors workers are *ratifying* their contract this afternoon.

1. likely + hood
2. steady + ly
3. heavy + ness
4. dismay + ing
5. handy + er
6. comply + ing
7. silly + ness
8. rely + able
9. flashy + ness
10. clumsy + ly

EXERCISE • 20

Follow the instructions for Exercise 19.

1. occupy + ing
2. hungry + ly
3. identify + able
4. dirty + er
5. wavy + er
6. defy + ing
7. pity + able
8. hearty + er
9. flurry + ing
10. silky + est

5. The Rule for Doubling the Final Consonant

This rule is divided into two parts: when you do double the final consonant and when you don't.

a. *Do* double the final consonant before an ending when the final consonant is preceded by a single vowel, and the word is accented on the last syllable. (An **accent** is the emphasis you place on part of the word.)

EXAMPLES:

admit + ed	-	admitted
drop + ing	-	dropping
glad + er	-	gladder
patrol + ed	-	patrolled

b. *Do not* double the final consonant before an ending when the final consonant is preceded by a single consonant or when the final consonant is preceded by two vowels.

EXAMPLES:

preceded by a single consonant

account + able	-	accountable
jolt + ing	-	jolting
predict + ed	-	predicted
wrench + ing	-	wrenching

preceded by two vowels

fail + ing - failing
loop + ed - looped
reveal + ing - revealing
seek + ing - seeking

EXERCISE • 21

Combine the following words with the endings indicated.

EXAMPLE:
lick + ing <u>licking</u>

1. wreck + ing ______________
2. confer + ed ______________
3. equip + ing ______________
4. allow + able ______________
5. recur + ing ______________
6. pit + ed ______________
7. droop + ing ______________
8. repair + ed ______________
9. commit + ed ______________
10. snap + ing ______________

EXERCISE • 22

Follow the instructions for Exercise 21.

1. control + able ______________
2. bar + ing ______________
3. submit + ed ______________
4. rank + ing ______________
5. flog + ed ______________
6. account + able ______________
7. incur + ed ______________
8. book + ing ______________
9. soil + ed ______________
10. mat + ed ______________

EXERCISE ◆ 23

Follow the instructions for Exercise 22.

1. propel + ed ____________________
2. star + ing ____________________
3. exhaust + ed ____________________
4. lend + ing ____________________
5. emit + ing ____________________
6. present + ed ____________________
7. quit + ing ____________________
8. forget + ing ____________________
9. heal + ed ____________________
10. hot + est ____________________

EXERCISE ◆ 24

Combine the following words with the endings indicated, and use them in sentences.

EXAMPLE:

dig + ing
Fred and I are *digging* for gold again.

1. stroll + ing
2. knot + ed
3. crack + ing
4. boot + ed
5. benefit + ing
6. permit + ed
7. gossip + ing
8. scoop + ing
9. pet + ed
10. gloat + ing

EXERCISE ◆ 25

Follow the instructions for Exercise 24.

1. conform + ing
2. rebel + ing

3. transfer + ed
4. clink + ing
5. host + ed
6. regret + able
7. begin + ing
8. murmur + ed
9. boat + ing
10. camp + ed

Item II: Words with Troublesome Spelling

Spelling rules cannot be applied to all words. Try to identify words with irregular spelling and memorize them.

abrupt
absence
absorbent
abundance
accede
acceptable
accessible
accessory
accommodate
accumulate
achievement
acknowledgement
acquaintance
acquire
acquittal
across
adequate
adjustment
admissible
admittance
advantageous
advertisement
advisable
affect
affiliate
aggressive
alignment
all right
allege
allotment
allotted
already
aluminum
analysis
analyze
anecdote
apologize
appearance
appropriate
architect
argument
arrangement
assess
asset
assignment
assistance
audible
authority
autumn
auxiliary

ballot
bankruptcy
banquet
bargain
basically
believable
beneficial
benefited
bookkeeper
boundary
brochure
bulletin
business

calendar

campaign
cancelled
careful
cashier
ceiling
champagne
clientele
collateral
collectible
column
commission
committee
competence
concede
conceivable
condemn
conducive
congratulate
conscience
conscientious
conscious
consecutively
convenience
correspondence
courteous
criticize
cylinder

decision
deductible
deficient
delinquent
dependent
despite
diagnosis
discrepancy
dissatisfaction
distinct

effect
efficient
eligible
embarrass
envelop
envelope
environment
equipped
equivalent
especially
exaggerate
exceed
excellent
exhaust
existence
extraordinary

facsimile
fascinate
February
financially
foreign
forfeit
forty
fourth
fulfill

gauge
genuine
gigantic
government
grammar
guarantee
guidance

handsome
harass
heavily
height
hindrance
humorous

illegal
illiterate
immediately
incidentally
independent
inhabitant
initiative
intentionally
interfere
irregular

justified

knowledge

laboratory
leisure
library
likable
livelihood
loneliness
luxury

maintenance

manageable
manoeuvre
marriage
mediocre
mileage
miniature
miscellaneous
misspell
mortgage
movable

necessary
necessity
ninety
ninth
nuisance

occasionally
occurred
omission
omitted

parallel
perform
precede
privilege
proceed

questionnaire
quizzical

realize
receipt
recipient
recommend
reconcile
recurrence
reimbursement
relevant
relief
relieve
reminisce
renown
ridiculous

safety
schedule
secretary
seize
separate
shining
siege
significance
skeptical
speech
stationary (adjective)
stationery (noun)
strength
subtle
succeed
successor
sufficient
summary
supersede
surprise
susceptible
suspicious
system

technique
temperament
temporary
terrible
their
theory
thoroughly
transferred
truly

unanimous
unique
unusual
usable
useful

vacuum
villain

weather
Wednesday
whether
writing
written
yacht
yield

"How do you remember all those words?"

EXERCISE • 26

Write sentences using the words indicated.

EXAMPLE:

relief

It was a *relief* to find out I passed the spelling test.

1. absence
2. condemn
3. recommend
4. harass
5. handsome
6. misspell
7. illiterate
8. courteous
9. grammar
10. ceiling

EXERCISE • 27

Follow the instructions for Exercise 26.

1. proceed
2. fascinate
3. lovable
4. relief
5. congratulate
6. separate
7. schedule
8. renown
9. fulfill
10. laboratory

EXERCISE • 28

Follow the instructions for Exercise 27.

1. equipped
2. Wednesday
3. bulletin
4. occurred
5. parallel
6. vacuum
7. usable
8. truly
9. argument
10. speech

EXERCISE • 29

Follow the instructions for Exercise 28.

1. receipt
2. hindrance
3. seize
4. unanimous
5. conscious

6. believable
7. calendar
8. absence
9. summary
10. February

EXERCISE • 30

Correct any spelling errors in the following sentences.

EXAMPLE:

interfere
Don't ~~interfear~~ with me again.

1. Take a night coarse; your grammer is terrible.
2. Who is saying their speach first?
3. I want a house, but I don't want a morgage.
4. How long have you been collecting miniture cars?
5. A fear of hights is a common phobia.
6. Don't forget to mark my birthday on your calender.
7. There is a great descrepency between my work and my pay.
8. Is fourty middle-aged or not?
9. It's a releaf to see that you're alright.
10. Did you mispell *preceed* again?

EXERCISE • 31

Follow the instructions for Exercise 30.

1. Of course, this is a genuwin goverment dockument.
2. Whoever started this arguement should appologize.
3. Soon you will be ninty, but you still need guidence.
4. You are two agressive.
5. There is no necesity to pay the bill yet.
6. Now he is both grumpy and iregular.
7. Your absense has made a big difference in our lives.
8. I find this theerie is very uneque.
9. Be carefull; bad spelling is unaceptible.
10. Only you think that this exercise is humerous.

Item III: Good Word Usage

Using the (right, write) word can be tricky. Because some words are similar in appearance, sound, and/or meaning, choosing the word you really want may be a problem.

Learning the spelling and meaning of these words will help you avoid choosing the wrong word and increase the clarity of your writing.

accept/except

Accept means to take willingly, to agree to, to consent to.

Except means not including, other than.

EXAMPLES:

The cheque was small, but they *accepted* it gratefully.
They invited everyone to the party *except* me.

advice/advise

Advice means an opinion given about something.

Advise means to give advice, to inform.

EXAMPLES:

I took your *advice* and asked her opinion.
She *advised* me to stay away from the racetrack.

affect/effect

Affect means to have an effect on, to influence.

Effect means a change produced by an action or cause, a result.

EXAMPLES:

The moon *affects* Morris badly; he's howling again.
The painkiller had no *effect* on the soccer player with the broken leg.

already/all ready

Already means before this time, as early as this.

All ready means completely prepared.

EXAMPLES:

I've *already* invited David to the party.
Myrna wishes she were *all ready* for Christmas.

all right/alright

All right means all correct, as desired, satisfactory.

Alright is an incorrect form of *all right*, but it is commonly used by the advertising media.

EXAMPLES:

I can't believe my answers are *all right*.

all together/ altogether

All together means in a group.
Altogether means entirely, wholly.

EXAMPLES:

The class went to see the play *all together*.
Your behaviour at the party last night was *altogether* inappropriate.

a lot/alot

A lot means a number of people or things of the same kind.
Alot is *a lot* misspelled.

EXAMPLE:

You have certainly collected *a lot* of books.

among/between

Among is used when referring to three or more things.
Between is used when referring to two persons only.

EXAMPLES:

It was difficult to divide the three doughnuts *among* the five children.
Between you and me, I really like vanilla ice cream.

amount/number

Amount means the total of anything, a quantity considered as a unit.
Number indicates things that should be counted individually.

EXAMPLES:

What *amount* of time have you spent on this essay?
The *number* of winners in yesterday's lottery is small.

angry/mad

Angry means feeling or showing anger.
Mad means insane, having a disordered mind.

EXAMPLES:

Erica was *angry* with the children for writing on the walls.
Roberto was *mad* with jealousy over his lost love.

awhile/a while

Awhile means for a short time.
A while means a period of time.

EXAMPLES:

Wait *awhile;* I'll be right with you.

In *a while*, the eclipse of the moon will be complete.

bad/badly

Bad is an adjective. It means unpleasant, not good.

Badly is an adverb. It means in a bad manner, very much, or to a great extent.

EXAMPLES:

What is that *bad* odour coming from the kitchen?

You spell as *badly* as I do.

This investment is *badly* financed.

breath/breathe

Breath is the air drawn into the lungs.

Breathe means to draw air in and out of the lungs.

EXAMPLES:

After the driving lesson, the instructor took several deep *breaths* of fresh air.

How can you *breathe* the air in this muffler shop?

can/may

Can means to have the ability or knowledge to do something.

May means to have permission.

EXAMPLES:

Can you tell me if this is Cantonese or Mandarin cuisine?

May I suggest that it's your turn to pay for lunch.

cite/site/sight

Cite means to quote or mention.

Site means the location at which something stands.

Sight is the faculty of seeing.

EXAMPLES:

Josh can *cite* passages from the Bible as easily as our minister.

I don't think that they've decided on the *site* for the new opera house.

Do rabbits really have better *sight* than other animals?

clench/clinch

Clench means to close teeth or fingers tightly.

Clinch means to fasten securely, settle conclusively.

EXAMPLES:

Thora *clenched* him by the shoulders and told him to smarten up.

By paying cash we were able to *clinch* our dream vacation.

complement/compliment

Complement means to make a thing complete.

Compliment means to express praise or admiration.

EXAMPLES:

Shoria's new glasses *complement* her appearance.

Wanda *complimented* Jan on his choice of wine for dinner.

conscience/conscious

Conscience is a person's sense of what is right and wrong.

Conscious means awake, aware of one's surroundings.

EXAMPLES:

Anyone who harms other individuals just for spite has no *conscience*.

Bob was not *conscious* that he kept saying "right" at the end of all his statements.

continual/continuous

Continual means something happens over and over again.

Continuous means without interruption.

EXAMPLES:

You could tell that Piotr's cold was bad by his *continual* sniffling.

In slow motion, the *continuous* beating of a hummingbird's wings is a wonder.

could of/could have

Could of is the mistaken expression for *could have,* or its contraction *could've.*

EXAMPLE:

You *could have* told me I needed a parachute.

council/counsel

A *council* is a legislative body or committee that advises, discusses, or organizes something.

Counsel is to give advice; as a noun, it means the suggestions given to someone.

EXAMPLES:

The *council* of reeves has made its recommendation for the new waste management plant.

An insurance agent can *counsel* you about the property damage.

decent/descent

Decent means proper, standard, and respectable.

Descent is the motion of going down.

EXAMPLES:

Esther, who lent me the money, is a *decent* person.

The eagle made a slow *descent* to the river's edge.

elicit/illicit

Elicit means to get, to draw out facts or information.

Illicit means against the law, improper.

EXAMPLES:

The police were able to *elicit* the names of the Korner Store Gang from one of its members.

Selling drugs to anyone is an *illicit* activity.

eminent/imminent

Eminent means famous, distinguished.

Imminent means about to occur, in the near future.

EXAMPLES:

Ms. Gorman is an *eminent* editor of classic books.

The midwife said that the birth of the baby was *imminent*.

farther/further

Farther means to a greater distance, literally.

Further is used less literally.

EXAMPLES:

Sidney has travelled much *farther* in his life than I.

He had no *further* need for the medication.

good/well

Good is an adjective.

Well is an adverb, except when it refers to health or appearance, in which case it is an adjective.

EXAMPLES:

I knew this would turn out to be a *good* night. (adjective)
My weedeater is not working as *well* as it did last summer. (adverb)
After 15 hours of sleep, you should feel *well*. (adjective)

ignorant/stupid

Ignorant implies lacking knowledge or information.
Stupid means lack of normal intelligence or contrary to common sense.

EXAMPLES:

Dale was *ignorant* of the new crosswalk law.
Drinking and driving is in the top ten of *stupid* things to do.

in/into

In expresses a *location* inside something.
Into expresses *movement toward* the inside.

EXAMPLES:

How much time did you spend *in* the mall on Saturday?
It's raining; come *into* the house.

inside of

The *of* here is unnecessary.

EXAMPLE:

What are you hiding *inside* that old chest?

irregardless/regardless

Irregardless is the mistaken expression for *regardless* or *irrespective of*.

EXAMPLE:

Amanda is not giving up *regardless* of your opinion.

it's/its

It's is the contraction for *it is* or *it has*.
Its is the **possessive** form of the personal pronoun *it* (that is, it shows ownership).

EXAMPLES:

It's not your turn yet.
It's been ten long years.
When did your dog injure *its* paw?

later/latter

Later means after a period of time.

Latter means the second of two in a list or comparison.

EXAMPLES:

Because of the snow, trains arrived an hour *later* than scheduled.

The first part of your story is believable, but the *latter* part is not.

loan/lend/borrow

Loan is a noun; it refers to the money lent, or to the fact (not the action) of lending it.

Lend means to give or allow the use of something to someone for a short period of time.

Borrow means to accept the use of something from someone for a short period of time.

EXAMPLES:

Give me a *loan*.

I wish I could *lend* you a thousand dollars.

Do you really want to *borrow* Doug's old sweatsocks?

less/fewer

Less refers to overall quantity or amount.

Fewer refers to number and things counted as individual items.

EXAMPLES:

It's strange, but each year I make *less* money.

The wolf told the shepherd that there were *fewer* sheep in the fields these days.

lessen/lesson

Lessen means to make less.

Lesson is a thing to be learned by a student of an amount of teaching given at one time.

EXAMPLES:

You're not going to *lessen* your workload by volunteering for more.

Jenny's dance *lessons* begin again next Thursday.

let/leave

Let means to allow or permit.

Leave means to go away.

EXAMPLES:

When I was young, my parents would *let* me stay up later on Friday nights.
What time did you *leave* Mohammed's party last night?

Let and *leave* have the same meaning when they are followed by a noun or pronoun and the adverb alone. There is, however, a difference in tone.

EXAMPLES:

Let him alone. (serious, demanding tone)
Leave him alone. (polite tone)

lie/lay

Lie means to recline one's body.
Lay means to place or put on a surface.

EXAMPLES:

It's not easy to *lie* on a bed of nails.
When did they *lay* the new carpet?

lightening/lightning

Lightening means becoming brighter or lighter.
Lightning is a flash of bright light produced by natural electricity.

EXAMPLES:

The sun streaming through the window is *lightening* the room considerably.
That *lightning* doesn't strike twice is a myth.

like/as

Like is a preposition and is followed by a noun or pronoun.
As is a conjunction and is usually followed by a subject and verb.

EXAMPLES:

This looks *like* stew, but doesn't taste *like* it.
The dance instructor said, "Do *as* I do."

lose/loose

Lose means to be deprived of or cease to have.
Loose means free from restraints.

EXAMPLES:

When did you *lose* your wisdom teeth?
My left shoelace is always *loose*.

may be/maybe

May be is a verb expressing a possibility.
Maybe is an adverb meaning perhaps or possibly.

EXAMPLES:

If I play the lottery, I *may be* a winner.
Sitting in the candlelight, Ron thought that *maybe* he should have paid the electric bill.

off of

The preposition *of* in this expression is not needed.

EXAMPLE:

Are you finished picking the lint *off* your pants?

passed/past

Passed is the past tense of the verb *pass*.
Past can be an adjective, an adverb, a noun, or a preposition.

EXAMPLES:

Paula said she *passed* me on the street yesterday, but I didn't see her. (verb)
Some *past* memories are painful to recall. (adjective)
Don't go *past* without saying hello. (adverb)
Sometimes I wonder what it would be like to live in different periods in the *past*. (noun)
I can mail your letter; I jog *past* the post office every day. (preposition)

peace/piece

Peace means a state of calm, stillness, or freedom from war.
Piece means one distinct portion of a thing.

EXAMPLE:

Will we live to see world *peace*?
Very few of us have complete *peace* of mind.
This *piece* of wrap is too small for the present.

principal/principle

Principal has several meanings: first in rank; a person with highest authority in an organization; the person who has the leading part in a play; a capital sum apart from interest.
Principle means a basic truth or doctrine.

EXAMPLES:

Paying the mortgage is Sally's *principal* concern this month.
Nora frequently reviews her ethical *principles*.

precede/proceed

Precede means to come before, go before, or be before.
Proceed means to advance or go forward.

EXAMPLES:
A green salad *preceded* the main course.
Are you going to *proceed* with your plans to buy a house this autumn?

refer back

The word *back* is redundant.

EXAMPLE:
Refer to page 121 for the answer.

rise/raise

Rise means to get oneself up.
Raise means to lift something up.

EXAMPLES:
The doctor said that Emma's temperature would *rise*.
Can you really *raise* that amount of money by tomorrow?

quiet/quite

Quiet means making little or no sound.
Quite means completely, entirely.

EXAMPLES:
The teacher is sleeping; please be *quiet*.
This new book by Erma Bombeck is *quite* amusing.

sensual/sensuous

Sensual refers to the pleasures and satisfaction of all physical appetites.
Sensuous refers to appreciation of perceptions through the senses.

EXAMPLES:
The late movie had some very *sensual* romantic scenes.
Martine has a *sensuous* appreciation of Ravel's music.

sit/set

Sit means to rest upright on the buttocks.
Set means to put, to place.

EXAMPLES:
Don't *sit* too close to the movie screen.
What time did you *set* the clock to ring?

stationary/stationery

Stationary means not moving, fixed.
Stationery means writing paper, envelopes.

EXAMPLES:

The hummingbird remained *stationary* over the garden flowers for only a moment.

I need some *stationery* supplies; I don't have any more envelopes or notepads.

teach/learn

Teach means to give knowledge.
Learn means to receive knowledge.

EXAMPLES:

Why doesn't anyone want to *teach* me how to drive?

What did you *learn* about driving after your first lesson?

than/then

Than is a conjunction used in comparisons.
Then means at that time or next.

EXAMPLES:

Karen always eats more *than* I.

First I spilled the coffee on my notes; *then* I dropped the jelly doughnut on my lap.

use to/used to

Use to is the mistaken expression for *used to.*

EXAMPLE:

I *used to* have more hair.

who's/whose

Who's is the contraction of *who is* or *who has.*
Whose is the possessive form of the pronoun *whose.*

EXAMPLES:

Who's supposed to be your replacement?

This is the photographer *whose* photograph won the national contest.

EXERCISE • 32

Underline the correct word in parentheses for the following sentences.

EXAMPLE:

Poi and Sam (use to, <u>used to</u>) be good friends.

1. First go to the market; (than, then) go to the post office.
2. Because of the nice weather, there were (fewer, less) students in class today.
3. Mirka always dresses so (good, well).
4. I must be gaining weight; my skirt is not as (lose, loose) as it (use to, used to) be.
5. My dream of owning a house seems to be getting (farther, further) and (farther, further) away.
6. Your friendship means (alot, a lot) to me.
7. (Whose, who's) in the mood for pizza?
8. After dinner, the waiter brought a magnificent (desert, dessert) cart to our table.
9. Xiang Zhao (already, all ready) has a Grade 12 certificate.
10. It is a very (quiet, quite) evening.

EXERCISE • 33

Follow the instructions for Exercise 32.

1. Marek laughed so hard watching television that he fell (off, off of) the couch.
2. This is starting to make my temperature (rise, raise).
3. Ljubo smiled for the photographer (irregardless, regardless) of the fact that he had a toothache.
4. The elevator operator is a (decent, descent) person.
5. Grazyna forgot to set her alarm and woke up two hours (later, latter) (than, then) usual.
6. The car was destroyed in the crash, but Olga and Jan are (alright, all right).
7. "(Maybe, May be) I do know how you feel," remarked Heiman.
8. The best way to (precede, proceed) is to apologize to Tomoko first.
9. Why does grandfather always (refer back, refer) to "the good old days"?
10. Try and remain (stationery, stationary) until I take all the photos.

EXERCISE • 34

Write sentences using the following words.

EXAMPLE:

lose

I seem to *lose* a pen every other day.

1. laid
2. stationery
3. set
4. inside
5. further
6. altogether
7. borrow
8. stupid
9. principle
10. angry

EXERCISE • 35

Follow the instructions for Exercise 34.

1. effect
2. all right
3. amount
4. lightening
5. passed
6. except
7. clinch
8. continued
9. breath
10. badly

EXERCISE • 36

Follow the instructions for Exercise 35.

1. complement
2. whose

3. number
4. awhile
5. elicit
6. sensuous
7. then
8. rise
9. like
10. let

Item IV: Articles

The words *a*, *an*, and *the* are usually not considered to be parts of speech. Their function, though, is similar to that of adjectives in that they modify nouns. They are referred to as **articles**.

Articles identify or designate nouns as being general or specific. *A* and *an* are the indefinite articles, and *the* is the definite article.

The use of these articles is often determined by the context in which you are stating a noun. This makes it a little tricky to master, especially if English is not your first language.

Here are some guidelines for the use of *a*, *an*, and *the*.

a. Use *a* before all words beginning with a consonant.

EXAMPLES:

a block parent
a hernia
a queen
a tourist
a xylophone

b. Use *an* before all words beginning with a vowel sound.

EXAMPLES:

an apology
an editor
an idiot
an outlet mall
an umbrella

c. Do not use *a* before the consonant *h* when the *h* is not pronounced. Use *an* instead.

EXAMPLES:

an honour
an honest person

d. Do not use *an* before the vowels *u* or *o* when the word is pronounced as though it began with *y* or *w*, as is the case with *you* and *one*.

EXAMPLES:

a utility belt
a Utopian existence
a one-ton truck
a once-in-a-lifetime opportunity

e. When the noun is the name of a letter of the alphabet, use *an* in front of *f*, *l*, *m*, *n*, *r*, *s*, *x*, and *a* in front of all others.

EXAMPLES:

Is there *an l* in salmon?
What does *an x* mean at the bottom of a birthday card?
Frank got *a* C on his final exam.

f. *A* refers to persons or things in a general way.

EXAMPLES:

I need *a* new life.
John lived in *a* bachelor apartment for three years.
Sherry is in *a* bad mood.

g. *A* may suggest the meaning of "one."

EXAMPLES:

I just want *a* chance.
In *a* year, my studies will be complete.

h. *The* refers to persons or things in a specific way.

EXAMPLES:

I like *the* way you dance.
Give me *the* book on *the* counter.
The door is open.

Here are some additional examples of the distinction between the general (*a* or *an*) and the specific (*the*) article.

EXAMPLES:

We need *a* good hammer. (general)
We need *the* good hammer. (specific)

They went to *a* museum. (general)
They went to *the* museum. (specific)

i. Use *the* with abstract nouns when giving a specific explanation.

EXAMPLES:

The beauty of her writing is evident.
I know *the* fears he has experienced.
Barb cherishes *the* love of her children.

j. Do not use *the* in front of an abstract noun when it is being discussed as a quality or emotion.

EXAMPLES:

Beauty is all around us.
Fear can be destructive.
They understand the importance of *love*.

k. *The* is often used in front of the names of geographical locations, buildings, and institutions.

EXAMPLES:

the Prairies
the Rockies
the United States
the CN Tower
the Church of St. Patrick

EXAMPLES:

Have you ever been to *the* Columbia Icefields in Alberta?
The mountain range known as *the* Alps is in Europe.

l. Do not use *the* in front of an academic course or subject.

EXAMPLES:

I am taking English 402.
How can you enjoy studying economics?

m. Do not use *the* in front of titles.

EXAMPLES:

I just read *Such Is My Beloved*.
Did you enjoy *O, River Remember* by Martha Ostenso?

EXERCISE • 37

Place *a, an,* or *the* in the space provided in the following sentences.

EXAMPLE:

When did you decide to become ___ teacher?
When did you decide to become _a_ teacher?

1. This is ____ unusual story.
2. Dino is ____ capable worker.
3. ____ dentist needs to take ____ x-ray.
4. Pass ____ pepper.
5. Did you see ____ mystery movie last night?
6. Give me ____ pipe wrench.
7. Did you hear about ____ accident?
8. Take ____ vacation.
9. Take ____ vacation I told you about.
10. There is ____ useful exercise on this page.

EXERCISE • 38

Follow the instructions for Exercise 37.

1. When did you see ____ Rockies?
2. What ____ idiot!
3. Did you you have ____ hernia operation?
4. Al should get ____ Ph.D. for all his hard work.
5. I need ____ opinion from ____ neutral party.
6. Did you get ____ A or ____ B on your English composition?
7. I'm in the mood for ____ burger.
8. ____ restaurant around ____ corner has ____ best burgers.
9. Is this ____ new couch?
10. This is ____ same couch we've had for years.

EXERCISE • 39

Follow the instructions for Exercise 38.

1. The car offer is ____ one-time opportunity.
2. Dale has ____ interesting occupation.

3. He is ____ osteopath.
4. Can you drive me to ____ hospital?
5. What ____ ugly painting!
6. ____ job should be completed in ____ day.
7. Ben has ____ fear of ____ dark.
8. Arthur Miller wrote ____ *Death of a Salesman*.
9. ____ harp is not ____ common household musical instrument.
10. This is ____ unbelievable coincidence.

EXERCISE • 40

Follow the instructions for Exercise 39.

1. How long have you been ____ Girl Guide leader?
2. Did you see ____ full moon last night?
3. That is ____ outrageous suggestion.
4. Neil is definitely ____ honest man.
5. You have chosen ____ unique gift for someone.
6. Did ____ teacher forget ____ *r* in *regret*?
7. I want to taste ____ cake you baked.
8. ____ way out is through ____ basement.
9. We all need ____ little appreciation.
10. ____ compromise is an important ingredient in ____ marriage.

EXERCISE • 41

Follow the instructions for Exercise 40.

1. Are you having ____ x-ray today?
2. ____ article on ____ proper use of articles is confusing.
3. Did you read ____ "Ode to the West Wind" by Percy Bysshe Shelley?
4. Are you going to ____ United States this summer?
5. Oh, do I ever have ____ bad headache!
6. Did you find ____ new apartment yet?
7. ____ apartment I saw last night was too small.
8. They gave Ed ____ heartfelt thank-you present.
9. Steve wanted ____ A; anyone can get ____ B.
10. Did you enjoy ____ swim class?

Item V: The Apostrophe

The apostrophe can be a nuisance to use. This is especially true when we write sentences in which its use seems questionable.

The correct use of the apostrophe is not difficult to learn. The apostrophe is a punctuation mark that has three basic functions:

1. To indicate the possessive form of nouns and pronouns
2. To indicate contractions
3. To indicate the plural of short symbols such as letters and numbers, and of certain words

1. The Possessive Form of Nouns and Pronouns

a. To indicate the possessive form of a singular noun or pronoun, add *'s*. Also add *'s* for singular nouns that end in *s*. (However, some writers prefer to add the apostrophe alone. Both forms are correct. Choose the form that is easier for you to use.)

EXAMPLES:

Ann's sweater is beautiful. (the sweater of Ann)
Everyone's book orders are here. (the orders of everyone)
Carlos's home-made wine is excellent.
Carlos' home-made wine is excellent.

b. To indicate the possessive form of all plural nouns that end in *s*, add an apostrophe.

EXAMPLES:

The administrators' conference is next Tuesday.
Several of the parents' recommendations have been addressed.

c. To indicate the possessive form of plural nouns that do not end in *s*, add an *'s*.

EXAMPLES:

The children's clothes are on the bed.
The committee's votes have been counted.

d. To indicate that two or more persons together own the same thing, add *'s* to the last word expressing ownership.

EXAMPLES:

This is Gisella and Arnold's new apartment.
Sung, Brian, Oliver, and Susan's variety store is doing quite well.

e. To indicate separate ownership of the same kind of thing, add *'s* to each noun.

EXAMPLES:

Doreen's and Kip's parents know each other.
James's and George's photos are on display in the school gym.

f. To indicate the possessive of compound nouns, add *'s* to the last noun even if the compound noun is plural.

EXAMPLES:

My sister-in-law's (singular) book is on the table.
My sisters-in-law's (plural) books are on the table.

EXERCISE • 42

Change the noun or pronoun indicated into the possessive form.

EXAMPLE:

the teacher advice   teacher's

1. a good day work ____________________
2. someone books ____________________
3. Harris attitude ____________________
4. a deer antlers ____________________
5. a mother love ____________________
6. the players cards ____________________
7. the children toys ____________________
8. Xiao Ping new friends ____________________
9. the kittens mother ____________________
10. the chocolate bar flavour ____________________

EXERCISE • 43

Follow the instructions for Exercise 42.

1. the skunk scent ____________________
2. ladies old shoes ____________________
3. the insurance agent offer ____________________
4. Patrick and Andrew apartments ____________________
5. Ioana and Jia apartment ____________________
6. a judges chambers ____________________

7. the elephants trunks ________
8. anybody guess ________
9. the government agenda ________
10. Delta dilemma ________

EXERCISE • 44

Change the noun or pronoun indicated into the possessive form. Then write sentences to complete the phrases.

EXAMPLE:

the principal office principal's

Fortunately, I've never been to the principal's office.

1. Fu Tian glasses ________
2. Cecilia and Nora dentists ________
3. Miron misconception ________
4. the student last words ________
5. Ross novels ________
6. Doreen and Stan cottage ________
7. the psychiatrists offices ________
8. the baby first tooth ________
9. the politicians promises ________
10. Moira new sandals ________

2. Contractions

When letter(s) are omitted to make an expression shorter, an apostrophe must be used in place of the missing letter(s).

EXAMPLES:

cannot	-	can't
do not	-	don't
did not	-	didn't
does not	-	doesn't
I am	-	I'm
it is it has	-	it's
it will	-	it'll

I had / I would	-	I'd
they are	-	they're
they have	-	they've
they will	-	they'll
we are	-	we're
we have	-	we've
will not	-	won't
who is / who has	-	who's

EXAMPLES:

It's been a year since *they've* last been here. (*it has, they have*)
We *won't* know *who's* coming to the party until we get there. (*will not, who is*)

EXERCISE • 45

Change the following words into contractions.

EXAMPLE:
it will it'll

1. cannot ____________
2. who is ____________
3. has not ____________
4. we will ____________
5. who has ____________
6. does not ____________
7. who will ____________
8. are not ____________
9. I am ____________
10. do not ____________

EXERCISE • 46

Follow the instructions for Exercise 44.

1. it is ____________
2. she will ____________
3. he is ____________

4. will not ____________________
5. we are ____________________
6. who has ____________________
7. should not ____________________
8. you will ____________________
9. they have ____________________
10. it will ____________________

EXERCISE • 47

Change the following words into contractions, and use them in a sentence.

EXAMPLE:

he is

Leroy is convinced that *he's* the winner.

1. they will
2. we are
3. would not
4. are not
5. who will
6. she is
7. are not
8. will not
9. we have
10. could not

3. The Plural of Letters, Numbers, and Certain Words

To form the plural of letters, numbers, and certain words, add *'s*.

EXAMPLES:

Did you say that there are two *i*'s in your last name?

You need to place the decimal point after the three 0's.

There are too many prepositions in your short story; in fact, there are more than ten *in*'s on your first page.

For some expressions involving time, add *'s* if they are singular, and add an apostrophe alone if they are plural.

EXAMPLES:

singular	*plural*
one day's wait	two days' wait
one year's delay	three years' delay

EXERCISE ♦ 48

Use apostrophes in the following sentences as required.

EXAMPLE:

Last nights baseball game was great.
Last *night's* baseball game was great.

1. Whos in charge here?
2. I wasnt there last night.
3. It was a 50s dance.
4. There was a twenty minutes subway delay.
5. Its not what you think.
6. Hanna doesnt know what colour to choose.
7. Were there more yess or nos in yesterdays vote?
8. Ted never crosses his *t*s.
9. Im not sure its the one you want.
10. The futures always uncertain.

EXERCISE ♦ 49

Follow the instructions for Exercise 48.

1. The *but*s in your brochure against smoking are misspelled.
2. Youve always made time to see us.
3. These are my last two 5s.
4. The bridge repair caused an hours delay to downtown traffic.
5. You wont believe your eyes.
6. Who said two wrongs dont make a right?
7. The motorbikes rear tire is flat.
8. I cant believe that this essay is hers.
9. Adam wanted to achieve straight As, but got 3 Bs and 2 Cs.
10. Giselle always ends her sentences with a couple of *right*s when she speaks.

4. Common Apostrophe Usage Errors

a. Never add the apostrophe or *'s* to the noun being owned.

EXAMPLES:

Jills antique bottle's are very rare. (incorrect)
Jill's antique bottles are very rare. (correct)

b. In contractions, always put the apostrophe in the place of the missing letter(s).

EXAMPLES:

incorrect	*correct*
is'nt	isn't
did'nt	didn't

c. Never use apostrophes for the possessive form of a personal pronoun (use *hers, its, ours, theirs, yours*).

EXAMPLES:

This award should really be her's. (incorrect)
This award should really be hers. (correct)

Does the place card say this table is our's or their's? (incorrect)
Does the place card say this table is ours or theirs? (correct)

d. Avoid confusing possessive pronouns with "sound-alike" contractions.

EXAMPLES:

its (ownership)	-	it's (it is)
your (ownership)	-	you're (you are)
their (ownership)	-	they're (they are)

Their on their way to their new cottage. (incorrect)
They're on their way to their new cottage. (correct)

Your such a pessimist to think your going to fail again. (incorrect)
You're such a pessimist to think you're going to fail again. (correct)

EXERCISE • 50

Place apostrophes where they are required in the following sentences.

EXAMPLE:

Dont forget to buy a Mothers Day card.
Don't forget to buy a Mother's Day card.

1. Everyones here for Lourdes party.
2. Are there two or three *m*s in Sammys name?
3. Weve been told that therell be another ten minutes delay.
4. Because the blue jay is related to the crow, its not pleasant to listen to its call.
5. Whats your prediction on tonights game?
6. Phuong and Kens CD player was a gift from friends of theirs.
7. After this exercise, I could use a whole days sleep.
8. There are six *in*s in the opening paragraph of Hemingways *A Farewell to Arms*.
9. My four brothers-in-laws bathrooms all have bidets.
10. The coffees aroma permeated the house.

EXERCISE ◆ 51

Follow the instructions for Exercise 50.

1. Id be lying if I didnt admit that shes the one I love.
2. Their best friends Dalia and Kim always get 100s on their tests.
3. Wouldnt you like to fly to Paris for two weeks vacation?
4. Its hard to believe that Tims and Jays apartments are in the same building.
5. The junkyard dogs bite is much worse than its bark.
6. The long days wait was finally over for the new mother.
7. My sisters boyfriends brother is seven feet tall.
8. Ive been told that James ability to pick winning lottery numbers is amazing.
9. Sonia and Marks friendship has continued for more than twenty years.
10. My mother-in-laws chocolate cheesecake is the best Ive ever tasted.

EXERCISE ◆ 52

Follow the instructions for Exercise 51.

1. Youll feel better in the morning if you dont look in the mirror.
2. I dont think there are any fs in phobia.
3. Mel didnt like the look on the bank managers face.
4. Most of it is yours; the rest is hers.
5. Did you see Dorotas picture in Thursdays paper?
6. Because of this bill, I havent had a good nights sleep in days.

7. It would be better if you did not use ands and buts to start your sentences.
8. Theyre predicting rain for Bess wedding day.
9. Dorrel, Jose and Mahnazs cars are the same make.
10. There should be three more 0s before the decimal point on my paycheque.

Item VI: Capital Letters

There are probably only a few times when you stop to question whether a word needs a capital letter. We know, for instance, that the pronoun *I*, the name of a person, and the first word in a sentence must all be capitalized.

Sometimes, however, you might not know when to use a capital letter. For instance, do you know when the word *uncle* or *earth* is capitalized? When do you capitalize *north, south, east,* and *west*? Which words in a title should be capitalized?

In this Item, you will learn the answers to these and other questions concerning capital letters.

1. Proper Names, Titles, and Religious Terms

a. Capitalize all **proper names**. Capitalize titles when they accompany a proper name and are part of that name.

EXAMPLES:

Selina	Father Thomas (priest)
Marek	Sister St. Joseph (nun)
Ms. Shen	Judge Chu
Dr. Appleton	Pope John Paul II
Professor Filice	Prime Minister Chretien

However, do not capitalize titles preceded by a proper name as in the following examples.

EXAMPLES:

Kimberly Gill is a doctor.
The new English professor is David Robertson.

Capitalize words expressing relationships that are part of a proper name or that are used in place of the proper noun.

EXAMPLES:

I know Aunt Mary will be here soon. (with a proper name)

Is Uncle going to the hardware store sale? (in place of the proper name)

b. Religious names and terms are another variety of proper names and must be capitalized.

EXAMPLES:

God	Jehovah
Jesus Christ	Islam
the Virgin Mary	Buddha
the Saviour	Catholic
Allah	Jewish
the Koran	the Moonies
the Bible	

2. Days, Months, and Time Periods

a. Capitalize the names of days, months, and holidays, and the names of periods and historical events.

EXAMPLES:

Thursday	the Precambrian era
November	the Dark Ages
Christmas	the Renaissance
Yom Kippur	the Crusades
New Year's Eve	the War of 1812
Simcoe Day	Atlanta 96

b. Never capitalize the name of a season — *spring, summer, winter, fall, autumn* — unless it is the first word in a sentence.

EXAMPLE:

I enjoy walking in the woods and looking at the autumn colours.

3. Buildings, Institutions, and Organizations

Capitalize the names of buildings, institutions, and organizations.

EXAMPLES:

the Manulife Centre	Brother André High School
George Brown College	the Château Laurier
the Comfort Inn	Collins Bay Penitentiary
Canadian Tire Corporation	Centennial Hospital

4. Geographical Terms, Nationalities, and Languages

a. Capitalize the names of cities, towns, provinces, states, countries, continents, islands, lakes, oceans, mountains, parks, constellations, and planets.

EXAMPLES:

Sarnia	Lake Erie
Duck Lake, Saskatchewan	the Indian Ocean
China	Polar Bear Provincial Park
North America	Centaurus
Wolfe Island	Jupiter
the Milky Way	Earth

Note that *Earth* (when referred to as the planet) is not capitalized when preceded by *the*.

EXAMPLE:

I know that the earth is the third planet from the sun.

b. Capitalize *north, south, east,* and *west* when they refer to a section of a country or are part of the name of a street.

EXAMPLES:

I'm definitely going visit the South this winter.
The new CD store is at 104 Princess Street West.

c. Capitalize the names of racial groups and derived words.

EXAMPLES:

Canadian	West Indian
Italian	Jewish
Polish	German (as a language)
Chinese	Germany (the country)
Korean	Germanic (as an adjective)

5. Titles, Documents, and Subjects

a. Capitalize the title of any written work in the following manner: (1) the first word and all important words must begin with a capital letter; (2) do not capitalize prepositions and conjunctions that are less than five letters long, and do not capitalize articles (*a, an, the*).

EXAMPLES:

Lives of the Saints *The Mill on the Floss*	(novels)
The Journal of Canadian Literature	(journal)
Magna Carta Canadian Charter of Rights and Freedoms	(documents)

b. Do not capitalize a school subject unless it is the first word in a sentence, is the name of a language, or is followed by a number.

EXAMPLES:

Why is physics so easy for you and so hard for me?
I am enjoying Latin classes.
Is Biology 9000 being offered at night school?

EXERCISE • 53

Place capitals in the following sentences where they are required. If the sentence is correct, write "C" beside it.

EXAMPLE:

What are you doing on new year's eve?
What are you doing on New Year's Eve?

1. do you want a danish pastry or an english muffin?
2. molly likes to shop in downtown toronto for christmas.

3. did you know that uncle is moving to saskatoon, saskatchewan?
4. "i'm learning to speak cantonese," remarked jose.
5. What is the capital of New Brunswick?
6. i know that mars is the fourth planet from the sun.
7. is manitoulin island the largest fresh-water island in the world?
8. there is a reason lake superior is a superior lake.
9. will you arrive at the georgian court hotel in vancouver, british columbia on tuesday or wednesday?
10. marvin's favourite subject is lunch 101.

EXERCISE • 54

Follow the instructions for Exercise 53.

1. i think the church of st. patrick is on highway 7.
2. is halloween a holiday?
3. you should get the *concise oxford dictionary of quotations*.
4. winter hasn't started, and i'm already anxious for spring.
5. james herbert wrote the horror novel entitled *creed*.
6. why does cousin john act like such an idiot?
7. sometimes i think the dark ages aren't over.
8. when my english professor said my compound sentence needed a surgeon, i called dr. miller right away.
9. *words we use* is a book published by prentice hall.
10. the vietnamese long dress is made to measure only.

EXERCISE • 55

Follow the instructions for Exercise 54.

1. the bank of montreal is having another mortgage sale.
2. what is the mathematics homework assigned by ms. brackets?
3. it's almost june; father's day will be here soon.
4. the prairies in winter can appear bleak, but they are always beautiful.
5. polish food and west indian food and chinese food and all ethnic foods, to tell the truth, are my favourites.
6. do you have this month's copy of the *journal of commonwealth literature*?

7. i'm sure the salmon river runs into lake ontario.
8. are you visiting or residing in kingston penitentiary?
9. marjorie agrees that the freight trains along dupont street are noisy.
10. you should get a copy of the *concise oxford dictionary of proverbs* to find out what "nothing succeeds like success" means.

EXERCISE • 56

Follow the instructions for Exercise 55.

1. barbara was surprised to learn that otty lake has more than 400 cottages on it.
2. when olga retires, she's moving to the warm south.
3. ray really enjoys his visits to killarney provincial park.
4. jayne was born in vietnam, but i'm sure she is chinese.
5. do you have the current issue of the *journal of canadian studies*?
6. i hope that dr. selwin can help me to quit smoking.
7. when did alberta join confederation?
8. the special thing about yom kippur is that it is a time of deep reflection.
9. everyone should read "lines composed a few miles above tintern abbey."
10. are you familiar with any of the teachings of buddha?

EXERCISE • 57

Follow the instructions for Exercise 56.

1. how far is vancouver island from the mainland?
2. what did aunt ask you to buy?
3. yanyu thought that christmas day had come early when she scored 100% on her english test.
4. at the st. lawrence market in toronto, you can always find something good to eat.
5. is that judge vidicki?
6. i would like to visit the northwest territories.
7. when was the renaissance period?
8. take history 203; the professor is great.
9. haig said that he is ready to travel to venus.
10. turn east at the lights; go two blocks, and you'll reach simmons street.

UNIT • 1 • POST-TEST

If you have completed Unit 1 satisfactorily, you are ready for the Post-Test. The answers immediately follow the Unit 1 Post-Test.

Part A

The following sentences contain errors in spelling and/or usage. Make the necessary corrections in the space provided.

1. John was releived that the plane made a save decent.

____

2. Whose responsable for buying the stationary?

____

3. Heather laid down for a nap an hour longer then Murray.

____

4. Fred complemented me on my apperance this morning.

____

5. Robin said he use to be concieted, but now he's perfect.

____

6. That was quiet an lightening bolt!

____

7. Does this grammer book gaurantee me better English?

____

8. Who can best advice me about growing tomatos?

____

9. I can not beleive a sun has all ready risen.

____

10. Warren feels badly that you fell off of your latter.

____

11. Between the three of us, we can aviod bankrupcy.

____

12. Because of the snowstorm, the classes had less students.

____

13. That blemish on your face is hardly noticable.

____

14. Is that snake edable?

____

15. For the correct use of the word *council* refer back to page 20.

____

Part B

Place apostrophes and capital letters where required in the following sentences.

1. is this todays *toronto sun*?
2. didnt you say that the hospital for sick children is on university avenue?
3. did marvin light the hanukkah candle?
4. the provincial flower of the yukon territory is the fireweed.
5. after a good nights sleep, angies migraine attack subsided.
6. is chief justice morris car available?
7. two bears were sighted at the edge of jasper national park by the tourists.
8. is there a place left in chemistry 300?
9. the royal astronomical society of canada is located in toronto, ontario.
10. in chile, south america, independence day is in september.
11. *name your baby* was written by lareina rule.
12. does *across* have one or two *c*s?
13. paul was old, but he still wanted to see the west.
14. havent you tried korean food before?
15. thats not hers; its jerrys.

ANSWERS • TO • UNIT • 1 • POST-TEST

Part A

The following sentences contain errors in spelling and/or usage. Make the necessary corrections in the space provided.

1. John was relieved that the plane made a safe descent.
2. Who's responsible for buying the stationery?
3. Heather lay down for a nap an hour longer than Murray.
4. Fred complimented me on my appearance this morning.
5. Robin said he used to be conceited, but now he's perfect.
6. That was quite a lightning bolt!
7. Does this grammar book guarantee me better English?

8. Who can best advise me about growing tomatoes?
9. I cannot believe the sun has already risen.
10. Warren feels bad that you fell off your ladder.
11. Among the three of us, we can avoid bankruptcy.
12. Because of the snowstorm, the classes had fewer students.
13. That blemish on your face is hardly noticeable.
14. Is that snake edible?
15. For the correct use of the word *council* refer to page 20.

Part B

Place apostrophes and capital letters where required in the following sentences.

1. Is this today's *Toronto Sun*?
2. Didn't you say that the Hospital for Sick Children is on University Avenue?
3. Did Marvin light the Hanukkah candle?
4. The provincial flower of the Yukon Territory is the fireweed.
5. After a good night's sleep, Angie's migraine attack subsided.
6. Is Chief Justice Morris'(s) car available?
7. Two bears were sighted at the edge of Jasper National park by the tourists.
8. Is there a place left in Chemistry 300?
9. The Royal Astronomical Society of Canada is located in Toronto, Ontario.
10. In Chile, South America, Independence Day is in September.
11. *Name Your Baby* was written by Lareina Rule.
12. Does *across* have one or two *c*'s?
13. Paul was old, but he still wanted to see the West.
14. Haven't you tried Korean food before?
15. That's not hers; it's Jerry's.

U•N•I•T 2

SENTENCE IMPROVEMENT

In Unit 2 you will examine the sentence in detail. You'll examine the parts of a sentence, sentence types, and the methods for recognizing and correcting common sentence errors. This knowledge will enable you to write confidently and effectively.

UNIT•2•PRE-TEST

Complete this test to measure your knowledge of the material in Unit 2. The answers immediately follow the Pre-Test.

I. Underline the main subject once and the main predicate twice in the following sentences.

1. I know.
2. When are you leaving?
3. Buy some cheese too.
4. Some of the red wine spilled on the carpet.
5. Juan and George are visiting tonight.

II. In the space provided, identify the underlined clauses as main, adjective, adverb, or noun clauses.

1. I wanted to see the movie, but <u>I was too late</u>. ____________
2. <u>Unless you get here by five</u>, we won't be able to see the movie. ____________

3. She knows what I mean. ________________
4. They are the ones who donated the money. ________________
5. This is a wine that I really enjoy. ________________

III. Identify the following sentences as simple, compound, complex, or compound-complex in the space provided.

1. When you're ready, let me know. ________________
2. I think that the meaning of the story is obvious. ________________
3. Marco or Anni will drive you to the mall. ________________
4. Because you are late, we'll have to reschedule your appointment, and you will be charged a small cancellation fee. ________________
5. I left before noon, and I arrived by dusk. ________________

IV. Identify the following sentences as run-ons or fragments in the space provided.

1. The water is choppy however, we are going fishing nevertheless. ________________
2. Without reading the instructions. ________________
3. Of course, you are right and I am wrong. ________________
4. This movie not about life in the Carribean. ________________
5. You should see the Egyptian artifacts at the museum, they're spectacular. ________________

V. Combine the following sentences using the words indicated. (Answers may vary.)

1. for

   Hilary ordered an espresso.
   It is her favourite.

   ____

   ____

2. although

   My grandfather danced all night.
   He did not know all the latest steps.

   ____

   ____

3. then

   Veronica went to the market.
   She went to the department store.

   ____

   ____

4. in fact

   The laser printer was expensive.
   It cost almost as much as the computer.

   ____

   ____

5. since

   We were eager to try the Kim-Chee.
   We had never tasted it before.

   ____

   ____

VI. The following sentences contain misplaced or dangling modifiers, errors in parallel structure, and wrong shifts in tense. Make the necessary corrections. (Answers may vary.)

1. Brian almost ate the whole cheesecake.

   ____

2. Trying to open the pickle jar, the cat startled me.

   ____

3. This year I want to visit Morroco, Vienna, and see the pyramids.

   ____

4. Jenny got new rollerblades and tries them out right away.

   ____

5. You only need to make two more appointments.

   ____

6. Having heard the weather report, the umbrellas were taken.

   ____

7. Tony bought a ballpoint pen at the mall that was leak-proof.

   ____

8. My next car has to be black, fast, and low in cost.

   ____

9. Seth was on the phone when there is a knock at the door.

____

10. Linda gave the chocolates to Arthur with the soft centres.

____

ANSWERS • TO • UNIT • 2 • PRE-TEST

I. Underline the main subject once and the main predicate twice in the following sentences.

1. I know.
2. When are you leaving?
3. Buy some cheese too. (subject you understood)
4. Some of the red wine spilled on the carpet.
5. Juan and George are visiting tonight.

II. In the space provided, identify the underlined clauses as main, adjective, adverb, or noun clauses.

1. I wanted to see the movie, but I was too late. main
2. Unless you get here by five, we won't be able to see the movie. adverb
3. She knows what I mean. noun
4. They are the ones who donated the money. adjective
5. This is a wine that I really enjoy. adjective

III. Identify the following sentences as simple, compound, complex, or compound-complex in the space provided.

1. When you're ready, let me know. complex
2. I think that the meaning of the story is obvious. complex
3. Marco or Anni will drive you to the mall. simple
4. Because you are late, we'll have to reschedule your appointment, and you will be charged a small cancellation fee. comp-compl
5. I left before noon, and I arrived by dusk. compound

IV. Identify the following sentences as run-ons or fragments in the space provided.

1. The water is choppy however, we are going fishing nevertheless. run-on
2. Without reading the instructions. fragment
3. Of course, you are right and I am wrong. run-on
4. This movie not about life in the Carribean. fragment
5. You should see the Egyptian artifacts at the museum, they're spectacular. run-on

V. Combine the following sentences using the words indicated. (Answers may vary.)

1. for

   Hilary ordered an espresso.
   It is her favourite.

   Hilary ordered an espresso, for it is her favourite.

2. although

   My grandfather danced all night.
   He did not know all the latest steps.

   Although my grandfather did not know all the latest steps, he danced all night.

3. then

   Veronica went to the market.
   She went to the department store.

   Veronica went to the market; then she went to the department store.

4. in fact

   The laser printer was expensive.
   It cost almost as much as the computer.

   The laser printer was expensive; in fact, it cost almost as much as the computer.

5. since

   We were eager to try the Kim-Chee.
   We had never tasted it before.

   We were eager to try the Kim-Chee since we had never tasted it before.

VI. The following sentences contain misplaced or dangling modifiers, errors in parallel structure, and wrong shifts in tense. Make the necessary corrections. (Answers may vary.)

1. Brian almost ate the whole cheesecake.
   Brian ate almost the whole cheesecake.
2. Trying to open the pickle jar, the cat startled me.
   While I was trying to open the pickle jar, the cat startled me.
3. This year I want to visit Morroco, Vienna, and see the pyramids.
   This year I want to visit Morroco, Vienna, and the pyramids.
4. Jenny got new rollerblades and tries them out right away.
   Jenny got new rollerblades and tried them out right away.
5. You only need to make two more appointments.
   You need to make only two more appointments.
6. Having heard the weather report, the umbrellas were taken.
   Having heard the weather report, we took our umbrellas.
7. Tony bought a ballpoint pen at the mall that was leak-proof.
   Tony bought a ballpoint pen that was leak-proof at the mall.
8. My next car has to be black, fast, and low in cost.
   My next car has to be black, fast, and inexpensive.
9. Seth was on the phone when there is a knock at the door.
   Seth was on the phone when there was a knock at the door.
10. Linda gave the chocolates to Arthur with the soft centres.
    Linda gave Arthur the chocolates with the soft centres.

Item I: Subjects and Predicates

The **subject** and the **predicate** are the basic parts of a sentence. Each of these has two types, **main** and **complete**.

Complete subject | **Complete predicate**

This chocolate cake is delicious.

Main subject (cake) | **Main predicate** (is)

1. Subjects

a. The **main subject** is the noun or pronoun naming the doer of an action or the person or thing talked about. To find the main subject, ask yourself "Who?" (for persons) or "What?" (for things) is performing the action of the main predicate (verb). Remember, a noun with an apostrophe can never be a subject because it is in the possessive form.

EXAMPLE:

The small dog is chewing the large bone. (What is chewing the large bone? Answer: the dog.)

b. The **complete subject** is the main subject plus any other words, such as adjectives and phrases that relate to the subject.

EXAMPLE:

The small dog (complete subject)	is chewing the large bone.

2. Predicates

a. The **main predicate** is the main verb in the sentence. It indicates what the subject is doing. To find the main predicate, ask yourself what the main subject is doing or stating.

EXAMPLE:

The small dog is chewing the large bone. (What is the dog doing? Answer: it is chewing.)

b. The **complete predicate** is the main predicate as well as any other words, such as adjectives, adverbs, and phrases that relate to the verb.

EXAMPLE:

The dog	is chewing the large bone. (complete predicate)

Note the subjects and predicates in the following sentences.

EXAMPLES:

Complete subject | **Complete predicate**

Some days seem longer than others.

Main subject | **Main predicate**

Complete subject | **Complete predicate**

That man was sleeping on that park bench.

Main subject | **Main predicate**

Complete subject | **Complete predicate**

Her oral presentation will begin in five minutes.

Main subject | **Main predicate**

Try the following exercises to reinforce what you have just learned.

EXERCISE • 1

Underline the main subject once and the main predicate twice in the following sentences.

EXAMPLE:

My sister is driving me home.

1. Mija is visiting her aunt in Korea.

2. The French toast should be ready.

3. I need a new life.

4. The children are restless tonight.
5. They can see the full moon clearly.
6. You need a breath mint.
7. Cockroaches make me nervous.
8. Suad wished for a million dollars.
9. Mariola's stomach was grumbling in class today.
10. You worry too much about money.

EXERCISE ♦ 2

Follow the instructions for Exercise 1.

1. The vampire's nose is red.
2. I feel a pain in my neck.
3. The sink is full of dirty dishes again.
4. The air conditioning system only works in winter.
5. English grammar is Yen Tao's main phobia.
6. You should get a haircut soon.
7. These cookies are really hard.
8. Her kiss was soft but sad.
9. These chocolate-covered cherries were made in Switzerland.
10. Carmina was dreaming about winning the lottery.

EXERCISE • 3

Follow the instructions for Exercise 2.

1. I know the subject in this sentence.
2. The storm clouds have appeared.
3. We heard the loon on the lake last night.
4. Lizzeth wants to visit Australia some day.
5. Your hives seem worse after an English test.
6. This timetable is terrible.
7. Everyone needs more money.
8. Piotr never goes anywhere without his good luck charm.
9. Life can be complicated.
10. John has an extensive beer can collection.

EXERCISE • 4

Follow the instructions for Exercise 3.

1. Most Europeans have a six-week summer vacation.
2. The weather person predicted the snowstorm's arrival correctly.
3. Mirko is afraid of illness, not old age.
4. This bathroom scale must be broken.
5. Sonya misses her native country, Chile.
6. The Christmas catalogue has bathing suits in it.
7. The explosion was in Aldo's wine cellar.
8. Quebec is the largest province in Canada.
9. Gulnar saw the accident from the bus window.
10. The starlings were pecking in the snow for food.

EXERCISE • 5

Follow the instructions for Exercise 4.

1. Blueberry pie is my favourite dessert.
2. You lick postage stamps, not rubber stamps.
3. The firewood will be delivered on Friday.
4. You need a good back massage.
5. Aminul prefers black-and-white movies.

6. Pauline sings in the church choir.
7. The dice are rolling in your favour.
8. Khanh complains about everything.
9. Angie has bought a new car.
10. The complaint department is closed.

Item II: More Subjects and Predicates

The sentences you have looked at so far have been simple sentences that expressed simple ideas. Finding the subjects and predicates in these sentences has been easy. However, sometimes it is difficult to find subjects and predicates in sentences that express a command, ask a question, begin with the word *here* or *there*, contain prepositional phrases, or contain more than one subject or predicate.

Sentences That Express a Command, Ask a Question, or Contain Prepositional Phrases or More Than One Subject or Predicate

a. An **imperative sentence** expresses a command through its verb (predicate). In an imperative sentence, the subject *you*, though not present, is understood.

EXAMPLES:

(You) Leave me alone.
(You) Get a job!

b. An **interrogative sentence** asks a question rather than making a statement. When a sentence expresses a question, the main verb (predicate) is placed *before* the subject, or, if it has two parts, is split and the subject placed between the parts of the verb.

EXAMPLES:

Sharmila is your sister. (statement)
Is Sharmila your sister? (question)

Mel is baking a cake. (statement)
Is Mel baking a cake? (question)

You have ordered the furniture. (statement)
Have you ordered the furniture? (question)

c. In sentences that begin with *here* or *there*, the subject usually follows the verb (predicate). Note that *here* and *there* are never subjects; only nouns and pronouns can be subjects.

EXAMPLES:

Here is my report.
There can be only one winner.

d. Do not mistakenly identify part of a **prepositional phrase** as the subject of a sentence. Though prepositional phrases may contain nouns and pronouns, they never contain the subject of a sentence. (For further information about prepositional phrases see Addendum A, Item VI.)

In the following examples the prepositional phrases are shown in parentheses.

EXAMPLES:

This jar (of jam) is hard to open.
A few (of the stories) are scary.

e. In the examples you have looked at so far, there has been only one subject and predicate in each sentence. Many simple sentences, however, contain multiple (or compound) subjects and predicates.

EXAMPLES:

I know. (simple subject and predicate)

Igani and you should buy a house. (compound subject)

Caridad writes and sings her own songs. (compound predicate)

Timo and Eva own and operate a small doughnut shop in Sarnia. (compound subject and compound predicate)

EXERCISE • 6

Underline the main subject once and the main predicate twice in the following sentences. To avoid confusion, place the prepositional phrases in parentheses.

EXAMPLE:

The joke (of the day) was not funny.

1. All of your friends are here.
2. What is the difference between a city and a town?
3. The view from Spy Rock in Westport, Ontario is spectacular.

4. There are no prerequisites.
5. Who is your favourite politician?
6. Start your engines!
7. Why do men hate asking for directions?
8. Here are your compact discs and tapes.
9. The light at the end of the tunnel is growing dimmer.
10. There is never a subject of a verb in a prepositional phrase.

EXERCISE ◆ 7

Follow the instructions for Exercise 6.

1. Count your blessings!
2. How does a bat catch mosquitoes?
3. Some of the nuts are hard to crack.
4. Here is the key.
5. Melissa made a wish and blew out the candles.
6. Leave it on the table.
7. Every one of your dishes is dirty.
8. Are you going to Nova Scotia this summer?
9. There were four cupcakes on the table before lunch.
10. Much of her wealth comes from her mother?

EXERCISE ◆ 8

Follow the instructions for Exercise 7.

1. The mood of the teacher was cool.
2. Are you dating Elwood?
3. Have Nora and you been to the new dentist yet?
4. Don't say another word.
5. When is the baby due?
6. There are many large snakes at the reptile exhibit.
7. Tell Susan and Marie the truth.
8. You should see your face.
9. Wojciech and Anna went to Egypt and saw the office buildings.
10. Did you visit Eduardo and his pet monkey?

EXERCISE • 9

Follow the instructions for Exercise 8.

1. I know more English now.
2. Did you go to the Billy Joel concert?
3. Have you counted and rolled all the pennies in the jar?
4. The value and importance of a good friendship should be cherished.
5. Pick a card, any card.
6. Some mornings Dorin feels like staying home but goes to school anyway.
7. Why did the man throw the butter out the window?
8. He wanted to see butter fly.
9. In this sentence the subject is the fifth word.
10. On the detour, a car and a boat collided.

EXERCISE • 10

Follow the instructions for Exercise 9.

1. Is John Mellencamp a singer or a recreation park?
2. Never pick your teeth in public.
3. One of the hot-air balloons was shaped like a cola can.
4. Jean-Paul Sartre and Boris Pasternak declined the Nobel Prize for literature.
5. Here is a sentence with one subject and one predicate.
6. A receding hairline has nothing to do with rabbits.
7. Maria and Carlos were chosen as the best dancers in the "Do the Twist" competition.
8. Guy folded the sweater and put it on the shelf in his closet.
9. Some of the teachers are more effective than a tranquilizer.
10. Have you read or studied any of Irving Layton's poetry?

Item III: Clauses

Clauses help us to determine sentence types. There are two types of clauses — main (independent) and subordinate (dependent).

1. Main Clause

A **main clause** is a group of words that contains a subject and a verb. It expresses a complete thought and makes sense by itself. In fact, *main clause* is another name for a simple sentence.

EXAMPLES:

Robert took the other road.
When you are sure, let me know.
Carly said that the linen was a gift from her mom.

2. Subordinate Clause

A **subordinate clause** is also made up of a subject and verb, but it does not express a complete thought and does not make sense by itself. It cannot stand alone, and *it is never a simple sentence.*

Subordinate clauses depend on main clauses to complete their meaning. Subordinate clauses connect with main clauses via a **relative pronoun** (see Addendum A, Item II) or a **subordinating conjunction** (see Addendum A, Item VI).

There are three types of subordinate clauses: **adjective**, **adverb**, and **noun**. Most adjective clauses are introduced by relative pronouns, and adverb and noun clauses by subordinating conjunctions.

Look at these examples of subordinate clauses as they appear in a sentence.

EXAMPLES:

Robert took the other road which was more scenic. (subordinate adjective clause)
When you are sure, let me know. (subordinate adverb clause)
Carly said that the linen was a gift from her mom. (subordinate noun clause)

EXERCISE • 11

Identify the following clauses as main or subordinate.

EXAMPLE:

when you pay attention   subordinate

1. since I last saw you ________
2. the blimp sailed into the sky ________
3. not that I can remember ________

4. if your hands are clean ______________
5. meet me at the bakery ______________
6. are you sick ______________
7. because of his bad breath, she fainted ______________
8. whenever you and Eugene are ready ______________
9. although this sentence is not complete ______________
10. name your price ______________

EXERCISE • 12

Follow the instructions for Exercise 11.

1. don't go ______________
2. unless you are convinced about it ______________
3. it's easy for you ______________
4. on my last visit, I saw it ______________
5. as we were arriving from Calgary ______________
6. that you lost ______________
7. before you burst ______________
8. when he dropped the cake ______________
9. the dress is too large ______________
10. it is clear now ______________

a. Adjective Clauses

Adjective clauses usually begin with a relative pronoun (*who, whose, whom, which, that*) and describe the noun or pronoun that precedes. Like an ordinary adjective, an adjective clause answers the question "What kind of"?

Remember, since a relative pronoun must be preceded by a noun or pronoun in order to introduce an adjective clause, it can never be the first word in a sentence.

EXAMPLES:

Michelle Wright is the Canadian country singer *who was on television last night.*

The birthday cake *that you ordered* is ready.

The woman *whose purse was found* is here now.

Note that sometimes an adjective clause divides a main clause. In general, when searching for clauses, look for the main clause last.

EXERCISE • 13

Underline the adjective clauses in the following sentences.

EXAMPLE:

This is the car <u>that I told you about</u>.

1. This is the tutor who is helping me with adjective clauses.
2. The antique chair that Stan ordered was delivered in a modern truck.
3. Have you ever read *College Business English* which is published by Prentice Hall?
4. Thelma, who is a surgical nurse, is always telling us funny stories from work.
5. Where is the meat in this mince pie that you ordered?
6. Buy some wine that everyone likes.
7. I would never date a man who flosses his teeth in a restaurant.
8. Where are the clothes that you wore this morning?
9. This perfume has a fragrance which is very pleasant.
10. Is this the cheese that you tried last night?

EXERCISE • 14

Follow the instructions for Exercise 13.

1. Linguini is the pasta that Norbert likes best.
2. Unfortunately, the apartment that is infested with cockroaches is mine.
3. I can't read the writing manual that you gave me.
4. This water has a colour which cannot be defined.
5. The individual whose dentures were lost is offering a reward.
6. Is this the computer disk that has the most storage space?
7. Joseph was able to listen to a broadcast that came from Korea on his short-wave radio.
8. Did you get the parts which you needed to repair the toaster oven?
9. You are the one who has always loved me most.
10. There are so many things that I still have to learn.

EXERCISE • 15

Write original sentences containing adjective clauses using the relative pronouns indicated. Underline the adjective clauses for your teacher.

EXAMPLE:

that
I want an order of chicken wings <u>that is extra hot</u>.

1. which
2. who
3. that
4. whom
5. whose
6. that
7. which
8. whom
9. who
10. whose

b. Adverb Clauses

Adverb clauses usually begin with a subordinating conjunction such as *because, if, provided that, since, when*. Like adverbs, they describe verbs, adjectives, and other adverbs, and give information about time, place, condition, and amount.

Here is a list of subordinating conjunctions that express these functions in a sentence.

time
when, before, while, since

place
where, wherever

condition
if, so, unless, provided that

manner
as, as if, as though

cause
because, as, since

purpose or result
in order that, so that, so … that

degree or comparison
than, as much as, as ... as, just as

Note that, in English, many words often have more than one function. A subordinating conjunction only begins a subordinate adverb or noun clause if it is immediately followed by a subject and verb.

EXAMPLES:

I have had a toothache *since* yesterday. (*Since* in this sentence is followed by a noun and is a preposition.)

Since you weren't coming, Ida cancelled the dinner reservations. (*Since* in this sentence is followed by a subject and verb and is a subordinating conjunction introducing a subordinate clause.)

Adverb clauses can occur anywhere in a sentence; however, an adverb clause that begins a sentence must be separated from the rest of the sentence by a comma.

EXAMPLES:

Because my breath was always bad, I received a bottle of mouthwash for my birthday.

They went to the autumn fair even though it was raining.

Miranda applied for a part-time job so that she could have some extra money for Christmas shopping.

EXERCISE • 16

Underline the adverb clauses in the following sentences.

EXAMPLE:

Cam was so tired that he fell asleep in class.

1. When it is two o'clock, we can leave.
2. If you pay, I will go out with you.
3. Karen washed the dishes while you were at the store.
4. How long has it been since you last looked in a mirror?
5. The supervisor treated her employees as if they were part of her own family.
6. When you finish this exercise, go to the next one.
7. Since you last visited, four homes have been sold on this street.
8. Orland acted as if he had just seen a ghost.

9. Before you start complaining, let me explain everything.
10. The students needed a break because they had been studying so hard.

EXERCISE • 17

Follow the instructions for Exercise 16.

1. We arrived at the cabin just as the thunderstorm began.
2. Alex was running as fast as he could just to keep up with the other joggers.
3. Ramon is acting that way because he is in love.
4. If you want some dessert, you have to eat all your spinach first.
5. How much did an ice cream cone cost when you were little?
6. The government will sponsor these students provided that they attend regularly.
7. Last night it snowed so much that most schools were closed the next day.
8. I'm going to call before she asks me again.
9. You need to hang it properly so that it won't wrinkle.
10. Don't be disappointed because this is the last sentence.

EXERCISE • 18

Write original sentences containing adverb clauses using the subordinating conjunctions indicated. Underline the adverb clauses for your teacher.

EXAMPLE:

as much as

Jordan enjoys lamb <u>as much as he enjoys beef</u>.

1. since
2. as if
3. so that
4. unless
5. when
6. provided that
7. although
8. while
9. before
10. just as

c. Noun Clauses

Noun clauses, like adjective and adverb clauses, contain a subject and a predicate and cannot stand alone as sentences. They are called noun clauses because they have the same function in a sentence as a noun; for this reason a noun clause can be the **subject of a verb,** the **subject complement,** the **object of a verb**, or the **object of a preposition.**

Noun clauses often begin with the following subordinating conjunctions.

how	where
that	which
what	who
whatever	whoever
when	why

Some of these words also begin adjective and adverb clauses. Don't worry; you won't be confused if you keep in mind the function of each kind of clause.

EXAMPLES:

His behaviour disturbed us. (The noun *behaviour* is the subject of the verb.)

How he behaved disturbed us. (The noun clause *how he behaved* is the subject of the verb.)

A vacation for Linda is a necessity. (The noun *necessity* is a subject complement.)

A vacation for Linda is what is necessary. (The noun clause *what is necessary* is a subject complement.)

I know the answer. (The noun *answer* is the object of the verb.)

I know what the answer is. (The noun clause *what the answer is* is the object of the verb.)

Sam will help you with your plan. (The noun *plan* is the object of the preposition *with*.)

Sam will help you with whatever you plan. (The noun clause *whatever you plan* is the object of the preposition *with*.)

EXERCISE • 19

Underline the noun clauses in the following sentences.

EXAMPLE:

Whatever he wants is fine with us.

1. Why you feel this way is a mystery to all of us.
2. Jibril said that you knew the answer.
3. His only fault is that he has really bad breath.
4. We will buy whichever computer you recommend.
5. That he had no money was no surprise.
6. I agree with how Troung responded to him.
7. One fact to keep in mind is that you should never give up.
8. Vanessa understood why he had to leave her.
9. Did anyone ask Claire what was moving in the soup?
10. The double chocolate cheesecake is what Norman wants for his birthday.

EXERCISE • 20

Follow the instructions for Exercise 19, but this time identify in the space provided if the noun clause is the subject of a verb, a subject complement, the object of a verb, or the object of a preposition.

EXAMPLE:

The rumour is that noun clauses are easy to understand. subject complement

1. Don't tell me how I look. ____________
2. What you need to do is eat more beans. ____________
3. The new cinema is around the corner from where you live. ____________
4. That she beat you at chess is a testament to her ability. ____________
5. There is a lot of sense in what Syed says. ____________
6. What a person can achieve under duress is amazing. ____________
7. A new husband is what Heather really wants for Christmas. ____________
8. What Sean did with the whipped cream cannot be mentioned in this sentence. ____________

9. George explained to me why you suffer from extreme body odour. _______________

10. Don't be discouraged by what you have just read. _______________

EXERCISE • 21

Write original sentences containing noun clauses using the words indicated. Underline the noun clauses for your teacher.

EXAMPLE:

that

That I admire you is no secret.

1. what
2. why
3. how
4. when
5. that
6. whatever
7. where
8. who
9. which
10. whoever

EXERCISE • 22

In the space provided, indicate whether the underlined clauses are main, adjective, adverb, or noun clauses.

EXAMPLE:

After you finish supper, let's go to the movies. adverb

1. Because the elevator is being repaired, we have to walk up to the seventh floor. _______________
2. I don't think you know what you are saying. _______________
3. The wallpaper that you put up in your family room is beautiful. _______________
4. The vanilla hazelnut coffee is delicious. _______________
5. Suzanne said that a car raced through the puddle and splashed her. _______________

6. These were the books that were left behind by the movers. ____________
7. Did you know that this sentence has one noun clause and one main clause? ____________
8. When Genet slept in this morning, she knew it was going to be a bad day. ____________
9. Please be sure to sign the form at the bottom before you take your copy. ____________
10. Even if Paul won the lottery, he wouldn't be happy. ____________

EXERCISE • 23

Follow the instructions for Exercise 22.

1. This is the teacher who can best help you to understand clauses. ____________
2. After her car accident, Judy viewed life differently. ____________
3. If you are what you eat, you are in big trouble. ____________
4. Why are those mice coming this way? ____________
5. Because you are an administrator, you have more pay and more pain. ____________
6. My sister thinks that music from the eighties should be called "oldies" music. ____________
7. When Zenate looked over her shoulder, the full moon was looking back. ____________
8. I just want a car that has four wheels. ____________
9. Juan is always nervous before he speaks in front of a large group. ____________
10. This is the movie that always makes Savita cry. ____________

EXERCISE • 24

Follow the instructions for Exercise 23.

1. When Linda gets on the dance floor, people give her a wide berth. ____________
2. Li-Fen, whose mother owns a pottery store downtown, is making some wine goblets for our wedding anniversary. ____________
3. Before you go into the pool, be sure to shower. ____________

4. You said that the answer is 116, but it's 611. ________
5. The manual which is supposed to tell me how to assemble the gas barbecue is missing. ________
6. Thu is interested in upgrading her English, but she also wants to learn about computers. ________
7. Marek, who is from Poland, is studying to be a dental technician. ________
8. The weather is perfect; let's go worm-picking. ________
9. The song that I sang from my heart was not supposed to make you laugh. ________
10. A job is what I really need. ________

EXERCISE • 25

Follow the instructions for Exercise 24.

1. Slow down, or you'll get hurt. ________
2. Since the rainstorm began this morning, there have been numerous road closures. ________
3. Being unemployed is depressing; you feel like sleeping until it's over. ________
4. Esmine said that she wanted a new coat; this is a goat. ________
5. This picture is scary; it can't really be you. ________
6. It's hard to disagree with what Iwona says about phobias. ________
7. Provided that the washing machine repair person is finished by noon, I'll be able to meet you for lunch. ________
8. The snake that we saw at the zoo this morning is more than four metres long. ________
9. Whatever carpet you choose is all right with me. ________
10. If you're not sure, don't do it. ________

EXERCISE • 26

Follow the instructions for Exercise 25.

1. What's the matter with my haircut? ________
2. Every time the driver in front of us lowered his window, he threw out some litter. ________

3. Celine worried me for a moment when she said that she had chicken fingers. ____________
4. All these words and songs and places are special for me because we shared them together. ____________
5. The fruit trees that you planted last spring have really grown. ____________
6. Glenna accidentally mixed some baby formula instead of creamer into her coffee. ____________
7. When the oven stopped working, we decided to finish baking the pizza on the barbecue. ____________
8. Willie was so tired that he went to bed without his supper. ____________
9. I prefer the oak furniture that has the light veneer. ____________
10. Nature was very special for the English poet William Wordsworth; he wrote many famous poems expressing his feelings about it. ____________

Item IV: Sentence Types

So far you have studied only the simple sentence and its variations. In this section you will examine compound sentences, complex sentences, and compound-complex sentences. Before you begin, have another look at the simple sentence.

1. The Simple Sentence

A **simple sentence** is a group of words that expresses a complete thought and contains a subject and a predicate. A simple sentence may contain a compound subject, a compound predicate, and one or more prepositional phrases.

Remember that a simple sentence can also be expressed by one word in a command.

EXAMPLES:

Stop! (The subject *you* is understood.)
These socks smell.
Tonya marinated and barbecued the flank steak.
The donkey, goats, and sheep were in the children's petting zoo.
Can Frank and Judy speak and write Filipino?

Try these exercises before moving on to compound sentences.

EXERCISE • 27

Write original simple sentences as indicated. Underline the main subjects once and the main predicates twice. Place parentheses around all prepositional phrases.

EXAMPLE:

compound subject

July and October are two (of my favourite months).

1. simple subject and predicate
2. compound predicate
3. compound subject and predicate
4. simple subject in interrogative sentence
5. simple subject and prepositional phrase
6. *here* and compound subject
7. simple subject and compound predicate
8. compound predicate in interrogative sentence
9. *there* and compound predicate
10. compound predicate and prepositional phrase

EXERCISE • 28

Follow the instructions for Exercise 27.

1. simple subject and compound predicate
2. imperative with simple predicate
3. simple subject and prepositional phrase
4. compound subject and simple predicate
5. compound subject and compound predicate
6. simple subject in interrogative sentence
7. compound predicate and prepositional phrase
8. *here* with simple subject
9. compound predicate in interrogative sentence
10. imperative with compound predicate

2. The Compound Sentence

A **compound sentence** contains two or more simple sentences (main clauses). You can use coordinating conjunctions and a variety of other words to join simple sentences or main clauses in a compound sentence.

a. **Coordinating** or **correlative conjunctions** can be used to join main clauses to form compound sentences. When coordinating conjunctions are used in this way, they must always be preceded by a comma.

, and	, for
, but	, yet
, or	, so
, nor	

EXAMPLES:

Wash your hands, *and* wash your feet.
You can buy the emerald ring, *but* it is very expensive.
The children had a large lunch, *yet* they were still hungry an hour later.

b. **Conjunctive adverbs** are joining adverbs. When they are placed between two main clauses, they must be preceded by a semicolon (;). In most cases they are followed by a comma.

; accordingly	; however,	; namely
; also	; incidentally	; nevertheless
; anyway	; indeed	; otherwise
; besides	; instead	; similarly
; consequently	; likewise	; still
; finally	; meanwhile	; then
; furthermore	; moreover	; therefore
; thus	; undoubtedly	

Note that *however* must *always* be followed by a comma when it is used as a conjunctive adverb.

EXAMPLES:

Francis asked for $10*; then* she suddenly asked for another $10.
They wanted to see the movie*; however,* the lineup was too long.
Bernice hated admitting that she was wrong*; nevertheless,* she apologized to her friend.

c. **Transitional phrases**, like conjunctive adverbs, must be preceded by a semicolon and are always followed by a comma when placed between two main clauses.

; after all,	; generally speaking,	; in the meantime,
; as a result,	; if not,	; in the second place,

; at any rate,	; in addition,	; on the contrary,
; at the same time,	; in fact,	; on the other hand,
; by the way,	; in my opinion,	; that is,
; for example,	; in other words,	; to tell the truth,

EXAMPLES:

Carmen needed this vacation; *in my opinion,* he should have taken it months ago.

Rachelle will eat anything; *to tell the truth,* I saw her eating a peanut butter and hot pepper frozen yogurt yesterday.

d. Main clauses in a compound sentence can also be separated by a semicolon alone. (See Unit 4, Item V for more information about the semicolon.)

EXAMPLES:

Buy a thesaurus; you're going to need it in this course.

My favourite radio station has a new morning person; she's great.

EXERCISE ♦ 29

Identify the following sentences as simple or compound.

EXAMPLE:

Take off your shoes, and sit here. <u>simple</u>

1. Have some chocolate mousse, but don't eat it all. ________________
2. Why is your credit card so warm? ________________
3. Cough; you'll feel better. ________________
4. You and Fred need some time alone. ________________
5. I have a fear of heights; however, I applied for the window cleaning job anyway. ________________
6. The tickets for the new musical were expensive; nevertheless, they were worth it. ________________
7. The moon is full; you need a shave. ________________
8. Gem walked down to the lake, dipped her foot in the water and walked back up to the cottage. ________________
9. The golfer swung at the ball and watched it fly into the seventh hole. ________________
10. Ice wine is very delicious; unfortunately, it is also very expensive. ________________

EXERCISE ◆ 30

Follow the instructions for Exercise 29.

1. Should I watch the hockey game, or should I wash the kitchen floor? __________
2. These batteries should have lasted longer. __________
3. First she laughed; then she cried; then she laughed again. __________
4. By the time the party was over, the sun had already risen. __________
5. These ruby earrings are beautiful. __________
6. Julio's taxes have gone up; unfortunately, his salary has not. __________
7. Maya accidentally spilled the beans. __________
8. Why did you buy an alarm clock with a two-hour snooze button? __________
9. Kiri kept repeating her story; she was really upset. __________
10. This leather jacket is very supple; yet, it is also very durable. __________

EXERCISE ◆ 31

Follow the instructions for Exercise 30.

1. I'm worried; my piano tuner used to be a drummer in a rock band. __________
2. The Iranian New Year coincides with the first day of spring. __________
3. You can never have too much chocolate in the house. __________
4. A second full moon in the same month is often called a "blue moon." __________
5. The moose dipped its head into the lake and pulled up some tender reeds. __________
6. Marco enjoys watching wrestling on television, but Sophie can't stand it. __________
7. Would you like a bagel, or would you prefer a fibre bun for breakfast? __________
8. This has to be a simple sentence. __________

9. I put the eggs away, but the milk is still in the bedroom. ______
10. It's true; I took all the jelly beans. ______

EXERCISE • 32

Follow the instructions for Exercise 31.

1. Don't eat that green bean; I saw it move. ______
2. What is the difference between a rock and a hard place? ______
3. The world's largest underground railway tunnel is more than 50 km long in Japan. ______
4. Not all the sentences will be as bad as this one. ______
5. Wish upon a star, and make one for me too. ______
6. This bestselling novel has a weak plot and poor writing, but it also has a great cover. ______
7. The pig and the cow wanted to play cards, but the donkey wanted to listen to old records. ______
8. Are the stories about earwigs really true? ______
9. I wanted a kiss; this is a fish. ______
10. Why do you like to play tiddly winks so much? ______

EXERCISE • 33

Follow the instructions for Exercise 32.

1. Doug would rather have a tooth pulled than study verbs. ______
2. Why are you making the bungee cord longer for me? ______
3. Cyril was going to pay the water bill on time; however, he was going to take a shower first. ______
4. A day on the planet Jupiter lasts 9 hours and 50 minutes. ______
5. Rush-hour traffic can be stressful; in the same way, so can Christmas shopping. ______
6. These are strange-tasting mushrooms. ______
7. Dilp was a little nervous; the Szechuan noodle dish was served with a fire extinguisher. ______

8. Mohammed painted our whole apartment for less than $300. ________________
9. You're wrong; Syed is a vegetarian not a veterinarian. ________________
10. Pat and Lois are thinking of buying a cottage with their lottery winnings. ________________

EXERCISE ◆ 34

Write ten compound sentences using the punctuation mark or word indicated.

EXAMPLE:

or

Jacques has to leave for work by 6 a.m., *or* he will be late.

1. and
2. for example
3. ;
4. for
5. in fact
6. anyway
7. however
8. but
9. on the other hand
10. therefore

EXERCISE ◆ 35

Follow the instructions for Exercise 34.

1. also
2. or
3. finally
4. in the meantime
5. so
6. incidentally
7. as a result
8. yet
9. to tell the truth
10. in addition

3. The Complex Sentence

A **complex sentence** contains one simple sentence (main clause) and one or more subordinate clauses. Usually the main clause completes the idea expressed by the subordinate clause (see Item III).

Remember that though a subordinate clause contains a subject and a predicate, it cannot stand alone as a sentence. For its meaning to be complete, a subordinate clause must be attached to one or more main clauses with a subordinating conjunction or relative pronoun.

EXAMPLES:

since I ordered the pizza (subordinate clause)
It has been an hour *since I ordered the pizza.* (complex sentence)

while you were shopping (subordinate clause)
While you were shopping, the parcel arrived. (complex sentence)

who needs a new coat (subordinate clause)
My sister is the one *who needs a new coat.* (complex sentence)

EXERCISE ◆ 36

Identify the following sentences as simple, compound, or complex.

EXAMPLE:

When you're finished with the paper, may I read it? complex

1. You could be taller if you stood up more for yourself. ____________
2. Fish bite more when the barometric pressure is low. ____________
3. Always look into your heart before you propose marriage. ____________
4. The green jacket is nice, but Mercedes really wanted the blue one. ____________
5. You know what I mean. ____________
6. Danuta spent a week in Greece and $1000 on souvenirs. ____________
7. Count on me; I'll be there. ____________
8. You should never scratch your head when the teacher is asking questions. ____________
9. Two of the credit cards have melted. ____________
10. Muktar didn't win the prize; nevertheless, he learned a lot from the experience. ____________

EXERCISE • 37

Follow the instructions for Exercise 36.

1. The St. Lawrence River is 1352 km long. __________
2. Drink your juice; then eat your cereal. __________
3. When I was your age, I had to walk 15 km to school barefoot in the winter. __________
4. As long as you can look forward to something, you will always have something on which to look back. __________
5. Don't cry; it's only an English test. __________
6. You act as if you have never met Cecil before. __________
7. While you barbecue, I'll set the table. __________
8. I knew that he wasn't telling the truth. __________
9. Stephanie will eat strawberry cheesecake, but she prefers chocolate. __________
10. I couldn't have installed the dishwasher without your help. __________

EXERCISE • 38

Follow the instructions for Exercise 37.

1. Even if it is a good investment, Nicholas doesn't have the money to invest in a used toupee store. __________
2. Because Greg hurt his leg, he had to walk with crutches. __________
3. Doesn't Ernie look different without his moustache? __________
4. When the students heard Young's speech, they couldn't stop laughing at her clever jokes. __________
5. If your blouse shrank after only one wash, return it. __________
6. The Canada geese which are flying over my house are returning from their summer vacation. __________
7. The professor is not familiar with some English idioms. __________
8. Are you familiar with the philosophy of Ed Moran? __________
9. A horse can be brought to water, but a pencil must always be lead. __________
10. James and Andrew are hiking tomorrow even if it rains. __________

EXERCISE ◆ 39

Write original complex sentences using the subordinating conjunction or relative pronoun indicated.

EXAMPLE:

that (relative pronoun)

The essay *that* you wrote on the Cree Indians was excellent.

1. which
2. why
3. although
4. when
5. in order that
6. who
7. because
8. whose
9. since
10. that (conjunction)

EXERCISE ◆ 40

Follow the instructions for Exercise 39.

1. how
2. before
3. where
4. whom
5. as if
6. which
7. unless
8. who
9. that (pronoun)
10. that (conjunction)

4. The Compound-Complex Sentence

A **compound-complex sentence** has elements of both a compound and a complex sentence. It contains two or more main clauses and at least one subordinate clause.

EXAMPLES:

The water ride at the amusement park had several steep drops, and we were really splashed when we went down them. (compound-complex sentence)

analysis

The water ride at the amusement park had several steep drops (main clause)
we were really splashed (main clause)
when we went down them (subordinate clause)

After the party is over, is Maya returning the lawn chairs, or is Adolpho looking after them? (compound-complex sentence)

analysis

After the party is over (subordinate clause)
is Maya returning the lawn chairs (main clause)
is Adolpho looking after them (main clause)

EXERCISE • 41

Identify the following sentences as simple, compound, complex, or compound-complex.

EXAMPLE:

You shouldn't scratch a mosquito bite; it won't help even though it feels better momentarily. compound-complex

1. That is a funny place for a phone number. ____________
2. Don't go on that ride unless you know where the washrooms are. ____________
3. Grind the tomatoes, and add the salt before you drain them. ____________
4. Bozena has a VCR that talks. ____________
5. I know the car that I want, but I just can't afford it right now. ____________
6. Don't worry; no problem is that great. ____________
7. When you finish painting your foyer, you can do the one in my house. ____________
8. Kiri is leaving Canada tomorrow; she's going to Mexico. ____________
9. You said that English class wasn't canceled. ____________
10. When Kaila said that her braces cost more than $5000, I was impressed. ____________

EXERCISE • 42

Follow the instructions for Exercise 41.

1. Sometimes Ravinder brings home some pastries from the bakery where he works nights. ____________
2. Fortunately, Khan discovered the flat tire when he stopped for gas on the freeway, and he was able to have it repaired before he continued his journey. ____________
3. Your joke about the chicken and the plumber was not very funny. ____________
4. This bed is so hard; it's like lying in a parking lot. ____________
5. Rhonda knew that she had dialed the wrong number when she reached New Zealand instead of Ottawa. ____________
6. I'm in trouble again; I've lost my keys. ____________
7. Try again. ____________
8. Of course it's my own hair; I paid for it. ____________
9. Keung deserves the job; to tell the truth, he is the most qualified. ____________
10. Your hearing is good, but you don't listen. ____________

EXERCISE • 43

Follow the instructions for Exercise 42.

1. Order the flowers when you're downtown; tomorrow is Rose's birthday. ____________
2. What kind of cheese is on this pizza that you ordered? ____________
3. The porcupine that was crossing the road made it safely to the other side. ____________
4. Take a moment, and look over my essay. ____________
5. The antibiotics that the doctor prescribed should be kept in the refrigerator. ____________
6. Are you drinking Scotch, rye, or tea? ____________
7. Before you devour that eclair, let me have a bite. ____________
8. There must be more cookies in the cupboard. ____________
9. These poems that are by T. S. Eliot are not easy to interpret. ____________
10. The cream has gone sour; don't use it in your coffee when you have breakfast. ____________

EXERCISE • 44

Complete the following phrases and clauses to make the sentence types indicated.

EXAMPLE:

complex
when the train finally arrives
I will be relieved when the train finally arrives.

1. *complex*
   even if you were rich
2. *compound*
   think carefully
3. *simple*
   in the morning for breakfast
4. *compound*
   it's possible that
5. *compound*
   the colour is right
6. *complex*
   provided that you study
7. *simple*
   chicken soup and fresh bread
8. *compound*
   the last apartment was
9. *compound-complex*
   of course it smells when you
10. *complex*
    before you go

EXERCISE • 45

Write sentence types as indicated.

EXAMPLE:

compound
The hockey game is tonight, and I have tickets to see it.

1. complex
2. simple
3. compound-complex

4. compound
5. simple
6. complex
7. compound-complex
8. simple
9. compound
10. compound-complex

Item V: Correcting Run-On Sentences

A **run-on sentence** is an error that occurs when two main clauses, each of which is a simple sentence, run into each other because of an incorrect punctuation mark or connector word. The most common type of run-on sentence results from a **comma splice**, in which two main clauses (simple sentences) are joined by a comma.

There are several ways in which run-on sentences can be corrected. Learn the following methods, and apply them to your writing.

a. Use a period to make two separate sentences from the clauses.

EXAMPLE:

This salsa is spicy, it burned my mouth. (incorrect — comma splice)
This salsa is spicy. *I*t burned my mouth. (correct)

b. Use a coordinating conjunction preceded by a comma to join main clauses.

EXAMPLE:

Sam saw the robbery she never told anyone. (incorrect)
Sam saw the robbery, *but* she never told anyone. (correct)

c. Use a semicolon (;) to separate sentences with related ideas.

EXAMPLE:

The lumberyard fire was terrible you could see the flames and smoke on the other side of town. (incorrect)
The lumberyard fire was terrible; you could see the flames and smoke on the other side of town. (correct)

d. Use a semicolon with a conjunctive adverb or transitional phrase. (See Item IV for a list of common conjunctive adverbs and transitional phrases.)

EXAMPLES:

It rained on the day of the garage sale, many persons came. (incorrect)

It rained on the day of the garage sale; *nevertheless*, many persons came. (corrected by using conjunctive adverb)

Madra likes red wine, she enjoys white wine as well. (incorrect)

Madra enjoys red wine; *on the other hand*, she enjoys white wine as well. (corrected by using transitional phrase)

e. Change one of the main clauses to a subordinate clause, and use a suitable joining word.

EXAMPLE:

Stephanie was really tired she had studied until four o'clock this morning. (incorrect)

Stephanie was really tired *because* she had studied until four o'clock this morning. (corrected by using subordinating conjunction)

It is important to keep in mind that run-on sentences can be corrected in a variety of ways. Always choose the correction that makes your writing clearer or more effective.

"There was an enormous pothole in the road. Unfortunately, I found out the hard way."

Here is a sentence that has been corrected using the methods you have just learned.

EXAMPLES:

Emma is a good friend she always has time to listen to my problems. (incorrect)

Emma is a good friend. She always has time to listen to my problems. (corrected by making two sentences)

Emma is a good friend, *for* she always has time to listen to my problems. (corrected by using a coordinating conjunction preceded by a comma)

Emma is a good friend; she always has time to listen to my problems. (corrected by using a semicolon)

Emma is a good friend; *furthermore,* she always has time to listen to my problems. (corrected by using a conjunctive adverb)

Emma is a good friend; *in fact,* she always has time to listen to my problems. (corrected by using a transitional phrase)

Emma is a good friend *because* she always has time to listen to my problems. (corrected by using a subordinate clause)

EXERCISE • 46

Use one of the methods you have learned to correct the following run-on sentences. Write "C" beside the sentence if it is correct.

EXAMPLE:

The blueberry pie is almost baked, you can have some this afternoon for a snack. (incorrect)

The blueberry pie is almost baked; you can have some this afternoon for a snack. (corrected)

1. Andrew and Patrick are not the same age, Patrick is almost two years older.
2. Baby toads are cute in fact they look like adult toads.
3. Ed never asks any questions he just signs the cheques.
4. Line dancing is a lot of fun but it has nothing to do with fishing.
5. Herman shouldn't have said anything; instead, he accidentally mentioned the surprise party to Gladys.
6. The college campus is downtown unfortunately, I live in the suburbs.
7. Some collective nouns for animals sound strange for instance, a group of starlings is called a "murmuration."
8. My dog thinks that she is a cat; instead of barking, she meows.
9. Where did you buy these chocolate-coated coffee beans and how much did they cost?

10. Every Christmas the same mysterious thing happens we open the boxes of ornaments and find that several are broken.

EXERCISE • 47

Follow the instructions for Exercise 46.

1. The moon doesn't always hit you in the eye like a big pizza pie when you fall in love it just feels like it.
2. Dinosaurs are very popular, my favourite is the stegosaurus.
3. The number 13 doesn't worry Joanne, undoubtedly, she doesn't have triskaidekaphobia.
4. Invest in a food bank the return is great.
5. We were temporarily lost in the woods even our guide couldn't find the trail at first.
6. The fortuneteller had bad news, and she had good news.
7. The good news was that I was going to win the lottery today, the bad news was that I wouldn't be able to buy a ticket.
8. Spending money is too easy and saving it is too hard.
9. You mixed up the cans, this tuna is for cats only.
10. The Bank of China is high after all, it has 72 storeys.

EXERCISE • 48

Follow the instructions for Exercise 47.

1. Miguel doesn't understand life, every time he gets some unexpected money, he also gets some unexpected bills.
2. Renata always wanted to fly in space, so she entered the astronaut program.
3. Bourbon is a whiskey but it's also the name of our cat.
4. Pyramids began appearing around 2700 B.C., now that's a long time ago.
5. It rains about three days a year in Málaga, Spain, but Salvatore tries not to complain.
6. Daria really enjoys horror films however, she never watches them alone.
7. The past tense of "burst" is "burst," and the past participle is "burst" too.
8. Jay wants to be a professional sprinter, to tell the truth, he's hoping to enter the Olympics.
9. MSG is a flavour enhancer for food not a skin treatment so don't rub it into your face any more.

10. Some people feel that Father's Day is unnecessary it was created to benefit merchants first and fathers second.

EXERCISE • 49

Follow the instructions for Exercise 48.

1. English is so confusing, "storm" and "worm" have very similar spelling but very different pronunciation.
2. In the light of the rising moon, Abram leaned over to kiss Adele unfortunately, he was so nervous that his arm slipped, and he rolled down the hill and landed in the lake.
3. No, this is not a simple sentence; it is a compound sentence, and it is punctuated correctly.
4. The last day of vacation can be depressing, it can give you a funny feeling in the pit of your stomach.
5. Gene's sunflower plant is enormous, I'm sure that it is more than three metres high.
6. When you get to Humber College, ask for the dean, she will answer all your questions.
7. Make the popcorn but try not to burn it this time.
8. The parents were beaming with delight at the graduation exercises, they were so proud of their children.
9. This rollercoaster makes four loops then repeats the ride in reverse.
10. This is my favourite house on the street, it is my house.

EXERCISE • 50

Follow the instructions for Exercise 49.

1. Eric Clapton is a very popular musician on the other hand, Van Morrison is no slouch.
2. Don't give this teacher an apple, he's so crabby he'll turn it into applesauce just by looking at it.
3. Everything happened at once, the phone rang, the doorbell sounded, and the toaster popped.
4. Casey embarrassed himself during the spelling competition unfortunately, he spelled embarrassed with only one *r*.
5. The movie *Cape Fear* with Robert De Niro is good but the original with Robert Mitchum is better.

6. Jorge eats his meals too quickly consequently he is always complaining that his stomach hurts.
7. The thing that makes a possession so precious is simple to understand it was touched by some person or memory that is special to you.
8. The road sign read "40 km to Timmins" thank goodness we're almost there.
9. Gina helped me with my French homework otherwise I wouldn't have been able to complete it.
10. Simon was exhausted from his swim across Lake Ontario at the same time, he was exhilarated that he had completed the crossing.

Item VI: Correcting Sentence Fragments

Sentence fragments are pieces or parts of whole sentences that require a subject and predicate to make them complete. A fragment error occurs when sentence fragments are punctuated as if they form a whole sentence and express a complete thought.

Here are some examples of sentence fragments and methods of correcting them.

1. Incomplete Sentences

Sometimes a group of words appears to have a subject and a verb and to make sense by itself, but the subject, verb, or both are incomplete or missing.

EXAMPLES:

The movie beginning in twenty minutes. (incomplete verb)
The movie *is beginning* in twenty minutes. (correct)

Lying about the stolen money. (incomplete verb, no subject)
Jon was lying about the stolen money. (correct)

2. Subordinate Clauses as Fragments

A subordinate clause has a subject and a verb but cannot stand alone as a sentence. (See Item III.) A subordinate clause usually begins with one of the following words.

EXAMPLES:

after	in order that	when
although	just as	whenever
as	provided that	where

as … as	since	wherever
as if	so	whether
as though	so that	which
because	so … that	whichever
before	that	while
even if	unless	who
how	until	whoever
if	what	why

Look at the following examples of subordinate clauses as sentence fragments, and note how they are corrected by joining them to the ideas expressed in main clauses.

EXAMPLES:

That you gave me for my birthday. (subordinate clause fragment)
This is the sweater that you gave me for my birthday. (correct)

As he said goodbye. (subordinate clause fragment)
As he said goodbye, *a tear trickled down his cheek.* (correct)

EXERCISE • 51

Some of the following are fragments. Use the skills you have learned to form complete sentences. Write "C" if the sentence is correct.

EXAMPLE:

Until the game is over. (fragment)
I'm not leaving until the game is over. (correct)

1. Telling me about her new car.

____

____

2. As if he didn't know.

____

____

3. Unless I forget.

____

____

4. Having received the money.

____

____

5. That's all right.

6. The plane landing in North Bay.

7. If there is time.

8. The mountains in the distance.

9. Javinder thought that he seeing things.

10. Attach part B first.

EXERCISE • 52

Follow the instructions for Exercise 51.

1. No amount of scrubbing clean that carpet stain.

2. So that you understand.

3. Being superstitious about black cats.

4. You will know soon.

5. The person reading this sentence very special.

6. Working too hard again.

7. Provided that you phone first.

8. Every time I hear her sing.

9. Why you were late.

10. Being compassionate, David's best characteristic.

EXERCISE • 53

Follow the instructions for Exercise 52.

1. Until you are sure.

2. I couldn't resist.

3. Wow! What a mess.

4. Although you are sad about it.

5. By the time spring is here.

6. That I did not want.

7. The temperature was still rising.

8. Even if you are my friend.

9. Sitting still for more than five minutes.

10. Whatever was ordered.

EXERCISE • 54

Follow the instructions for Exercise 53.

1. Since the train won't be here for another hour.

2. Reading your palm.

3. Just another ten minutes of sleep.

4. Not unless you know the answer.

5. The latest fad nothing to do with chickens.

6. Achieve your goals first.

7. Is easier than you think.

8. Growing your own vegetables.

9. That you are happy about the decision.

10. Sneaking into the house after midnight.

EXERCISE • 55

Follow the instructions for Exercise 54.

1. Jiri developing new techniques in his sculpting.

2. Burning my shoulders on the beach.

3. The teacher still confusing me.

4. Having bought an extra ticket for Jack.

5. When people tell you to take a vacation.

6. That you have given all of this to me.

7. The pressure to achieve high grades too great.

8. As though she expected the gift.

9. Listening to the thunder at the cottage.

10. Waiting for you is no trouble.

For more practice, try the following exercises, which contain both run-on and fragment errors.

EXERCISE • 56

Indicate whether the following sentences are run-ons, fragments, or correct. Make changes to the incorrect sentences. Remember that some sentences can be corrected in a variety of ways.

EXAMPLE:

Write a thank-you note, he'll appreciate it.
Write a thank-you note; he'll appreciate it. (correct) run-on

1. Let's wait a few minutes, it's still raining. ______

2. Feeling the way you do. ______

3. Have you ever read *Pillars of the Earth* by Ken Follett? ______________

____

____

4. You are right, I shouldn't have said that. ______________

____

____

5. Call me. When you're in town again. ______________

____

____

6. Some people don't like cabbage; it gives them stomach gas. ______________

____

____

7. Upgrading his English skills to study sports management. ______________

____

____

8. The play was excellent in fact, the cast received a standing ovation for more than five minutes. ______________

____

____

9. Because it's three days old. ______________

____

____

10. The word *typhoon* is derived from the Chinese *tai fung*. Which means "big wind." ______________

____

____

EXERCISE • 57

Follow the instructions for Exercise 56.

1. Yolanda and Paul are dating however, their parents are not happy about it. ______________

____

____

2. You could go to the post office first and then meet me at the bank. ________

____

____

3. Vyny really enjoys seafood in fact, he has shrimp, scallops, and squid at least three times a week. ________

____

____

4. Realizing that life is short. ________

____

____

5. Mija said that nothing could get her to ride. In a hot-air balloon. ________

____

____

6. Morley Callaghan, a Canadian novelist, wrote *The Loved and the Lost*, it was published in 1951. ________

____

____

7. Fishing from the cottage dock. ________

____

____

8. Many of us are developing a fear of poverty, it is called "peniaphobia." ________

____

____

9. After the concert in the park ended. ________

____

____

10. Dari wanted to be a pediatrician; unfortunately he was not encouraged to pursue his goal. ________

____

____

EXERCISE • 58

Follow the instructions for Exercise 57.

1. While the moon was rising over the rippling waters of the lake.

2. Confession is good for the heart.

3. You ate so much cake, my stomach hurt watching you.

5. Why do you play that song, you know I hate it.

6. Take responsibility for your own actions instead, you blame everyone but yourself.

7. The blueberry muffins that you just took out of the oven.

8. Andrew is grumpy. When he gets out of bed.

9. This can't be a CD, it's square.

10. Knowing the ending of the movie beforehand.

EXERCISE • 59

Follow the instructions for Exercise 58.

1. The wishing well must be broken, I wished for water, but there was none. ______

______

______

2. Determined to have the highest grade point average, Ashi even studied Friday nights. ______

______

______

3. If you have inner peace; material possessions mean nothing. ______

______

______

4. This sharkfin soup is really fresh to tell the truth, I'm sure I saw a shark swimming in it. ______

______

______

5. I was happy when Ying stole my heart but I was sad when she gave it back. ______

______

______

6. Canadian literature professor Douglas Spettigue. Wrote the short story "The Haying." ______

______

______

7. A piece of Barb's apple pie like a slice of heaven. ______

______

______

8. Don't buy the snails instead get some squid. ______

______

______

9. Verbal abuse can be very cruel in fact, it can hurt more than physical abuse. ______

______

______

10. When you were busy learning about life. Did you learn anything about yourself? __________

EXERCISE ♦ 60

Follow the instructions for Exercise 59.

1. Dimitri hurt his neck in fact, he had to wear a neck collar after watching the air show. __________
2. No one would dance with me so I went home early. __________
3. When the smoke finally cleared. __________
4. Don't sing any more all the plants have died. __________
5. Quitting your job out of frustration. __________
6. That was how it ended. __________
7. Having received the notification about the accident. __________
8. What is the freshness date on the cream cheese? __________
9. Daydreaming about the cottage vacation next summer. __________

10. While you were putting up another false front. ________________

____

____

EXERCISE • 61

Make the necessary changes to the following paragraph to correct run-on and fragment errors.

Gus was very shy and soft-spoken one day. A continuing education calendar came from the local community college and it advertised a new course entitled "Assertiveness Training — Do It for You." Gus was interested in the course. Because he was tired of being reticent, he decided to enroll. Even though he was very nervous.

There was a terrible storm the night of the first class in fact thunder and lightning filled the sky. The registration slip which Gus clutched in his hand was so soaked. That he could not make out the room number of his class. He thought that it was Room E-366 and he knocked on the door. Within minutes, a warm glow came to Gus's cheeks. The instructor was positive, and the course was rich and invigorating.

Of course, Gus had found the wrong room however he was determined to finish "Wine Tasting 101" no matter how much homework he would have to do.

Item VII: Sentence Combining

You are already familiar with the basic principles of sentence combining. Effective sentence combining involves an awareness of how to join ideas through coordination and subordination, and an understanding of the structure of the four basic sentence types and the methods for correcting run-on sentences and sentence fragments. Effective sentence combining also requires a knowledge of the words (conjunctions, conjunctive adverbs, transitional devices) that are needed to join subordinate clauses to main clauses and main clauses to other main clauses. This is the knowledge that allows you to add details, descriptions, and ideas to improve your writing.

In this section you will examine coordination and subordination in detail.

1. Coordination

When you join words, phrases, and main clauses, you are establishing a relationship of like values between two or more ideas — you are **coordinating** them. Use the following coordinating or correlative conjunctions to join words, phrases, and main clauses.

and	nor	so	as ... as	neither ... nor
but	for	both ... and	so ... as	
or	yet	either ... or	whether ... or	

a. To expand the ideas in your sentences, combine nouns, pronouns, verbs, adjectives, and adverbs.

EXAMPLES:

Gil paints the kitchen. Agnes paints the kitchen.
Agnes and Gil paint the kitchen. (nouns joined)

Andrea wrote the children's story. Andrea illustrated the children's story.
Andrea illustrated and wrote the children's story. (verbs joined)

Juan ate his burger quickly. Juan ate his burger noisily.
Juan ate his burger quickly and noisily. (adverbs joined)

Heather enjoys swimming in a pool. Heather enjoys swimming in a lake.
Heather enjoys swimming in a lake and in a pool. (phrases joined)

b. Joining main clauses (simple sentences) tells your reader to consider them as one. You may join ideas that show similarities or differences.

Remember that a comma must precede a coordinating conjunction joining main clauses. Also, remember that when you use a conjunctive adverb or transitional device, it must be preceded by a semicolon, and in most cases it must be followed by a comma. (See Item III.)

EXAMPLES:

Peter is trying to lose weight. Some days it is not easy.
Peter is trying to lose weight, *but* some days it is not easy. (coordinating conjunction)

Georgia was encouraged to apply for the office manager's position. She was not interested.
Georgia was encouraged to apply for the office manager's position; *however,* she was not interested. (conjunctive adverb)

Carmina's mother is looking after the children. She really enjoys looking after her grandchildren.
Carmina's mother is looking after the children*; to tell the truth,* she really enjoys looking after her grandchildren. (transitional device)

EXERCISE • 62

Use the device indicated to combine the following sentences.

EXAMPLE:

coordinating conjunction
Marvin is a wonderful singer. He is always nervous in front of a large group.
Marvin is a wonderful singer*, but* he is always nervous in front of a large group.

1. *coordinating conjunction*

   The hairstylist cut too much off the sides. The customer was very upset.

   ____

   ____

2. *conjunctive adverb*

   Margaret Atwood is a Canadian novelist. Irving Layton is a Canadian poet.

   ____

   ____

3. *transitional device*

   Sam recently lost her job. She is happy about it.

   ____

   ____

4. *correlative conjunction*

   Arron is on an extended vacation. He is very ill.

   ____

   ____

5. *conjunctive adverb*

   House prices are very low. It will still require a large down payment to buy one.

   ____

   ____

6. *conjunctive adverb*

   Jenny doesn't enjoy reading murder mysteries. She does enjoy seeing them as films.

   ____

   ____

7. *transitional device*

   Ola's brother has an interesting hobby. He repairs porcelain dolls.

   ____

   ____

8. *conjunctive adverb*

   Dan forgot to pay his traffic ticket. Two police officers came to remind him.

   ____

   ____

9. *coordinating conjunction*

   Barbara volunteers at a literacy centre in the afternoon. She reads to elderly patients at the hospital in the evening.

   ____

   ____

10. *coordinating conjunction*

   Harjit is fascinated by snakes. Nora is not.

   ____

   ____

EXERCISE • 63

Follow the instructions for Exercise 62.

1. *conjunctive adverb*

   Timo has been eager to become a Canadian citizen. His dream has come true.

   ____

   ____

2. *transitional device*

   Darren will not eat a soft-boiled egg. He can't stand the soft glop in it.

   ____

   ____

3. *coordinating conjunction*

Edna seems to be very outgoing. She is really quite shy.

____

____

4. *conjunctive adverb*

Memorizing a poem can be tough. Repeating each line can help.

____

____

5. *correlative conjunction*

Sidney cannot dance. He cannot carry a tune.

____

____

6. *coordinating conjunction*

Prunes are tasty. Their side-effects are open to interpretation.

____

____

7. *transitional phrase*

Helena was at the last night. Someone stole her car.

____

____

8. *conjunctive adverb*

Jay holds the door open for everyone. He is courteous to everyone.

____

____

9. *coordinating conjunction*

Lian took the expressway home. She reached home in 20 minutes.

____

____

10. *correlative conjunction*

Stop at the dry cleaners. Stop at the window cleaners.

____

____

EXERCISE • 64

Follow the instructions for Exercise 63.

1. *transitional device*

The greeting card was very touching. It made me feel better.

2. *coordinating conjunction*

The Tequila Sunrise is a nice drink. She prefers Margaritas.

3. *conjunctive adverb*

Lam worked until 2 in the morning. He is going to class at 8 a.m.

4. *transitional device*

I'll be back in three hours. Finish vacuuming the hallway.

5. *transitional device*

Lorne surprised everyone by dancing on the table. He is usually quiet and reserved.

6. *coordinating conjunction*

You pay for the tickets. I'll pay for the dinner.

7. *coordinating conjunction*

Mel didn't have supper again. He doesn't get paid until Thursday.

8. *conjunctive adverb*

The school trip to the zoo was canceled. We studied grammar.

9. *coordinating conjunction*

   The CNE is in Ontario. The PNE is in British Columbia.

   ____

   ____

10. *coordinating conjunction*

    This bagel is great. Some cream cheese would make it better.

    ____

    ____

EXERCISE • 65

Expand the following sentences using suitable joining devices and punctuation.

EXAMPLE:

The dog has a loud bark.

<u>The dog has a loud bark, but it doesn't bite.</u>

1. I can't wait for December.

   ____

   ____

2. Some of this spinach is bitter.

   ____

   ____

3. The cows mooed at the same time.

   ____

   ____

4. There was a power failure.

   ____

   ____

5. The odour was bad.

   ____

   ____

6. The bulbs were planted in autumn.

   ____

   ____

7. The water at the cottage was ice-cold.

8. Are these your buns?

9. The train has left already.

10. The dentist was smiling at me.

EXERCISE • 66

Follow the instructions for Exercise 65.

1. My dictionary has pages missing.

2. The late show started an hour late.

3. This falchion is very sharp.

4. Anya doesn't like beans.

5. Moira was caught in the rainstorm.

6. Don't wear that tie in public.

7. This bakery is very popular.

____

____

8. Wash the dishes!

____

____

9. Jacques' face was red.

____

____

10. Rub the magic lamp three times.

____

____

2. Subordination

Subordination, like coordination, joins ideas together. However, in **subordination** the related ideas are unequal. Because subordination involves complex and compound-complex sentences, the emphasis is placed on the main clause (the clause that expresses the main idea).

Some commonly used subordinating conjunctions are *as if, provided that, although,* and *whenever.* (See Addendum A, Item VI for a list of subordinating conjunctions.) Use these words to introduce a subordinate clause in a complex or compound-complex sentence and to join a main clause to a subordinate one.

EXAMPLES:

Belzac was startled from his sleep. The phone rang.
Belzac was startled from his sleep *when* the phone rang.

Betty was going to the James Taylor concert. She had to borrow the money.
Betty was going to the James Taylor concert *even if* she had to borrow the money.

Another method for joining main clauses to subordinate clauses is to use a relative pronoun (*who, whose, whom, which, that*).

EXAMPLES:

The rain fell hard last night. The road was washed out.
The rain *that* fell hard last night washed out the road.

John Candy was a well-known Canadian comedian. He was also a very good actor.

John Candy, *who* was a well-known Canadian comedian, was also a very good actor.

EXERCISE • 67

Use the technique of subordination to join the ideas in the following sentences. Use the subordinating conjunction or relative pronoun indicated.

EXAMPLE:

that
Portia bought a new car
It is red.
Portia bought a new car *that* is red.

1. *which*

Lanark is a small town in eastern Ontario.

It is famous for maple syrup.

____

____

2. *because*

Miron was not allowed to leave the restaurant.

He did not pay the bill.

____

____

3. *although*

Fred is ninety-four.

He jogs 5 km every day.

____

____

4. *whose*

Jill hates to cook.

Her father is a chef.

____

____

5. *that*
   The nuts are very expensive.
   Hanna bought two kilograms.

   ____

   ____

6. *while*
   The toilet backed up again.
   You were at the bank.

   ____

   ____

7. *in order that*
   In her heart, Felice repeated her proposal many times.
   She wanted it to be perfect.

   ____

   ____

8. *which*
   The troll has red hair.
   It has brought me only bad luck.

   ____

   ____

9. *after*
   He ate six burgers.
   He drank four large colas.

   ____

   ____

10. *even if*
    We all love you.
    You are a little weird.

    ____

    ____

EXERCISE • 68

Follow the instructions for Exercise 67.

1. *where*
   I like to travel.
   The people are friendly.

   ____

   ____

2. *who*

Stephen Leacock was a well-known Canadian humourist.
He was born in 1869, in England.

____

____

3. *before*

Read the instructions.
Light the barbecue.

____

____

4. *if*

The barometric pressure is low.
I'm sure it will rain soon.

____

____

5. *even though*

Herman was the centre of attention on the dance floor.
He has never had a single dance lesson.

____

____

6. *whom*

Alexandre Dumas was a French novelist.
I admire him very much.
He wrote *The Count of Monte Cristo.*

____

____

7. *as … as*

The black mamba snake is fast.
It can run 33 km/h.

____

____

8. *unless*

You will end it all.
Tie the bungee cord to your ankles first.

____

____

9. *whenever*
Gary sings at parties.
Everyone cries.

____

____

10. *so that*
Louise inherited a great deal of money.
She never has to work again.

____

____

EXERCISE • 69

Use the technique of coordination or subordination to join the following sentences.

EXAMPLES:

The cheese tastes good.
It smells bad.
The cheese tastes good; *however,* it smells bad.

1. The accordian band played rock and roll.
It was hot.

____

____

2. Lizzeth is very zealous.
She really enjoys life.

____

____

3. Vito forgot his wallet at home.
He was unable to buy his lunch at work.

____

____

4. Morocco is located on the northwest coast of Africa.
Arabic is the official language.

____

____

5. Aldo wakes early in the morning.
He goes to bed late.

____

____

6. Ferehiwot agreed to marry Julius.
   He had to get a job first.

   ____

   ____

7. Charles washed the car.
   Jenna washed the children.

   ____

   ____

8. Dim went to the movie with her brother.
   She didn't want to go.

   ____

   ____

9. The H. J. Heinz Company makes ketchup.
   It also makes 9Lives cat food.

   ____

   ____

10. It was October.
    The weather was cool.
    Leaves fell from the trees.

    ____

    ____

EXERCISE • 70

Follow the instructions for Exercise 69.

1. Alyson poured the coffee.
   She sneezed suddenly.
   She made fresh coffee.

   ____

   ____

2. The spider rushed up the wall.
   Monica rushed out of the room.

   ____

   ____

3. The surgery was completed.
   Mary Anne had a new nose.
   It looked like her mother's nose.

   ____

   ____

4. The passport office was very busy.
   More than two hundred people were in the room.

   ____

   ____

5. The bus was a half-hour late.
   It had had a flat tire.

   ____

   ____

6. Connie played the ring-toss game at the carnival.
   She spent $40.
   She won a large plush ostrich.

   ____

   ____

7. Patrick fell asleep in class.
   His head banged against his desk.
   He startled himself, the other students, and the teacher.

   ____

   ____

8. The peaches were ripe.
   Some had already fallen.
   The farmer began harvesting.

   ____

   ____

9. The heron walked stealthily in the shallow water.
   It quickly speared a small bass.

   ____

   ____

10. Perry is very ticklish.
    He laughs very easily.

    ____

    ____

EXERCISE • 71

Follow the instructions for Exercise 70.

1. The grass was greener on the other side of the fence.
   Wilbur climbed the fence.
   The grass was the same colour.

   ____

   ____

2. Wai Lin wanted to meet her sister at the airport.
   She needed to leave work early.

   ____

   ____

3. The Colossus of Rhodes is one of the Seven Wonders of the World.
   It is a bronze statue of the sun god Helios.
   It was built in the early days of 200 B.C.

   ____

   ____

4. There were fresh bear tracks on the hiking trail.
   We decided to cancel our hike.

   ____

   ____

5. The cap fell off the pepper sauce bottle.
   The stew was extra spicy now.
   We ate it anyway.

   ____

   ____

6. Joel needed to study for his math test.
   He forgot his review material at school.

   ____

   ____

7. The roses arrived at Yvette's house.
   She was happy to receive them.
   She was glad Carl remembered her birthday.

   ____

   ____

8. Gordon is not a plumber.
He fixed the shower.
He wrenched his elbow.

____

____

9. The first Liberal prime minister of Canada was Alexander Mackenzie.
He was the second prime minister of Canada.
He was prime minister from 1873 to 1878.

____

____

10. Trevor parked at the meter.
He didn't have any change.
He decided to take a chance.
He received a $20 parking ticket.

____

____

Item VIII: Correcting Misplaced and Dangling Modifiers

A **modifier** is an adjective, adverb, phrase, or clause that describes or alters the meaning of another word. When a modifier is not placed near the word it describes, the meaning of the sentence often becomes unclear. To clarify the meaning, place the modifier as close as possible to the word it describes or alters.

1. Misplaced Modifiers

a. Adverbs

Almost, even, hardly, just, merely, nearly, only, precisely, and *practically* are examples of adverbs that can easily be misplaced in a sentence.

EXAMPLES:

Sarah *nearly* lost all her money at bingo. (Unclear — the misplaced adverb, *nearly,* suggests that Sarah almost lost her money but probably lost none.)

Sarah lost *nearly* all her money at bingo. (Clear — *nearly* now clearly refers to the amount of money lost.)

Cynthia *only* needs two more CD's to complete her Lawrence Welk collection. (The misplaced adverb, *only,* suggests that Cynthia has no other need in life than to have these two CD's.)

Cynthia needs *only* two more CD's to complete her collection. (Placing the adverb *only* beside the word it describes clarifies what Cynthia needs.)

b. Phrases

Phrases must be placed as close as possible to the words they describe for the intended meaning of the sentence to be clear.

EXAMPLES:

Tien bought an alarm clock from the salesperson *with a large snooze button*. (misplaced phrase)

Tien bought an alarm clock *with a large snooze button* from the salesperson. (clear)

I could see many people browsing *from my window* at the garage sale. (misplaced phrase)

From my window I could see many people browsing at the garage sale. (clear)

c. Clauses

Clauses must be placed near the word(s) they modify.

EXAMPLES:

On the blackboard, the instructor, *which was hard to discern*, wrote down the homework assignment. (misplaced clause)

On the blackboard, the instructor wrote down the homework assignment *which was hard to discern*. (clear)

My aunt said that the diningroom table belonged to her mother *that has the sturdy, ornate legs*. (misplaced clause)

My aunt said that the diningroom table *that has the sturdy, ornate legs* belonged to her mother. (clear)

EXERCISE • 72

Some of the following sentences contain misplaced adverbs, phrases, and clauses. Make the necessary changes to correct them. If the sentence is correct, write "C" beside it.

EXAMPLE:

She gave the egg to her daughter *that was boiled*. (misplaced clause)

She gave the egg *that was boiled* to her daughter. (clear)

1. Vanessa almost baked a hundred cakes for the party.
2. At the zoo we saw a reptile in a cage that had coarse scales.

3. He only cheated on tests.
4. Jung bought a house through a real estate agent with a large verandah in the rear.
5. I could see the rainwater rushing down the drain from my window.
6. Andy volunteers often to help his friends move.
7. The instructor frequently told jokes to his students that were really silly.
8. Beven almost swallowed two golf balls when he was demonstrating that he could hold six in his mouth.
9. Myrna gave the silverware to the rabbi that she had just polished.
10. Joannie bought two plane tickets for France with great excitement.

EXERCISE ◆ 73

Follow the instructions for Exercise 72.

1. He nearly drank the whole bottle of prune juice.
2. Pam approached the office with a bad attitude.
3. Shirin wanted really to eat a greasy burger with fried onions.
4. David visited his sister in the hospital that had a broken leg.
5. John doesn't understand even me.
6. Lance took the pizza from the delivery person which was loaded with pepperoni.
7. They picked up the birthday cake at the mall that had fudge topping and yellow flowers.
8. The stolen VCR was found in the trunk of an abandoned car by the police.
9. You often need to brush your teeth.
10. Judy bought a new cereal at the grocery store that was vitamin-enriched.

EXERCISE ◆ 74

Follow the instructions for Exercise 73.

1. You almost made me lose all hope.
2. A piece of dirt flew into my eye that came from the construction site.
3. We bought the tarts from the baker with the custard filling.
4. Dan gave his old suit to his brother that was striped.
5. Colin liked frequently to stay out late.
6. Men only have one bad habit.
7. They had cake in the kitchen that was stale.
8. Young Shin wanted merely to express her opinion.

9. She gave the sandwich to Robert that was loaded with chili peppers.
10. In the warehouse I saw the fire in my shorts.

EXERCISE • 75

Make up sentences using the following words correctly.

EXAMPLE:

only

Claire needs *only* one more card to complete her collection.

1. nearly
2. almost
3. hardly
4. often
5. merely
6. practically
7. with red stripes
8. that was made of gold
9. which smells like fish
10. just

EXERCISE • 76

The following passage contains misplaced modifier errors. Make the necessary corrections.

Ken said no rarely to a challenge. When a friend dared him in an old graveyard for English teachers to spend an entire night, only he could say yes.

He put on his heavy jacket and stepped out into the cool night with a hood. As he reached the graveyard, he thought he saw something moving at the edge of town. He cried, "It's the ghost who taught me in college of my English teacher."

Ken decided almost to run away, but the spirit spoke to him.

"Help me! I am forced always to roam the cemetery because someone wrote my epitaph with a misplaced modifier." The spirit pointed to the gravestone that read:

Here lies Fred.
He's really dead.
He never thought only
That he would be so lonely
In his final bed.

2. Dangling Modifiers

Dangling modifiers are ones that have no clear word to describe or modify. In most cases, the remedy is to add a suitable word for the dangling modifier to describe or modify.

EXAMPLES:

While fishing, the canoe glided through the reeds. (Dangling modifying phrase — did the *canoe* fish?)

While fishing, Glen glided the canoe through the reeds. (Clear — the subject *Glen* is added for the phrase to modify.)
OR
While Glen was fishing, he glided the canoe through the reeds. (Clear — the dangling phrase is changed into a subordinate clause.)

After looking at the map, it was still difficult to know where to turn. (Dangling modifying phrase — did *it* look at the map?)

After looking at the map, we still found it difficult to know where to turn. (Clear — the subject *we* is added for the phrase to modify.)
OR
After we looked at the map, we still found it difficult to know where to turn. (Clear — the dangling phrase is changed into a subordinate clause.)

To understand dangling modifiers better, listening to the teacher helps. (Dangling modifying phrase — who should be *listening*?)

To understand dangling modifiers better, you should listen to the teacher. (Clear — the subject *you* is added for the phrase to modify.)

Remember that to correct a dangling modifier you must insert an appropriate noun or pronoun for the modifier to describe. Two effective methods of correcting dangling modifiers have been demonstrated in the examples above:

1. Add an appropriate subject for the dangling modifier to describe.
2. Change the dangling modifier to a subordinate clause.

Here is another example showing how both methods are used.

EXAMPLE:

While baking the cake, the barking dog startled me. (dangling modifying phrase)

While baking the cake, I was startled by the barking dog. (corrected by adding subject *I*)

While I was baking the cake, I was startled by the barking dog. (corrected by changing dangling modifier to a subordinate clause)

EXERCISE • 77

Some of the following sentences contain dangling modifiers. Make the necessary changes to correct them. If a sentence is correct, write "C" beside it.

EXAMPLE:

Returning the library book, the bicycle had a flat tire. (dangling modifier)
While I was returning the library book, the bicycle had a flat tire. (clear)

1. After hearing the English assignment, it was hard to smile.
2. While drinking the wine, the parrot started talking.
3. Having found a cockroach in my cupboard, it made me sick.
4. To be a good dancer practising every day is required.
5. After eating ten bags of potato chips, my stomach hurt.
6. Excited about the trip, the maps were brought out.
7. While spitting out the watermelon seeds, several landed on the floor.
8. After milking the cow, it mooed, "Ah, that's better."
9. While I was daydreaming about winning the lottery, the radio announced my numbers.
10. To improve English grammar, a good usage text can help.

EXERCISE • 78

Follow the instructions for Exercise 77.

1. Since listening to you, trouble has become my friend.
2. Overburdened with debts already, another bill came.
3. While swimming at the lake, it began to rain.
4. Having announced the winner, the prize was handed out.
5. Daydreaming in class, the question was not heard.
6. When dining alone, a magazine can be a good companion.
7. While painting the fence, the sprinkler came on.
8. Sneaking into the house at 2 a.m., each stair creaked more than usual.
9. While baking bread, the oven stopped working.
10. Watching the late show, the commercials were amazing.

EXERCISE • 79

Follow the instructions for Exercise 78.

1. We saw the horses driving down the country road.
2. Having finished dessert, the coffee was served.
3. After complaining about all the rain, it snowed.
4. Going to the bathroom in the middle of the night, the bed creaked.
5. While visiting Poland, her second cousin was seen for the first time.
6. While we were waiting in line to ride the rollercoaster, someone fainted.
7. Buttering the toast, the cat meowed loudly.
8. After considering all the options, it was still difficult to make a decision.
9. To find happiness, it is necessary to look for it.
10. While looking out the window, the geese flew by.

EXERCISE • 80

Using two methods for each sentence, correct the dangling modifiers in the following sentences.

EXAMPLE:

While waiting in line at the bank, a robbery took place. (dangling modifier)
While I was waiting in line at the bank, a robbery took place.
OR
While waiting in line at the bank, I witnessed a robbery.

1. Rinsing with the mouthwash, the spider crawled out of the drain.
2. Having loaded the trunk, the vacation began.
3. Confused by the teacher, the lesson was difficult.
4. While visiting Fred, the dog became sick.
5. Watching the sunset, the sky was filled with beautiful colours.
6. After buying the cream, it was sour.
7. Having read the book, the movie was disappointing.
8. After consolidating all the debts, the payments were small.
9. While driving to work, the muffler fell off the car.
10. After entering the haunted house, the ghost appeared.

EXERCISE • 81

Follow the instructions for Exercise 80.

1. While dreaming about you, my heart pounded.
2. Having bowled all night, a rest was needed.
3. Having set the table, it was time to eat.
4. After reading this book, my outlook on life changed completely.
5. While putting peanut butter on the sandwich, the bread tore.
6. After finishing the report, it was necessary to get up and stretch.
7. Having cut the grass, it was time for a cold drink.
8. While thinking about the meaning of life, the baby started to cry.
9. After eating the bratwurst, the beer was refreshing.
10. Having cleaned the garage, there was now room for the car.

Item IX: Correcting Faulty Parallel Structure

Parallel structure, or **parallelism**, is the expression of similar ideas in similar grammatical constructions. Parallel structure gives clarity, balance, and flow to your writing.

Under each of the guidelines given below, study the examples of faulty parallel structure and how they have been corrected.

a. Words in a series should have the same construction.

EXAMPLES:

Erica *writes, records,* and *likes to perform her own music.* (faulty parallel structure)

Erica *writes, records,* and *performs* her own music. (correct)
OR
Erica likes *to write, to record,* and *to perform* her own music. (correct)

Shelly wants to be *an astronaut, a sailor,* or *care for animals.* (faulty parallelism)

Shelly wants to be *an astronaut, a sailor,* or *a veterinarian.* (correct)
OR
Shelly wants to *fly in space, sail on the water,* or *care for animals.* (correct)

b. Use the same construction on both sides of a coordinating conjunction (*and, but, or, nor, for*).

EXAMPLES:

Shoria's visit to Nova Scotia was wonderful and which she will never forget. (faulty parallel structure)
Shoria's visit to Nova Scotia was wonderful, and she will never forget it. (correct)

The monkeys at the zoo were silly and while we were there we saw the enormous elephants. (faulty parallelism)
The monkeys at the zoo were silly, and the elephants were enormous. (correct)

c. Use the same construction with both parts of a correlative conjunction (either ... or, neither ... nor).

EXAMPLES:

I am going either to break up with David, or I will marry him. (faulty parallel structure)
I am going either to break up with David or to marry him. (correct)

Domenic neither likes buying store-made pasta, nor does he like eating it. (faulty parallel structure)
Domenic likes neither buying store-made pasta nor eating it. (correct)

EXERCISE • 82

Some of the following sentences contain faulty parallel structure. Make the necessary corrections. If the sentence is correct, write "C" beside it.

EXAMPLE:

Jack likes backgammon, chess, and to play checkers. (faulty parallel structure)
Jack likes backgammon, chess, and checkers. (correct)

1. Katrina is self-determined, well educated, and she is self-centred.
2. Boris's new shoes are comfortable, soft, and they are expensive.
3. We neither ordered Greek food nor Chinese food.
4. Dino shouted at the football game with enthusiasm and loudly.
5. We could help you decorate the room, blow up balloons, and have the presents wrapped.
6. Claire likes to have blueberry muffins, chocolate doughnuts, or tarts for breakfast.

7. The rock climbers were hungry, tired, and had sores.
8. Steven is either a genius, or he is an idiot.
9. Last summer we visited Saskatchewan and went to see Fort Carlton.
10. Never underestimate the negative effects of gossip or the negative character of the gossiper.

EXERCISE ♦ 83

Follow the instructions for Exercise 82.

1. Either Jerry will sell his camera through the want ads or privately.
2. Fortina is going to visit Spain, study Spanish, and learn how to dance the lambada.
3. By getting a good night's sleep and because he eats a good breakfast, Fred is ready for Monday mornings.
4. You can be sure that Waldemar's home-made sausages are fresh, spicy, and full of juice.
5. Helen neither jogs nor will she walk to work.
6. Marco is a tireless volunteer and who is generous with his donations.
7. Traveling to Lake Superior and to touch its water was a thrill for Julie Ann.
8. We saw the blue jays at the feeder, and we saw them eating.
9. Teresa is a good friend and who listens to me.
10. To be happy, you need good health, enough money, and breath that is fresh.

EXERCISE ♦ 84

Follow the instructions for Exercise 83.

1. The rock band was raucous but who were entertaining.
2. Stephanie does not like going to the dentist nor working.
3. The smell from the kitchen made our eyes burn, and it hurt our throats.
4. Margaret Laurence wrote many Canadian novels and who portrayed complex characters in them.
5. She wired an extra electrical outlet, installed a new dishwasher, and she attached an electric fan.
6. Daniella lives in London, Ontario and who has become a Canadian citizen.
7. Bring the raspberries and strawberries and the bushels of snow peas into the house.
8. Unfortunately, neither was Fred very handsome nor too ugly.

9. Donald was either going to quit smoking or who was going to die trying.
10. Marcelina enjoys eating barbecued ribs, baked potatoes, and she also likes fresh vegetables.

EXERCISE • 85

Follow the instructions for Exercise 84.

1. Laurie came back from vacation with a new attitude, and she was eager to work.
2. Keith not only repaired the electric mixer but also the gas dryer.
3. By checking his compositions for spelling mistakes and because he looks out for run-on sentence errors, Bart always hands in excellent papers.
4. The doctor said Sid should either lose 20 kg or that he should buy larger clothes.
5. It's time to dig up the garden and plant new bulbs.
6. Bruce was convinced that Quebec is the largest province in Canada and with the largest population.
7. This evening dress is elegant, alluring, and costs a fortune.
8. She wanted her children to grow up with good health, with a good education, and that they have inner peace.
9. Either this sentence has a fault in parallel structure, or it is correct.
10. Emma is always worried about what her fortuneteller is going to predict and that she will charge too much.

EXERCISE • 86

Follow the instructions for Exercise 85.

1. My boss treats his employees with attention, consideration, and he is always patient with them.
2. Milk the cow; feed the chickens, and then clean the barn.
3. Yvette neither knows the names nor how old the children are.
4. Skipping stones, collecting shells, and to build sand castles are fun things to do on the beach.
5. Werner baked the bread, sliced the bread, and he put butter on it.
6. This pasta sauce is rich, spicy, and it is hot.
7. Neither the mystery novel nor the movie frightened Iwona.
8. These socks need washing, deodorizing, and they need to be bleached.

9. How rich he was, how much money he made, and his age were what his admirers wanted to know.

10. I need to be more like Mike who is compassionate, generous, and he is unselfish.

Item X: Correcting Shifts in Tense

It is important to be consistent in your use of tense in sentences. For instance, if you begin a sentence in the present tense, use the present tense for the remainder of the sentence (assuming the time frame being referred to is the same). Make no changes in tense unless there is a special reason. Following this simple rule will make your sentences more understandable.

EXAMPLES:

Martine *is buying* a new winter coat and *paid* cash for it. (Incorrect—there is a shift from **present progressive tense** to the simple past.)

Martine *is buying* a new winter coat and *is paying* cash for it. (Correct — both verbs are present progressive.)

OR

Martine *bought* a new winter coat and *paid* cash for it. (Correct — both verbs are **simple past tense**.)

The dog *barked* and *runs* after the car. (Incorrect shift from simple past to **simple present tense**.)

The dog *barked* and *ran* after the car. (Correct — both verbs are simple past tense.)

OR

The dog *barks* and *runs* after the car. (Correct — both verbs are simple present tense.)

EXERCISE • 87

Some of the following sentences contain incorrect shifts in tense. Make the necessary corrections. If the sentence is correct, write "C" beside it.

EXAMPLE:

Kich stayed up late and then wakes up late in the morning. (incorrect shift in tense)

Kich stayed up late and then woke up late in the morning. (correct)

1. Sara was biting into her burger when she sees one of her French fries move across the plate.

2. After Mario told the joke, no one laughs.
3. Jill turns her wheelchair around the corner and reached her class just in time.
4. The red-tailed hawk flew across the highway and rests on a hydro pole.
5. Carol studied so hard for the math test, but unfortunately, she fails it badly.
6. The old cat is resting on the verandah stairs and purrs.
7. Ellen read *The Cashier* by Gabrielle Roy and really enjoys it.
8. Wendell walked through the woods and is taking pictures.
9. She says she loves me but never showed it.
10. Winston bought a new leather belt, but it didn't fit properly.

EXERCISE • 88

Follow the instructions for Exercise 87.

1. Hector is happy when he sings in the shower; unfortunately, everyone else was unhappy when he does.
2. Once Alma made up her mind, she is determined to succeed.
3. Eun and Byeong need your help, but they were too embarrassed to ask.
4. The plane lifted into the sky just as the sun sets.
5. Tran met the woman of his dreams and asks her out.
6. It is hard to find a well-paying job that was suitable for someone like me.
7. I was so surprised that my brother comes from Europe to visit me.
8. The smell of coffee perking makes Philip feel good, but the smell of burning milk made him feel sick.
9. Inge put her glasses on the bed and then accidentally sat on them.
10. The whole class had a headache after the teacher explains "shift in tense."

EXERCISE • 89

Follow the instructions for Exercise 88.

1. Yolanta enjoyed the smoked salmon that she buys at the market.
2. The cyclist raced down the road, ran through the red light, and bumps into a police car.
3. Idalina left the house, but she couldn't remember if she turned the stove off.
4. They checked into the Holiday Inn in Ottawa and stays three days.
5. The snow fell very heavily and lasts until the next day.

6. Ursula is operating a small doughnut shop and was working long hours.
7. Print your first name first; then writes your last name next.
8. Roland was admiring his new Porsche when a motorcycle crashes into it.
9. The music was too loud, but the food is good at Fiona's party last night.
10. Those are the best cabbage rolls I have ever tasted.

EXERCISE • 90

Follow the instructions for Exercise 89.

1. During his wedding ceremony, Alex was so nervous he accidentally says "I don't know" instead of "I do."
2. It was sad to see that the geese is flying south already.
3. Mark wants to apply for a teaching position in Hong Kong, but his wife didn't want to leave Canada.
4. The shoes that Hilary bought at the discount mall were very expensive.
5. You need someone who was more like you.
6. We saw the diver enter the aquarium at the zoo and feeds the fish.
7. The Toronto radio station CFRB 1010 states that it had news every 30 minutes.
8. David is always meeting people who were absolutely no good for him.
9. You are doing work that you are not expected to do.
10. Melissa was so angry she pours the maple syrup over her boyfriend's head.

EXERCISE • 91

Follow the instructions for Exercise 90.

1. The two gunshots that were heard turns out to be two flat tires.
2. Kim's nose became so itchy she sneezes loudly several times.
3. John shouldn't wear that shirt; it looked as if he slept in it.
4. The big bad wolf huffed and puffed, and the three little pigs shiver in fear.
5. I want to see the air show and watches the biplanes.
6. After the test was over, Francis goes straight home to study some more.
7. Cynthia tasted the hot soup and burns her tongue.
8. Arnold is eating the raw meat; fortunately, he was a dog.
9. Susan embroidered the shirt and shows it to her sister.
10. Grazyna tried on the dress yesterday, and it fits perfectly.

UNIT • 2 • POST-TEST

If you have completed Unit 2 satisfactorily, you are ready for the Post-Test. The answers immediately follow the test.

Part A

Underline the main subject once and the main predicate twice in the following sentences.

1. Here is the first sentence.
2. Be more considerate.
3. One of your poems has been accepted for publication.
4. When you see Julian, say hello for me.
5. It was hot at the beach yesterday; all of us were sunburned.
6. Are you waiting for me or Sam?
7. Helen knows the ending of the mystery novel even though she hasn't finished reading it yet.
8. If you mail the parcel today, it should reach me by the end of the week.
9. Every piece of furniture in Chan's apartment is second-hand.
10. What are you doing now?

Part B

Write sentence types as indicated in the space provided.

1. simple

 ____

 ____

2. complex

 ____

 ____

3. compound-complex

 ____

 ____

4. simple (with two main predicates)

 ____

 ____

5. compound

____

____

Part C

The following sentences may contain run-on and fragment errors. Make the necessary corrections where required. If the sentence is correct, write "C" beside it.

1. Baseball is my favourite sport, I never miss a game.

2. We were going to stop in Kingston, Ontario instead, we drove all the way to Montreal, Quebec.

3. The car left idling in the garage too long.

4. Send me your short story. Even if it is a rough draft.

5. Playing squash looks easy, but I'm not so sure.

6. If you could help me. I would appreciate it.

7. The wallpaper in your kitchen looks great, it must have been expensive.

8. Not everything Jill says about me is true but most of it is.

9. Since you missed the last train. You can sleep here on the sofa bed.

10. Who is James Last, and where from?

Part D

Combine the following sentences using coordination or subordination.

1. The pileated woodpecker lives in mixed-forest regions.
   It is solid black with a red-and-white head.
   It is about 38 cm in length.

2. The party started at 8 p.m.
   It was a surprise party for Doug.
   The big surprise was that Doug never showed up.

3. T. S. Eliot is a very famous poet.
   He is a very famous playwright.
   He won the Nobel Prize for Literature in 1948.

4. Many wildflowers blossom in autumn.
   They are considered to be weeds.
   Several common ones are the common milkweed and the hoary vervain.

5. Mary Anne drove to Minneapolis, Minnesota from Toronto.
   The drive took two days.
   She stopped the first night in Gurney, Illinois.
   She arrived in the afternoon of the second day.

Part E

The following sentences contain misplaced or dangling modifiers, errors in parallel structure, and wrong shifts in tense. Make the necessary corrections where required.

1. We received the wall clock from Cindy with the big hands.

2. Whenever Gil speaks, his voice was so loud.

3. Having poured the coffee, the mouse jumped off the counter.

4. I neither like oatmeal nor bran for breakfast.

5. Finish the composition tonight, and hands it in tomorrow.

6. After tasting all the samples, it was difficult to choose one.

7. First Gene stained the chair; then he paints it.

8. Sadie asked the bookseller with a strong plot to recommend a horror novel.

9. Andrew raked the leaves, cut the grass, and he trimmed the bushes.

10. They were so hot that they ran to lake and jump in with their clothes on.

ANSWERS • TO • UNIT • 2 • POST-TEST

Part A

Underline the main subject once and the main predicate twice in the following sentences.

1. Here is the first sentence.
2. Be more considerate. (subject you understood)
3. One of your poems has been accepted for publication.
4. When you see Julian, say hello for me. (subject you of verb say understood)
5. It was hot at the beach yesterday; all of us were sunburned.
6. Are you waiting for me or Sam?
7. Helen knows the ending of the mystery novel even though she hasn't finished reading it yet.
8. If you mail the parcel today, it should reach me by the end of the week.
9. Every piece of furniture in Chan's apartment is second-hand.
10. What are you doing now?

Part B

Write sentence types as indicated in the space provided. (Answers will vary.)

Part C

The following sentences may contain run-on and fragment errors. Make the necessary corrections where required. If the sentence is correct, write "C" beside it. (Answers may vary.)

1. Baseball is my favourite sport; I never miss a game.
2. We were going to stop in Kingston, Ontario; instead, we drove all the way to Montreal, Quebec.
3. The car was left idling in the garage too long.
4. Send me your short story even if it is a rough draft.
5. C
6. If you could help me, I would appreciate it.
7. The wallpaper in your kitchen looks great; it must have been expensive.
8. Not everything Jill says about me is true, but most of it is.
9. Since you missed the last train, you can sleep here on the sofa bed.
10. Who is James Last, and where is he from?

Part D

Combine the following sentences using coordination or subordination. (Answers may vary.)

1. The pileated woodpecker, which lives in mixed-forest regions, is solid black with a red-and-white head and is about 38 cm in length.
2. The surprise party for Doug started at 8 p.m., but the big surprise was that Doug never showed up.
3. T. S. Eliot, a very famous poet and playwright, won the Nobel Prize for Literature in 1948.
4. Many wildflowers which are considered to be weeds, such as the common milkweed and the hoary vervain, blossom in autumn.
5. When Mary Anne drove to Minneapolis, Minnesota from Toronto in two days, she stopped the first night in Gurney, Illinois and arrived in the afternoon of the second day.

Part E

The following sentences contain misplaced or dangling modifiers, errors in parallel structure, and wrong shifts in tense. Make the necessary corrections where required. (Answers may vary.)

1. We received the wall clock with the big hands from Cindy.
2. Whenever Gil speaks, his voice is so loud.
3. Having poured the coffee, I saw the mouse jump off the counter.
4. I like neither oatmeal nor bran for breakfast.
5. Finish the composition tonight, and hand it in tomorrow.
6. After tasting all the samples, we found it difficult to choose one.
7. First Gene stained the chair; then he painted it.
8. Sadie asked the bookseller to recommend a horror novel with a strong plot.
9. Andrew raked the leaves, cut the grass, and trimmed the bushes.
10. They were so hot that they ran to lake and jumped in with their clothes on.

U·N·I·T 3

SENTENCE AGREEMENT

Agreement refers to the relationship of some words within a sentence to other words that follow. In Unit 3 you will examine the agreement of subjects with verbs, pronouns with their antecedents, and pronouns with each other.

UNIT·3·PRE-TEST

This Pre-Test will measure your knowledge of the material covered in this Unit 3. The answers immediately follow the test.

I. Underline the correct verb in parentheses in the following sentences.

1. Edna or Charisse (is, are) coming to the party.
2. A number of cars (was, were) involved in the accident.
3. Each of the musical instruments (contribute, contributes) to the harmony of the arrangement.
4. Two weeks of summer vacation (go, goes) too quickly.
5. Sally, together with Paul and Patrick, (is, are) going to the basketball game.

II. Underline the correct pronoun in the parentheses.

1. Neither Irwin nor Jim likes (his, their) new coach.
2. Everyone has (her/his, their) team jacket.
3. The students and staff are having (his/her, their) year-end picnic in the city park.

4. Alice or Carol is bringing (her, their) special dessert.
5. The kitchen staff have donated (her, their) time to the food drive.

III. The following sentences contain errors in pronoun form. Underline the mistake and make corrections in the space provided.

1. The next contestant will be her. ______________
2. Do you remember we students from high school? ______________
3. I wish I were as clever as him. ______________
4. Yen Tao and him are good friends. ______________
5. Tell Henry and she what you think. ______________

IV. Correct the errors in pronoun usage in the following sentences.

1. A person should know when they should be discreet.

   ____

   ____

2. She told her mother that her eyes were bloodshot.

   ____

   ____

3. Tonya heard the new CD in the record store and wanted it.

   ____

   ____

4. One can pass any test if they study hard enough.

   ____

   ____

5. Gary told his brother that the phone was for him.

   ____

   ____

ANSWERS • TO • UNIT • 3 • PRE-TEST

I. Underline the correct verb in parentheses in the following sentences.

1. Edna or Charisse (<u>is</u>, are) coming to the party.
2. A number of cars (was, <u>were</u>) involved in the accident.
3. Each of the musical instruments (contibute, <u>contributes</u>) to the harmony of the arrangement.

4. Two weeks of summer vacation (go, goes) too quickly.
5. Sally, together with Paul and Patrick, (is, are) going to the basketball game.

II. Underline the correct pronoun in the parentheses.

1. Neither Irwin nor Jim likes (his, their) new coach.
2. Everyone has (her/his, their) team jacket.
3. The students and staff are having (his/her, their) year-end picnic in the city park.
4. Alice or Carol is bringing (her, their) special dessert.
5. The kitchen staff have donated (her, their) time to the food drive.

III. The following sentences contain errors in pronoun form. Underline the mistake and make corrections in the space provided.

1.	The next contestant will be her.	she
2.	Do you remember we students from high school?	us
3.	I wish I were as clever as him.	he
4.	Yen Tao and him are good friends.	he
5.	Tell Henry and she what you think.	her

IV. Correct the errors in pronoun usage in the following sentences.

1. A person should know when she/he should be discreet.
2. She said to her mother, "Your eyes are bloodshot."

   OR

   She said to her mother, "My eyes are bloodshot."
3. Tonya heard the new CD in the record store and wanted the compact disc.
4. One can pass any test if he/she studies hard enough.
5. Gary said to his brother, "The phone is for you."

   OR

   Gary said to his brother, "The phone is for me."

Item I: Subject-Verb Agreement

The principle of **subject-verb agreement** is simple. With singular subjects (one), use the singular forms of verbs. With plural subjects (more than one), use the plural forms of verbs.

EXAMPLES:

The *monkey is* happy. (singular subject, singular verb)
These *dishes are* still dirty. (plural subject, plural verb)

In some sentences, however, it may be difficult to determine the correct subject and verb agreement. Avoid common subject-verb agreement errors in your writing. Examine the following sentence constructions and the correct subject-verb agreement patterns.

a. Use a plural verb for compound subjects (more than one) joined by the coordinating conjunction *and*.

EXAMPLES:

The *counsellor* and *the teacher are* good friends.
Paris, Vancouver, London, and *Vienna are* a few of my favourite cities.

b. For subjects followed by *or*, *either ... or*, or *neither ... nor*, the verb must agree with the subject closest to the verb.

EXAMPLES:

Neither the *singers* nor the *dancer is* here yet. (singular subject closest to verb, singular verb)
Neither the *dancer* nor the *singers are* here yet. (plural subject closest to verb, plural verb)

c. Use a singular verb with compound subjects beginning with *each* or *every*.

EXAMPLES:

Each peach, pear, and pineapple *is* fresh.
Every dress, skirt, and coat *is* on sale today.

d. For singular subjects followed by *along with*, *as well as*, *in addition to*, *including*, *together with*, and *with*, the verb remains singular, no matter what the number of the noun that follows.

EXAMPLES:

The *rent*, in addition to the credit card bill, *makes* this an expensive month. (singular subject, singular verb)
The *goose*, as well as her goslings, *is swimming* across the pond. (singular subject, singular verb)

e. Use a singular verb after a **collective noun** if the noun seems to refer to a single unit. Use a plural verb if the collective noun refers to the individuals that make up a group.

EXAMPLES:

army	crowd	jury
audience	faculty	mob
band	family	number
bunch	fleet	public
class	flock	swarm
club	group	team
committee	herd	

EXAMPLES:

The rock band *is* finally on stage. (*Band* refers to a unified whole.)

The rock *band are adjusting* their instruments. (*Band* refers to the individual members.)

f. Some nouns look plural but are singular and require a singular verb.

EXAMPLES:

economics	news
mathematics	physics
measles	politics
mumps	

Mathematics is not my favourite subject.

Mumps is a contagious disease.

g. **Indefinite pronouns** can be singular or plural. Use the verb form that agrees with the form of the indefinite pronoun. (See Addendum A, Item II for a complete list of the indefinite pronouns.)

EXAMPLES:

Everybody wants more cake.

Some of the coffee cups *are* broken.

Some of the cheese *is* mouldy.

h. It is usual to use a singular verb with nouns which express sums of money and measurement of time, distance, or quantity.

EXAMPLES:

Four *tests* in three days *is* no fun.

Seventy *dollars is* the ticket price per couple.

Sometimes, however, nouns that express quantity are considered as items within a whole and require a plural verb.

EXAMPLES:

Three-quarters of the men *agree* with the opinion poll.
Two of my cousins *are* in the medical profession.

i. Use a singular verb when the word *number* is preceded by *the*. Use a plural verb when the word *number* is preceded by *a*.

EXAMPLES:

The number of participants in the walkathon *is* small. (singular)
A number of windows at the school *were replaced*. (plural)

j. Use a singular verb with the singular title of an article, book, play, song, or work of art even when it looks plural.

EXAMPLES:

"The Dream Songs" is a poem by John Berryman.
Literary Lapses by Stephen Leacock *is* very humorous.

EXERCISE • 1

Choose the verb that agrees with the subject in the following sentences.

EXAMPLE:

Regina or Bill (<u>is waiting</u>, are waiting) for you.

1. The class (is, are) ready for this test.
2. Jung Ah and Derrick (is learning, are learning) line dancing.
3. Many of you (know, knows) me.
4. Myrna, along with her brothers, (is visiting, are visiting) Israel in May.
5. The news from the relatives (was, were) about Uncle Andrew's new dentures.
6. *Over Prairie Trails* (is, are) a collection of short stories by F. P. Grove.
7. Two years of unemployment (is, are) enough.
8. The number of wrong answers (was, were) excessive.
9. The staff (is discussing, are discussing) their new social contract.
10. The backpack, as well as the hiking boots, (cost, costs) less than $200.

EXERCISE • 2

Follow the instructions for Exercise 1.

1. Neither Alexandra nor her sisters (is going, are going) to the cottage this weekend.
2. Each cigarette and drink (is bringing, are bringing) me closer to the end.

3. Glenda or Paula (is meeting, are meeting) you at the bus station.
4. The swarm of bees (has, have) left the hive.
5. Some of Nenita's suggestions (is printed, are printed) in this report.
6. Two-thirds of the computer paper (has been used, have been used).
7. The committee (is, are) unable to make any recommendations until next week.
8. "Crow Jane's Blues" (is, are) a short story by Barry Callaghan.
9. Everyone of importance (was, were) at the reception last night.
10. The colour in these photos (is starting, are starting) to fade.

EXERCISE • 3

Follow the instructions for Exercise 2.

1. None of his sons (play, plays) golf.
2. "Bermudas" (was written, were written) by the English poet Andrew Marvell.
3. Two of Al's six horses (has been entered, have been entered) in the Kentucky Derby.
4. Pediatrics (is, are) the branch of medicine that interests Maxine the most.
5. Either the Polish sausages or the Italian salami (is, are) left over from the business luncheon.
6. A number of deer at the petting zoo (was, were) very hungry.
7. Each butterfly and moth (is, are) on display in the science lab.
8. Blanca, together with her husband and two daughters, (is traveling, are traveling) to Portugal in September.
9. Some of this zucchini (is, are) bitter.
10. You know these numbers (don't, doesn't) add up.

EXERCISE • 4

Follow the instructions for Exercise 3.

1. The jury (has, have) not made a decision yet.
2. Everyone (know, knows) that Armini hates slugs.
3. Much of what the lecturer said about becoming a millionaire (is, are) hard to believe.
4. By halftime, our football team (was losing, were losing).
5. "The Murders in the Rue Morgue" (is, are) a good short story by Edgar Allan Poe.

6. Both of the polar bears (is, are) asleep.
7. The large coffee, in addition to the three muffins (cost, costs), only four dollars.
8. Neither chicken liver nor goose liver (appeal, appeals) to Julie Ann.
9. A covey of quail (is crossing, are crossing) the path.
10. The ski team (is discussing, are discussing) their trip to the top.

EXERCISE • 5

Follow the instructions for Exercise 4.

1. One thousand, nine hundred forty-one joggers (has completed, have completed) the marathon.
2. Every duck, goose, and swan in the pond (is flying, are flying) south for the winter.
3. The rites of passage (is, are) now popular with many young people.
4. Neither Lake Huron nor Lake Michigan (is, are) as large as Lake Superior.
5. The toast but not the jam (is, are) on the table.
6. The faculty of the college (is complaining, are complaining) to their chairs about classroom conditions.
7. "Thirteen Ways of Looking at a Blackbird" (was, were) written by Wallace Stevens.
8. None of this (mean, means) anything to me.
9. Six hundred dollars (is, are) a lot of money for a used computer.
10. Either the vocabulary test or the composition assignment (is scheduled, are scheduled) for next Thursday.

Item II: Pronoun-Antecedent Agreement

In addition to subject-verb agreement within a sentence, there must be **pronoun-antecedent agreement** — that is, all pronouns must agree with the nouns or pronouns they refer to or replace (their **antecedents**). Pronouns and nouns must agree in *number*, *person*, and *gender*.

1. Number

Number is the grammatical term that identifies a noun or pronoun as singular or plural. Always use a singular pronoun when referring to a singular antecedent and a plural pronoun when referring to a plural antecedent.

EXAMPLES:

I sang *my* favourite song. (*My* refers to the first person singular pronoun *I*.)

We sang *our* favourite songs. (*Our* refers to the plural antecedent *we*.)

2. Person

In English, there are three **persons**: **first person**, **second person**, and **third person**.

a. Use the first person (*I, my, me, we, our[s], us*) when you talk about yourself.

EXAMPLE:

I sang *my* favourite song.
(*My* refers to the first person singular pronoun *I*.)

b. Use the second person (*you, your[s]*) when referring to someone you are talking to.

EXAMPLE:

You sang *your* favourite song. (*Your* refers to the second person singular pronoun *you*.)

c. Use the third person (*he, she, it, his, her[s], its, him, they, their[s], them*) when you are talking about someone other than yourself or your listener.

EXAMPLE:

They sang *their* favourite song. (*Their* refers to the third person plural pronoun *they*.)

3. Gender

Pronouns must agree in **gender** (sex) with their antecedents. In most cases, this identification is easy, since female (*she, her*, etc.) and male (*he, him*, etc.) designations are obvious.

Traditionally, the third person singular possessive pronoun *his* has been used to refer to both males and females when the gender of the singular antecedent is unclear (as with indefinite pronouns).

EXAMPLES:

No one finished *his* homework.
Everybody ate *his* dessert.

However, it is important to note that the trend today is to move away from this kind of usage and to use *her/his* or *his* or *her* instead. Since this solution tends to be stylistically awkward, here are some more suitable alternatives.

a. If you know definitely whether the antecedent is feminine or masculine, use the appropriate personal pronoun.

EXAMPLES:

Everyone made *her* own sandwich.
No one wound *his* watch.

b. Make both the antecedent and the pronoun plural.

EXAMPLE:

They made *their* own sandwiches.

c. Use an indefinite article instead of a personal pronoun.

EXAMPLE:

Everyone made *a* sandwich.

4. Pronoun-Antecedent Rules

Examine the following rules for pronoun-antecedent agreement.

a. Use a plural pronoun for antecedents joined by *and*.

EXAMPLES:

Gloria and Marlene are visiting *their* grandmother in Timmins, Ontario.
Claire, Jim, and Max are cleaning *their* rooms.

b. Use a singular pronoun for antecedents joined by *or, either … or,* or *neither … nor.*

EXAMPLES:

Either Stephanie *or* Jenny is growing *her* own vegetables.
Sean *or* Eugene will donate *his* coin collection to charity.

c. When a singular antecedent is joined to a plural antecedent by **or** or **nor**, the pronoun takes the number of the antecedent closest to the verb.

EXAMPLES:

Either the jugglers *or* the magician will perform *his/her* act at the children's party.

Either the magician *or* the jugglers will perform *their* act at the children's party.

d. Use a singular pronoun when a singular indefinite pronoun is used as an antecedent, and use a plural pronoun when a plural indefinite pronoun is used as an antecedent.

EXAMPLES:

No one wants to lose *her/his* job. (singular)
Several of the students are presenting *their* science projects. (plural)

e. Use a singular pronoun when a collective noun is used as an antecedent and when the collective noun refers to a single group or unit. Use a plural pronoun when a collective noun refers to the individuals or parts within a group or unit.

EXAMPLES:

The *committee* was seated for *its* weekly meeting.
The *committee* were discussing *their* agenda.

Try the following exercises to see if you've mastered the rules for pronoun-antecedent agreement.

EXERCISE • 6

Underline the correct pronoun form in parentheses.

EXAMPLE:

Neither Erroll nor Dwayne brought (<u>his</u>, their) homework to school.

1. The gerbils and hamsters are in (its, their) cages.
2. Helen or her niece will send (her, their) recipe to us.
3. Everybody has signed (his/her, their) contract.
4. The class has (its, their) own computer room.
5. Anyone can forget to wear (his/her, their) dentures.
6. Neither of the twins is in (his/her, their) room.
7. I know that my aunt or my cousins are having (his/her, their) garage sale this Saturday.
8. A few of the employees have (her/his, their) own parking spots.
9. The farmers were outstanding in (his/her, their) fields.
10. Not one of Elmer's friends owns (her/his, their) own car.

EXERCISE • 7

Follow the instructions for Exercise 6.

1. Some of the train passengers have had (his/her, their) luggage misplaced.
2. Limes, quinces, and pomegranates all have (its, their) own special taste.
3. Not only Frieda but also Miriam raises funds for (her, their) favourite charity.
4. The association of chicken farmers is having (its, their) meeting tonight to unscramble some myths about eggs.
5. The flames in a fireplace have (its, their) own special soothing affects on a weary soul.
6. Both of the professional hockey players still have all (his, their) own teeth.
7. One of the triplets wants (his/her, their) own room.
8. Last weekend Kristen or Jill placed first in (her, their) swimming competition.
9. Why do some of these pigeons have (its, their) wings clipped?
10. Everyone seems to have (her/his, their) share of woes.

EXERCISE • 8

Follow the instructions for Exercise 7.

1. Some of these liquor bottles have had (its, their) duty labels removed.
2. The college has heard the bad news that (its, their) funding has been cut.
3. I discovered that one of my nephews has sold (his, their) comic book collection.
4. Who said that neither Mary nor her sisters have (her, their) dental appointments until next week?
5. All of these old postcards have had (its, their) postage stamps removed.
6. Bella and Angie said that (her, their) electrical power was shut off for two hours yesterday.
7. Either George or Brad is going to visit (his, their) mother this weekend.
8. Have the doctors or the nurse seen (her/his, their) patients yet?
9. Did Vittorio or Tony sell (his, their) Trans Am?
10. The passengers on the salmon charter were having difficulty holding onto (her/his, their) fishing rods.

EXERCISE • 9

Follow the instructions for Exercise 8.

1. Don't be fooled; neither Esther nor Zelda like to have (her, their) cake without icing.

2. Much of the hawk's food comes from (its, their) immediate environment.
3. The priest, the minister, and the rabbi made (his, their) pleas for peace at City Hall.
4. Some of the passersby were inconsiderate in (his/her, their) choice of words to the beggar.
5. Felice, as well as her peers, saw (her, their) opportunity to define (her, their) job description.
6. Any one of the protesters could have vented (his/her, their) anger at the housing committee.
7. Wally and his colleagues should make up (his, their) minds about what college (he, they) want to attend.
8. Either Afshin or Sorial scored the first goal in (his, their) qualifying soccer game.
9. Some of the students were discussing the importance of (his/her, their) studies.
10. Neither Marta nor Linda wants to extend (her, their) lease in this cockroach-infested apartment.

EXERCISE ♦ 10

Follow the instructions for Exercise 9.

1. Much of Joseph's attitude toward authority comes from (his, their) childhood experiences.
2. A vacation in Alberta or Saskatchewan is special in (its, their) own way.
3. Everybody except Daigle wants (her, their) workload increased.
4. The old rowboats need (its, their) oars replaced.
5. The women's auxiliary set the date for (its, their) annual dinner and dance.
6. Songs of the heart are at (its, their) best at Valentine's.
7. These two students should have (her/his, their) tests reassessed.
8. One of my second cousins is getting (her, their) degree in English literature.
9. Either George or Brad is going to visit (his, their) mother this weekend.
10. Ed, as well as Mel, is on (his, their) way to Bob's house.

Item III: Pronoun Reference

1. Person Problems

As stated in Item II, pronouns must be consistent in person with other pronouns or nouns in our writing. It is important to avoid mixing them. Let us repeat the rules.

1. Use the first person (*I, we*) when talking about yourself or a group that includes you.
2. Use the second person (*you*, singular and plural) when talking about the person(s) you are speaking to in the sentence.
3. Use the third person (*he, she, anyone, one, someone, they*) when talking about a "third person" — that is, neither yourself nor the listener.

EXAMPLES:

No one would say that *they* don't want to be loved. (mixed persons)

No one would say that *she/he doesn't* want to be loved (third person singular used consistently — notice change to *doesn't*)
OR
They would not say that *they* don't want to be loved. (third person plural used consistently)

A *student* should work hard if *they* want to achieve academic success. (mixed persons)

A *student* should work hard if *she/he* wants to achieve academic success. (third person singular used consistently)
OR
Students should work hard if *they* want to achieve academic success. (third person plural used consistently)

While more than one method of correction is acceptable, avoid the awkward repetition of the indefinite pronoun *one*.

EXAMPLE:

One should express how *they* feel. (mixed persons)
One should express how *one* feels. (correct but not recommended)
One should express how *she/he* feels. (corrected without repetition of *one*)

2. Reference Problems

a. Ambiguous Reference

If the pronoun in your sentence is vague, the meaning of your sentence becomes unclear. In most cases, the simplest method of

Ralph told his grandfather that he was working too hard.

correcting sentences with ambiguous pronoun reference is to change the wording to direct speech.

EXAMPLES:

Sylvia told *her* that *she* was happy with her new wheelchair. (unclear who is happy, *Sylvia* or *her*)

Sylvia said, "I am happy with my new wheelchair." (clear)
OR
Sylvia said, "You are happy with your new wheelchair." (clear)

He told *him* that *he* needed a haircut. (unclear which *he* needs a haircut)

He said, "I need a haircut."
OR
He said, "You need a haircut."

b. Unclear Reference

Unclear pronoun reference occurs when a pronoun refers to a phrase or clause within a sentence instead of a specific antecedent.

EXAMPLES:

Michael was so impressed with the breeders at the cat show that he wanted to become one. (unclear reference — to what is *one* referring, the breeders or the cat show?)

Michael was so impressed with the breeders at the cat show that he wanted to become a breeder of cats as well. (clear — corrected by removing pronoun *one* and rewording sentence for clarity)

Knowing that Lana cares for me, it has made all the difference. (unclear reference — to what is *it* referring exactly?)

Knowing that Lana cares for me has made all the difference. (clear — corrected by removing the pronoun *it* so that no reference is required)

When the driver sped and crashed into my car, this is what upsets me. (unclear reference — to what is *this* referring: the driver, the speeding, or the crash?)

That the driver sped and crashed into my car upset me. (clear — corrected by removing pronoun *this* so that no reference is required)

EXERCISE ♦ 11

Correct the person or pronoun reference errors in the following sentences. If the sentence is correct, write "C" beside it.

EXAMPLE:

A person is usually more sympathetic after they have had a similar experience. (incorrect)

A person is usually more sympathetic after *she/he* has had a similar experience. (correct)

1. No one in school can be certain that they will get a job after graduating.
2. Dominic told his brother that he was confused.
3. After two months Jack changed the cat's litter box which made the air fresh again.
4. One can imagine the difficulties they might encounter if they have their wallet stolen.
5. She told her that her eyebrows were crooked.
6. A student with this much determination knows that they will succeed.
7. After watching the Olympic track meet, Boris wanted to become one.
8. Persons like Fred know the answers before the questions are even asked.
9. One is often sad that they have lost their youth.
10. She remarked to her sister that her slip had slipped.

EXERCISE • 12

Follow the instructions for Exercise 11.

1. Wanda saw the kitten at the animal shelter and wanted it.
2. He should get a second opinion before he has his cosmetic surgery.
3. If they really try, anyone can find the error in this sentence.
4. Running out of money just before the rent is due, it makes me crazy.
5. Celine told Raquel that her attitude had to change.
6. If you are not sure, one should check in the dictionary.
7. After walking by the ice cream store, we wanted two.
8. He told his uncle that he was the best.
9. A person like him would always say that they are right.
10. I copied the notes from yesterday's class, and it is appreciated.

EXERCISE • 13

Follow the instructions for Exercise 12.

1. Anyone can say that they saw Elvis Presley in a doughnut shop.
2. The ventriloquist told Duncan that he spoke out of both sides of his mouth.
3. She told her mother that she did not know whether to boil or broil the liver.
4. One of them said that they would wash the car.
5. The dog ate some mushrooms on the lawn which explains why it is not feeling well.
6. A person should follow their head as well as their heart when he has an important decision to make.
7. An individual can have a tremendous impact on other people if they give themselves a chance.
8. After listening to the country CD, Kiley wanted to become one.
9. Steven told him that he had rhinoceros breath.
10. If a person worries too much over matters of little consequence, they could develop an ulcer.

EXERCISE • 14

Follow the instructions for Exercise 13.

1. Joseph told Bill that he resembles a goose from the neck down.
2. One should see the manager before they lodge a complaint.

3. He will get a copy of the short story when they arrive.
4. Irwin saw the photographer working with the bride and groom at the wedding and wanted to become one.
5. All of the aliens in the space ship said that he thought Earth was a nice place to visit.
6. If she wanted more potatoes, she could have had some.
7. The police officer said that she was in the wrong place at the wrong time.
8. When Jeff saw the commercial for the burger sale, he wanted to eat one badly.
9. When one of the relatives said that they wanted hair replacement, and the other said that they wanted hair removal, everyone laughed.
10. They all know that they can receive only three wishes from the genie.

EXERCISE • 15

Correct the pronoun person and reference errors in the following passage.

One of the food critics at a newspaper said that they had heard that a new Chinese restaurant had opened, and that they were serving great food. He told his editor that he was going to try it. As soon as he opened the door, it was clear that the food smelled wonderful.

He was seated at a corner table, and this pleased him. He looked over the menu, but it was too difficult to decide what to order. He told the waiter that he was poor at making decisions and needed a little more time.

However, he eventually ordered a large, satisfying meal and told the waiter that a person knows they have had a great meal after eating in this restaurant.

In fact, the writer was so impressed with the food and service at the restaurant that he decided to quit his job and become one.

Item IV: Pronoun Usage Problems

Choosing the correct pronoun is not difficult when you learn the forms of the personal pronoun and when to use them.

The following is a list of pronouns in their **subject** and their **object** forms. (Note that the pronouns *you* and *it* retain the same form.)

subject form	*object form*
I	me
we	us

you	you
he	him
she	her
it	it
they	them

The conditions under which each form is used are discussed below.

1. Pronouns as Subjects

Use personal pronouns from the subject group to replace nouns that are the doers of an action or are the persons or things talked about. Always use the subject form of the personal pronouns when a noun and a pronoun or two pronouns are used as subjects.

EXAMPLES:

The Shaws and (they, them) are going to the hockey game.
Norman and (I, me) saw the accident.

Sometimes you can determine the correct form by mentally removing the other noun or pronoun in a sentence.

EXAMPLE:

Alison and (I, me) need to talk.
~~Alison and~~ (I, me) need to talk.

2. Pronouns after Non-action Verbs

Use personal pronouns from the subject group to replace nouns that follow non-action verbs (forms of the verb *to be*: *is, are, was, will be,* etc.) and refer to the subject. (See Addendum A, Item III for more information about non-action verbs.)

EXAMPLES:

The master of ceremonies is (she, her).
One of the newly hired shippers is (he, him).

Note that in daily speech, an expression such as "It's me" is the norm. In formal writing, however, we always use the subject form of the personal pronoun after all forms of the verb *to be*. Therefore, the spoken expression "It's me" becomes "It is I" in formal writing.

3. Pronouns as Objects of a Verb

Use personal pronouns from the object group to replace nouns that are acted upon by an action verb. Always use the object form of the personal pronoun when a noun and pronoun or two pronouns receive the action.

EXAMPLES:

Desceyln really surprised Duane and (she, her).

The security guard escorted Gloria and (I, me) to the bus stop.

4. Pronouns as Objects of the Preposition

Use personal pronouns from the object group to replace a noun and pronoun or two pronouns that complete a prepositional phrase. (See Addendum A, Item VI for more information on prepositions and prepositional phrases.)

EXAMPLES:

Pasquale was worried about Margaret and (she, her).

Veronica disagreed with the committee and (he, him).

Remember that the personal pronouns that end a prepositional phrase are objects of the preposition and must be in the object form.

5. Pronouns with Appositives

An **appositive** is a word or group of words that gives additional information about the noun or pronoun beside it. If the appositive is a subject, use the subject form of the personal pronoun. If the appositive is an object, use the object form of the personal pronoun.

In the first example below, the appositive *citizens* is a subject; therefore *we* is chosen.

EXAMPLES:

(We, us) citizens know for whom to vote.

This company always gives (we, us) employees a generous vacation bonus.

If you are having difficulty selecting the correct pronoun form, mentally remove the appositive.

EXAMPLE:

Tell (we, us) students if there will be any extra homework for the weekend.

Tell (we, us) if there will be any extra homework for the weekend.

6. Pronouns with *Than* and *As*

To determine the correct form of the personal pronoun after *than* and *as*, always add a word or two to complete the meaning of the sentence.

EXAMPLES:

Dawn is certainly as good a writer as (she, her).
Dawn is certainly as good a writer as she *is a good writer.*

Kim likes to wash cars more than (I, me).
Kim likes to wash cars more than *I like to wash cars.*

EXERCISE • 16

Choose the correct pronoun form in the following sentences.

EXAMPLE:

Have another cup of coffee with Abe and (I, me).

1. You and (I, me) should see this movie.
2. Do you really think that Erin and (she, her) should try this rice pudding?
3. Moira was disappointed; the winner was not (she, her).
4. Is Cecily really as young as (he, him)?
5. When are you going to give (we, us) customers a refund?
6. I wish I were as smart as (she, her).
7. (We, Us) heard the news this morning.
8. As a team (we, us) players need to do better.
9. Why did Nick tell (he, him) to get an oil change?
10. Kelly and (he, him) are going around the bend.

EXERCISE • 17

Follow the instructions for Exercise 16.

1. Do you want to see Laurie or (she, her)?
2. What are you going to tell Tina and (they, them)?
3. Luzuiminda and (she, her) are cutting the grass.
4. How could it have been (he, him)?
5. I always like to visit Marilyn and (he, him) in Newfoundland.
6. Agatha believes in (they, them).
7. Let (we, us) workers know when the social contract days will be taken.
8. You know I love you as much as (he, him).

9. Why don't you come with Larry and (I, me) tonight?
10. If I were as rich as Bruce and (she, her), I'd quit my job.

EXERCISE • 18

Follow the instructions for Exercise 17.

1. Does this magazine belong to Tonya or (he, him)?
2. Greg saw Paolo and (he, him) crying.
3. Do you think that Ned or (she, her) ate the last muffin?
4. The next group to enter the dinosaur park should be (they, them).
5. These peaches are not as fresh as the ones (we, us) have.
6. How much did you pay for (they, them)?
7. (We, Us) taxpayers are worn out.
8. Marcel likes spicy foods as much as (I, me).
9. There is an empty seat between Olive and (he, him).
10. My real friend has always been (she, her).

EXERCISE • 19

Follow the instructions for Exercise 18.

1. The Trolls and (they, them) live in the enchanted forest.
2. Carol can't stand being near snakes or (we, us).
3. After Pat dances with Tong Wei, she will dance with (he, him).
4. These tortoises have more energy than (I, me) today.
5. It is interesting that Blanca and (he, him) like the same things.
6. I'm sure she shoveled as much snow as (he, him).
7. Berndt greeted (she, her) with a hug.
8. Lois and (he, him) need more time alone.
9. No one could be as silly as (they, them).
10. Make your travel arrangements with Gorgio or (she, her).

EXERCISE • 20

Follow the instructions for Exercise 19.

1. Where can (we, us) visitors park?
2. The next chairperson could be (she, her).
3. The cat and the parrot and (he, him) are asleep on the couch.

4. Ryan and (they, them) are sharing the cottage next week.
5. I really wish it were (she, her) instead of (he, him) who was conducting the interview.
6. Give the last two pieces of fudge to Katherine and (she, her).
7. Jayne was so angry she screamed at Rocco and (he, him).
8. It was because of (I, me) that Laura was late.
9. This math problem was not so easy for (we, us) to understand.
10. Glenda told Jamie and (she, her) that love hurts.

EXERCISE • 21

Follow the instructions for Exercise 20.

1. This movie was directed by Xiaoping and (she, her).
2. I didn't notice (they, them) when (they, them) walked by us.
3. Dorian seems to be a better basketball player than (I, me).
4. Kyle, John, and (she, her) have been friends since grade school.
5. Shawna was tired of Monday-night football and tired of (he, him).
6. Depending on the time of the appointment, it may be (I, me) who takes you to the dentist.
7. One of his problems is that David is jealous of (he, him).
8. (We, Us) cooks are boiling mad about the new work schedule.
9. The Lintons and (they, them) have been to the Stratford Festival many times.
10. Rubina is tired; don't bother (she, her).

EXERCISE • 22

Follow the instructions for Exercise 21.

1. They gave the leftover food to (we, us) caretakers to take home.
2. Yuri realized a long time ago that he was not as clever as (he, him) thought he was.
3. Frank cried that he couldn't live without Gerta or Daniella or (she, her).
4. That actor is not as tall as (she, her).
5. You know that (we, us) nurses are overworked and underpaid.
6. Did you say that Jerome or (I, me) should lose fifteen pounds?
7. Why are (we, us) so lucky?
8. The dog jumped over the hedge and almost gave Gena and (I, me) a heart attack.

9. The exterminators who will solve all your rodent troubles will be (we, us).
10. I wouldn't admit to Carl or (she, her) that I don't like licorice.

EXERCISE • 23

Follow the instructions for Exercise 22.

1. This road is leading (we, us) tourists nowhere.
2. The camera you loaned to Thoria and (she, her) has autofocus.
3. The owner of this beautiful but empty wallet is (I, me).
4. With help from Inge and (he, him), Sarah will be able to complete her assignment.
5. I'm not as sure as Helga and (she, her) that Deborah is innocent.
6. The chef teacher asked (we, us) new students the correct time and temperature to roast a 4 kg turkey.
7. After he slipped, the boys laughed at (he, him).
8. At the parade, Jean was not as close as (I, me) to Santa Claus.
9. I hope it is (he, him) and not Simon who is chosen as our representative.
10. What are they saying about Gerry and (we, us)?

EXERCISE • 24

Follow the instructions for Exercise 23.

1. Ron doesn't know the writings of Gabrielle Roy as well as (I, me).
2. Are you considering Jira or (he, him) for the new job?
3. Physics, chemistry, biology, and (I, me) don't always get along.
4. Dahlia was so happy that she hugged Marcella, Andrea, and (he, him).
5. "Virtual reality" is not for Ed and (I, me); (we, us) haven't mastered "actual reality" yet.
6. A glass of wine, a glowing fire, and (he, him) make the day special.
7. Give (they, them) what they deserve.
8. You will be able to dance as well as (she, her) by the end of the course.
9. Some of (we, us) students are still writing our tests.
10. We will pay for the pizza for Carol and (she, her).

EXERCISE • 25

Follow the instructions for Exercise 24.

1. Morgan would rather go to a dentist than be seen with (they, them).
2. None of (they, them) remembered that it was (I, me) who helped them.
3. If it is not (she, her), I will be surprised.
4. Last night, Steve and (she, her) heard a coyote howling.
5. The punchline of the joke had no effect on (they, them).
6. The smell from your locker has been having a negative effect on (we, us).
7. Justine and (he, him) thought that *Know More English* meant "no more English."
8. It was Debbie and (she, her) who complained that the handicapped parking spot was being misused.
9. Nothing is more beautiful in the morning than the sunrise and (she, her).
10. The first to fall off the wagon was (I, me).

UNIT • 3 • POST-TEST

If you have completed Unit 3 satisfactorily, then you are ready for the Post-Test. The answers immediately follow the test.

Part A

Underline the correct pronoun or verb form in parentheses in the following sentences.

1. Most of the pottery (has been, have been) hand-painted.
2. Terry or Brad (is, are) available if the need arises.
3. Everyone wants (his/her, their) share of the credit.
4. The aquarium, including some fish, a water pump, and lights, (is, are) included in the set.
5. Either Carly or her sisters have (her, their) own catering business.
6. The army of ants is trying to protect (its, their) queen.
7. Andrea or Mathew received (her/his, their) medals for skating last night.
8. The donkey and the pig were complaining about the conditions in (his/her, their) barn.
9. The sound of the winds (is, are) haunting.
10. Neither Larry nor Frank and Heather will allow (his/her, their) children to toboggan down Dead Man's Drop.

Part B

Correct the errors in pronoun form or pronoun usage in the following sentences. If the sentence is correct, write "C" beside it.

1. Each of my friends knows that they are appreciated.

2. Why would you wish to be as rich as her?

3. Ed and him have been friends for 12 years.

4. If one is patient, they will be rewarded.

5. Ever since Philip saw a real operation, he wanted to become one.

6. Murray told him that he was becoming forgetful.

7. A few of the teachers are allowing their students to leave early because of the snowstorm.

8. One of the six counsellors is leaving their job today.

9. A person like Donna always has their heart in the right place.

10. Linda and the children are going to visit their grandparents.

ANSWERS • TO • UNIT • 3 • POST-TEST

Part A

Underline the correct pronoun or verb form in parentheses in the following sentences.

1. Most of the pottery (**has been**, have been) hand-painted.
2. Terry or Brad (**is**, are) available if the need arises.
3. Everyone wants (**his/her**, their) share of the credit.
4. The aquarium, including some fish, a water pump, and lights, (**is**, are) included in the set.
5. Either Carly or her sisters have (her, **their**) own catering business.
6. The army of ants is trying to protect (**its**, their) queen.
7. Andrea or Mathew received (**her/his**, their) medals for skating last night.
8. The donkey and the pig were complaining about the conditions in (his/her, **their**) barn.
9. The sound of the winds (**is**, are) haunting.
10. Neither Larry nor Frank and Heather will allow (his/her, **their**) children to toboggan down Dead Man's Drop.

Part B

Correct the errors in pronoun form or pronoun usage in the following sentences. If the sentence is correct, write "C" beside it.

1. Each of my friends knows that he/she is appreciated.
2. Why would you wish to be as rich as she?
3. Ed and he have been friends for 12 years.
4. If one is patient, she/he will be rewarded.
5. Ever since Philip saw a real operation, he has wanted to become a nurse.
6. Murray said, "You are becoming forgetful."

   OR

   Murray said, "I am becoming forgetful."
7. C
8. One of the six counsellors is leaving his/her job today.
9. A person like Donna always has her heart in the right place.
10. C

U • N • I • T 4

PUNCTUATION PERFECTION

Punctuation marks are the symbols you use to define, control, and clarify your writing. In this Unit you will expand your knowledge of basic punctuation rules, and you will learn some new ones as well. You will soon find punctuation marks easy to use.

UNIT • 4 • PRE-TEST

Complete this Pre-Test to measure your knowledge of the material in Unit 4. The answers immediately follow the test.

I. Place a period, question mark, or exclamation mark where required in the following sentences.

1. This is the correct address
2. You can't be serious
3. Don't touch that wire
4. Aren't you feeling well
5. Your MA degree is in what subject

II. Place commas where required in the following sentences.

1. Of course how could I have forgotten.
2. One sheep two sheep three sheep or four hundred sheep won't help me to sleep tonight.
3. The moon is full tonight but my heart is empty.

4. Yes I am a magician.
5. Were you born on March 8 1981 in Sarnia Ontario?

III. Place colons and semicolons where required in the following sentences.

1. This perfume is expensive however, it's worth it.
2. Remember what mother said be on time, and be polite.
3. What is Act II iii about?
4. Are you familiar with these three plays by Anton Chekhov *The Seagull*, *The Three Sisters*, and *The Cherry Orchard*?
5. I was so embarrassed I didn't notice the rip until I got home.

IV. Place quotation marks, commas, capitals, and closing punctuation marks where they are required in the following sentences.

1. You are a kind person stated Alec
2. Did Jimmy really ask are you divorced yet
3. Most of the jewelry boxes replied the salesperson are on sale this week
4. Did Hanna say you look ten years younger
5. Have you read the Australian short story Borrowed Light by Alan Moorehead

ANSWERS • TO • UNIT • 4 • PRE-TEST

I. Place a period, question mark, or exclamation mark where required in the following sentences.

1. This is the correct address.
2. You can't be serious.
3. Don't touch that wire!(.)
4. Aren't you feeling well?
5. Your M.A. degree is in what subject?

II. Place commas where required in the following sentences.

1. Of course, how could I have forgotten.
2. One sheep, two sheep, three sheep(,) or four hundred sheep won't help me to sleep tonight.
3. The moon is full tonight, but my heart is empty.
4. Yes, I am a magician.
5. Were you born on March 8, 1981(,) in Sarnia, Ontario?

III. Place colons and semicolons where required in the following sentences.

1. This perfume is expensive; however, it's worth it.
2. Remember what mother said: Be on time, and be polite.
3. What is Act II:iii about?
4. Are you familiar with these three plays by Anton Chekhov: *The Seagull*, *The Three Sisters*, and *The Cherry Orchard*?
5. I was so embarrassed; I didn't notice the rip until I got home.

IV. Place quotation marks, commas, capitals, and closing punctuation marks where they are required in the following sentences.

1. "You are a kind person," stated Alec.
2. Did Jimmy really ask, "Are you divorced yet?"
3. "Most of the jewelry boxes," replied the salesperson,"are on sale this week."
4. Did Hanna say, "You look ten years younger"?
5. Have you read the Australian short story "Borrowed Light" by Alan Moorehead?

Item I: The Period

1. Completion

The **period (.)** is the most common form of closing punctuation. It comes at the end of almost every indicative sentence. An **indicative sentence** is one that states a fact.

EXAMPLES:

This is your lucky day. (simple)
Agatha finished her breakfast; however, she was still hungry. (compound)
Because the coffee was too hot, I burned my tongue. (complex)
Maureen swam across the bay, but before she swam back, she rested a moment. (compound-complex)

2. Abbreviation

Use the period to indicate that a word is an abbreviation of a longer word.

EXAMPLES:

Dr.	-	Doctor
i.e.	-	*id est* (that is)

Wed.	-	Wednesday
M.A.	-	Master of Arts

Note that agencies, organizations, and scientific or technical terms widely recognized by their initials do not require a period.

EXAMPLES:

ESP	-	extrasensory perception
BTU	-	British Thermal Units
RCMP	-	Royal Canadian Mounted Police

Item II: The Question Mark and the Exclamation Mark

1. The Question Mark

Use the **question mark (?)** at the end of all direct questions (interrogative sentences).

EXAMPLES:

Are you praying for a miracle? (direct)
What is his last name? (direct)

Note that all questions do not require a question mark. A **rhetorical question** is asked to make a point and does not expect an answer.

EXAMPLES:

Why wasn't I born rich. (rhetorical)
Who wouldn't like a few extra vacation days. (rhetorical)

2. The Exclamation Mark

Use the **exclamation mark (!)** after interjections or sentences that express a forceful command, strong emotion, or surprise.

EXAMPLES:

Ouch! That really hurt.
Oh, no! It's too late.
Don't touch that switch!

EXERCISE • 1

Place periods, question marks, or exclamation marks where required in the following sentences.

EXAMPLE:

Are you sure

Are you sure?

1. Say what you mean
2. Fr Al is still here
3. He voted for the losing party
4. This pasta is wonderful
5. What will they think of next
6. When does your train arrive
7. What's the use
8. You should have seen all the onion rings they ordered
9. Does Dave have a BA or an MA in English literature
10. Take a hike

EXERCISE • 2

Follow the instructions for Exercise 1.

1. Let's go
2. Moira enjoyed her week in Spain
3. What can you tell me about earwigs
4. You are strange
5. Set the clock
6. What a surprise this is
7. Yikes I forgot to turn the steaks over on the barbecue
8. What is OXFAM
9. *Etc* is the abbreviation for *et cetera*
10. Do you know what the plural of *Ms* is

EXERCISE • 3

Follow the instructions for Exercise 2.

1. Don't slam the door
2. Is the whole world going crazy

3. Say it
4. Since you're so clever, what is the capital of Saskatchewan
5. Byron wants to be an OPP officer
6. That is good news
7. Where did you see the UFO
8. What a mess
9. This is extra special
10. This is not what I expected in Ontario

EXERCISE • 4

Follow the instructions for Exercise 3.

1. In 1812, the United States declared war on the British
2. Did you know that the first American invasion to Upper Canada was defeated by Indian leader Tecumseh
3. Brenda likes all kinds of wines, eg Chablis and Chardonnay
4. I think Sr St Joseph wanted to see you
5. Why is George under the coffee table again
6. Don't ask me to spell *potpourri*; I can't even pronounce it
7. What is the good of being spiteful
8. Please, slice it thickly
9. Gen Smith told us about the new army manoeuvres
10. Shoot I forgot to pay the gas bill

EXERCISE • 5

Follow the instructions for Exercise 4.

1. I'm sure that Harold lives on Macklem Blvd in Cambridge, Ontario
2. How did you know I like pirogi
3. I thought about what he said
4. Did Dr Edwards tell you to drink more water
5. Nuts I hate pistachios
6. Close your eyes, and make a wish
7. That's it; I've had enough
8. The puppy we saw at the pound became the puppy at our house
9. I hate it when that happens
10. Do you mind I'm still eating

Item III: The Comma

Many people misuse the **comma (,)**. Some use too few commas; others use too many, and some use the right amount. Study the following rules, and you will soon be able to join the last group.

1. Commas in a Series

Use the comma to separate a series (three or more) of words, phrases, or clauses.

Note that the use of the comma that precedes the final conjunction is optional. Choose the method you prefer, but remember to be consistent throughout your piece of writing.

EXAMPLES:

The fruit stand had *peaches, pears(,) and plums* for sale. (series of words)

You need to *wash the floor, dust the furniture(,) and vacuum the carpet.* (series of phrases)

Jill asked him *where he was going, how long he would be (,) and when he would be back.* (series of clauses)

Note that the entire series may be joined by **and** for special emphasis. In this case, do not use commas to separate items.

EXAMPLE:

The fruit stand had peaches *and* pears *and* plums for sale.

2. Commas with Introductory Words, Phrases, and Clauses

Use a comma to separate direct words of address from the rest of the sentence. Note that the portions of the sentences that follow introductory words form complete sentences and can stand alone.

Do not use a comma when the first word in a sentence is a proper name and is part of the sentence.

EXAMPLES:

Yes, you are the winner.

Thus, the movie ended.

Personally, I think you eat too much fibre.

Sandy, you are an exceptional dancer. (introductory word)

Sandy received an award for her dancing. (subject of the sentence)

In view of your age, you may move to the front of the line. (introductory phrase)

If you don't feel well, stay home. (introductory clause)

3. Commas with Coordinating Conjunctions

Use a comma before a coordinating conjunction that joins main clauses.

EXAMPLES:

Steve saw the help-wanted sign in the window, *and* he applied for the job.

The chicken is burned, *but* the potatoes are all right.

EXERCISE • 6

Some of the following sentences require commas. Place commas where necessary. If the sentence is correct, write "C" beside it.

EXAMPLE:

These doughnuts muffins and rolls are stale. (incorrect)

These doughnuts, muffins (,) and rolls are stale. (correct)

1. Those cheese balls onion rings and potato chips are for the party.
2. No the mouthwash doesn't work.
3. When you deliver the pizza don't ring the doorbell; knock instead.
4. Hank you know the rules.
5. Of all the kind-hearted people I know, you are the best.
6. Margaret Atwood wrote *The Robber Bride* and Nino Ricci wrote *In a Glass House.*
7. On the desk by the phone you will find my notes.
8. Come in for a minute and sit down.
9. By saving some money every day Erin was able to save up for a new wallet.
10. Cassandra should write the thank-you note today.

EXERCISE • 7

Follow the instructions for Exercise 6.

1. Get a loaf of bread from the freezer and put it on the kitchen counter.
2. Mice rats and weasels give Ida the shivers.
3. Yes I did spill the beans.
4. Since your last visit nothing has changed.
5. Where to stay what to see and where to eat are the items highlighted in this brochure.
6. In Iran in China and in Canada the New Year begins on a different day.

7. When you burst out laughing I knew that I did not translate "I love you" properly in Japanese.
8. The moon the sun and all the stars are not as bright as your eyes.
9. Instead of complaining do something about the problem.
10. Walnuts and pecans and hazelnuts were used to make the Christmas cookies.

EXERCISE • 8

Follow the instructions for Exercise 7.

1. Donna when will the coffee be ready?
2. Not only does Cindy have a degree in economics but she also runs a financial planning firm.
3. Because of the heavy rains some of the roads were washed out.
4. Did you say you wanted to order a rice dish or a nice fish?
5. The monks nuns and friars were in the habit of rising early for prayers.
6. That you can speak French that you understand Polish and that you can write Yiddish is mind-boggling.
7. Hold your breath and then let go.
8. Matt don't do that to the cat.
9. By drawing premature conclusions you made a fool of yourself.
10. Why do words hurt more than sticks bricks and stones?

EXERCISE • 9

Follow the instructions for Exercise 8.

1. Dennis was so angry with himself for being forgetful that he wanted to cry yell and scream at the same time.
2. Knowing how you feel about snails I did not make escargots for supper.
3. "A little learning is a dangerous thing" is a line from Alexander Pope's poem "Essay on Criticism."
4. Have they arrested the person who gave you that terrible haircut yet or are they still looking for the culprit?
5. This is my college diploma and I am very proud of it.
6. "Face the music" and "sing a different song" are expressions that annoy me.
7. Well what do you think of my new apartment?
8. Sid the phone is for you.

9. The table was set and the supper was served but no one said thank you to the host.
10. By the time he was four Joseph had already had the worst day of his life.

EXERCISE • 10

Follow the instructions for Exercise 9.

1. The music the food and the wine were not just memories.
2. Yes a male buffalo can weigh as much as a metric ton and can grow as tall as two metres.
3. With the wind and the snow and the hail howling against him Murray was unable to cross the street.
4. Glen is this really your car?
5. Look in the mirror and then tell me that you don't need a vacation.
6. While Dimitri was in the bank it was robbed.
7. Serena sanded stained and varathaned the antique chair.
8. Read the small print sign the document and give me the money.
9. Perhaps I will attend the lecture on making positive decisions and perhaps I won't.
10. Hey it's only money.

4. Commas with Parenthetical Expressions and Appositives

a. Parenthetical Expressions

Parenthetical expressions are additional thoughts or modifiers within a sentence. These expressions are not necessary to the meaning of the sentence but tend to make it flow more smoothly.

The following are some commonly used parenthetical expressions.

as we said	I might add	on the contrary
at any rate	in addition	on the other hand
besides	in short	perhaps
for example	it is true	still
generally speaking	naturally	that is
however	nevertheless	to tell the truth
I believe	of course	

Such expressions are usually set off with commas. Note that they can appear at the beginning, the middle, or the end of a sentence.

EXAMPLES:

Of course, this is genuine leather.
This, *of course*, is genuine leather.
This is genuine leather, *of course*.

b. Appositives

An **appositive** is a word or group of words that gives additional information about a noun or pronoun in a sentence. It may include a prepositional phrase. (See Unit 3, Item III.)

Use commas to separate an appositive from the rest of the sentence.

EXAMPLES:

Henry Hudson, *an English explorer*, discovered Hudson Bay in 1610.
The cicada, *a large insect with wings*, may remain burrowed in the ground four to twenty years before emerging as an adult.

5. Commas with Units

Use commas within dates, addresses, geographical locations, and weights and measures to separate details. Generally, you must separate the smaller units from the larger, and the larger units from the rest of the sentence.

EXAMPLES:

William Lyon Mackenzie, the first mayor of Toronto, Ontario, was born in Dundee, Scotland. (city from province; city from country)
Eva's birth weight was 3 kg, 56 g. (kilograms from grams)
On July 1, 1867, Canada came into being made up of Ontario, Quebec, Nova Scotia, and New Brunswick. (day of month from year; year from sentence)

Note that if only the month and year are mentioned in a sentence, the use of the comma is optional.

EXAMPLES:

In February 1896 Winnipeg won the Stanley Cup from Montreal. (correct — no commas used)
In February, 1896(,) Winnipeg won the Stanley Cup from Montreal. (also correct — commas used after month and year — second comma optional)

EXERCISE • 11

Some of the following sentences require commas. Place commas where necessary. If the sentence is correct, write "C" beside it.

EXAMPLE:

The sun is shining but the sky is hazy. (incorrect)
The sun is shining, *but* the sky is hazy. (correct)

1. Doris the head nurse at St. Martin's Hospital is my cousin.
2. Fred I might add also collects stickers from fruit.
3. I know there is a Toronto Ontario but I didn't know there was an Ontario California.
4. Henri said that he was born on March 5 1972 in Hull Quebec.
5. Doreen without question is the luckiest person I know.
6. Mail it to the town clerk at 45 Hillside Dr. N. Elliot Lake Ontario.
7. The passport tickets and money are on the table.
8. The fish weighed 4 kg 37 g.
9. In spite of a bad cold Ms. Hill was still able to teach our class.
10. Voula where did you learn to tap-dance so well?

EXERCISE • 12

Follow the instructions for Exercise 11.

1. On the contrary Ben likes milk chocolate but he won't eat white chocolate.
2. Ms. Junn the new science teacher was born in Brooks Alberta.
3. Mount Saint Vincent University St. Francis Xavier University and St. Mary's University are in Nova Scotia.
4. Can Marco or Peter or Carol help you tonight?
5. You my dear friend need more than a facelift.
6. Gil you know was born in 1901 five years before my grandfather.
7. Before you go out don't forget to turn off the stove.
8. The play begins October 4 1993 and should continue until 1998.
9. Bea our accountant thinks we should buy some mutual funds.
10. Pumpkins squashes and gourds covered the vegetable stand.

EXERCISE • 13

Follow the instructions for Exercise 12.

1. The oatmeal was cold, but the service was warm.
2. The Great War Memorial Hospital is located at 33 Drummond St. W. Perth Ontario.
3. No this is not my last chance.
4. What do the words *gnaw gnat knead* and *knout* have in common?
5. Because this is your first day on the job someone will be here to assist you.
6. These chocolate chip cookies I think are made with real chocolate.
7. On July 20 1871 British Columbia became Canada's sixth province.
8. Dr. Cassidy our veterinarian knows our pets well.
9. After eating the chili my stomach felt strange.
10. The ceramic tile store is located on 2161 Dumont St. E. Brighton Ontario.

EXERCISE • 14

Follow the instructions for Exercise 13.

1. Yes the temperature is still below zero.
2. Even though he forgot his tickets Ivan was allowed into the theatre.
3. Well, things could be worse.
4. Peter an avid fisher is always looking for the best spot on the lake.
5. What is the day month and year of your birth?
6. To tell the truth I was convinced that Cecil was wrong but he was right.
7. The police wanted to know where she was last night what time she left work and what time she arrived home.
8. Before you say another word read this.
9. None of these nuts bolts and washers match.
10. Cloudy not sunny days are best for photographing autumn colours.

EXERCISE • 15

Write original sentences using the comma rules indicated.

EXAMPLE:

introductory word
Martha, you're a great skier.

1. in a series

2. introductory word
3. appositive
4. day, month, year
5. parenthetical expression
6. introductory clause
7. coordinating conjunction
8. street, city, province
9. month, year
10. unit of measurement

Item IV: The Colon

The **colon (:)** is similar in appearance to the **semicolon (;)** but has a different function. Use the colon in the following ways: (1) to introduce lists, explanations, and formal salutations; and (2) to separate hours from minutes, titles from subtitles, and acts from scenes in a play.

1. Use a colon to introduce lists, explanations, and formal salutations.

   a. With lists, be sure your sentence includes wording that suggests a list is to follow (*the following*, *these*, and *thus*).

   EXAMPLES:

   The movers misplaced the following items: an antique mantle clock, a Persian carpet, and a Picasso painting.

   To spice up the sauce use these ingredients: chili peppers, white pepper, and cayenne pepper.

   Never use a colon after the expressions *such as*, *for example*, *for instance*, and *that is*.

   EXAMPLES:

   He has visited some very famous deserts in the world, *for instance:* the Gibson, the Thar, and the Sahara. (incorrect)

   He has visited some very famous deserts in the world, *for instance these:* the Gibson, the Thar, and the Sahara. (corrected)

   OR

   He has visited some very famous deserts in the world, *for instance,* the Gibson, the Thar, and the Sahara. (corrected)

   Never use a colon after *are* and *were* when a simple list follows.

Please arrange for the following gifts to be delivered to the Queen: a pound of Swiss chocolate, a bottle of French cognac, and a copy of *Know More English.*

EXAMPLES:

Thoriah knows the new classmates *are:* Carmen, Hanna, and Lin Yin. (incorrect)

Thoriah knows the new classmates *are* Carmen, Hanna, and Lin Yin. (corrected)

b. Use a colon after a statement which is followed by an explanatory expression or clause.

EXAMPLES:

The supermarket advertised two specials*: lettuce for 69 cents and cantaloupe for 89 cents.*

The president of the aluminum ladder company made two important announcements*: She wanted all staff to have higher sales, but she also wanted to have a decrease in commission.*

Note that the explanatory clause in the second example begins with a capital letter because it is a complete sentence.

c. Use a colon at the end of a *formal* salutation.

EXAMPLES:

Dear Ms. Henricks*:* (formal)
Dear Kelly, (informal)

2. **Use a colon to separate hours from minutes, titles from subtitles, acts of plays from their scenes, and chapters of the Bible from their verses.**

EXAMPLES:

The train will be here at 9*:*35 p.m. (hour and minutes)
In *Henry IV, Part I,* Act V*:*i, Falstaff gives an interesting account of "honour." (act and scene)
I like *Look It Up: An Alphabetical Reference for Writers* by H. Read. (title and subtitle)
What is Matthew saying in Matthew *24: 23–31*? (chapter verses in Bible)

EXERCISE ◆ 16

Place colons where they are needed in the following sentences. If the sentence is correct, write "C" beside it.

EXAMPLE:

There are two persons named Carmen where I work, one is from Malta; the other is from Ecuador. (incorrect)
There are two persons named Carmen where I work: One is from Malta; the other is from Ecuador. (corrected)

1. Meet me at 630 p.m., and we'll work on the newsletter.
2. There are two nice things about Jim in particular he is determined, and he is innovative.
3. Whose photograph is taken in *The Wild Duck* I iv?
4. Karen's favourite butterflies in her collection are the painted lady, the giant swallowtail, and the mourning cloak.
5. Eduardo made these points at the staff meeting he stated that there were longer hours, fewer benefits, and little thanks.
6. The passage John 4 34–38 is very comforting.
7. Oh, these knives, forks, and spoons are still crusted with bits of food.
8. Rhonda understood his problem he was a big spender, but he had little money.
9. I'm only up to Act II i of *The One Day of the Year* by Alan Seymour, but I'll finish it by tomorrow.
10. You've already complained that the apartment has the following flaws little heat, loud neighbours, and healthy mice.

EXERCISE • 17

Follow the instructions for Exercise 16.

1. Martin's favourite breeds of dog are fox terriers, cocker spaniels, and Weimaraners.
2. Why does the teacher use the following words when he talks about me *lugubrious*, *perspicacious*, and *peccadillo*?
3. You know that Farid is interested in only two things money and more money.
4. Jana is disappointed in her mathematics, chemistry, and history grades.
5. Before you start taking pictures, check two things that the camera has film and that the lens cap is off.
6. Cynthia thinks that these apples are Courtland, MacIntosh, or Empire.
7. In Shaw's *Heartbreak House*, Lady Utterwood says that there are only two classes in good society in England the equestrian and the neurotic.
8. *Nova Scotia The Lighthouse Route and the Annapolis Valley* is an exceptional picture book by Sherman Hines.
9. Ida suggested the following times for the meeting 1030 a.m. on Monday, 1100 a.m. on Tuesday, or 230 p.m. on Thursday.
10. The winning numbers are 112539, 481737, and 994728.

Item V: The Semicolon

Use a **semicolon (;)** to separate main clauses, to separate two main clauses joined by conjunctive adverbs or transitional phrases, and to separate several long series which have commas within them.

1. With Main Clauses

Use a semicolon to separate main clauses.

EXAMPLES:

Hand me the matches; I'm going to start the fire.

Sang never gets tired of rereading *Pillars of the Earth* by Ken Follet; it's her favourite novel.

2. With a Conjunctive Adverb

Use a semicolon before a conjunctive adverb to separate main clauses. (See Unit 2, Item III.)

EXAMPLES:

Agnes won the lottery Saturday night; *naturally,* she won't be coming to work on Monday.

This is only a 5 kg turkey; *nevertheless,* it will feed all of us.

3. With a Transitional Phrase

Use a semicolon before a transitional phrase to separate main clauses. (See Unit 2, Item III.)

EXAMPLES:

Jose's résumé was poorly written; *as a result,* it hindered his employment prospects.

You can wait for the movie to come out; *on the other hand,* you could read the book now.

4. With a Long Series

For clarity, use a semicolon to separate a series in which commas are used.

EXAMPLES:

This autumn Sylvester became so motivated to upgrade his cooking skills that he enrolled in several evening cooking classes including Chinese Cooking, Cooking with Garlic, Secrets of Summer Grilling, and Magnificent Marinades and Sauces of Spain. (unclear)

This autumn Sylvester became so motivated to upgrade his cooking skills that he enrolled in several evening cooking classes including Chinese Cooking; Cooking with Garlic; Secrets of Summer Grilling; and Magnificent Marinades and Sauces of Spain. (clear)

Several similar-sounding pairs of words really confuse me, such as *contemptible, contemptuous, continual, continuous,* and *tortuous, torturous.* (unclear)

Several similar-sounding pairs of words really confuse me, such as *contemptible, contemptuous; continual, continuous;* and *tortuous, torturous.* (clear)

EXERCISE • 18

Place semicolons where they are required in the following sentences. If the sentence is correct, write "C" beside it.

EXAMPLE:

The phone call is from Italy it's for you. (incorrect)
The phone call is from Italy; it's for you. (correct)

1. Steve finally cut the grass it was up to his knees.
2. Warren entered the essay-writing contest unfortunately his paper was not one of the winning entries.
3. Look in the mirror your problem is obvious.
4. Meet me downtown otherwise we'll never make it to the theatre on time.
5. Don't bet on that horse it hasn't won a race in 15 years.
6. Lawrence Sterne wrote *Tristram Shandy*, and Henry Fielding wrote *Tom Jones*.
7. Believe me, you need an oil change you've driven this car over 10,000 km since the last one.
8. We arrived at the county fair late in addition, we forgot our free passes.
9. Pauline kissed her son Matthew consequently, her daughter Melissa wanted one too.
10. This lettuce wasn't cleaned properly it still has soil in its leaves.

EXERCISE • 19

Follow the instructions for Exercise 18.

1. Dorothy was so excited at the hockey game to tell the truth, she jumped up and down as she cheered her team.
2. Buy some milk tonight otherwise we won't have any for breakfast tomorrow.
3. Ian said he had a bad headache after doing Exercise 18 however, he feels better now.
4. The pet owner taught his three parrots to sing "The Bird Dance Song" in harmony everyone laughed when the birds sang.
5. "Alliteration" is a figure of speech in which the first sound in a group of words is repeated an example is "lovely little lake."
6. Darian ate his pomegranate unfortunately, no one told him to peel it first.
7. Albert always asks interesting questions yesterday he wanted to know if sour cream ever went bad.
8. This algebra problem is impossible to solve in fact, I think the answer in the back of the book is wrong.

9. First you didn't like my appetizer then you complained about my main course now you're holding your stomach after eating my dessert.
10. Doug quit smoking to tell the truth, I didn't think he could do it.

EXERCISE • 20

In this exercise place colons and semicolons where they are required. In some instances capital letters may be required. If the sentence is correct, write "C" beside it.

EXAMPLE:

The store manager said that she needed these three pieces of identification a driver's licence, a birth certificate, and a credit card. (incorrect)

The store manager said that she needed these three pieces of identification: a driver's licence, a birth certificate, and a credit card. (correct)

1. This is my advice follow your head, and follow your heart.
2. Michelle would like a pet for Christmas for instance, she would like a hamster, a kitten, or a puppy.
3. Call me I could use a friend.
4. Glenda has been everywhere she has been as far as Singapore, the Philippines.
5. The dental hygienist recommended two things to keep my teeth healthy brush after every meal, and floss before bed.
6. Are you familiar with these Patsy Cline songs "I Fall to Pieces," "Crazy," and "Don't Ever Leave Me?"
7. Derrick agreed to the blind date unfortunately when she opened the door, he discovered that it was his ex-girlfriend.
8. At 730 p.m., the drama group will be rehearsing Act III iv of *Richard III.*
9. Tara needs a break she's been studying more than five hours.
10. Are you sure that these shoes, jackets, slacks, and skirts are on sale?

EXERCISE • 21

Follow the instructions for Exercise 20.

1. There are some interesting vocabulary words in *Street Talk The Language of Coronation Street.*
2. I hate hospitals however, I will go with you to visit Shelly.
3. It must be a bad day I arrived at work an hour early.
4. Can you buy me the following fishes sole, salmon, and swordfish?

5. You can use the semicolon with main clauses, with a conjunctive adverb between main clauses, and with a transitional phrase between main clauses.
6. The bartender gave this advice to his heartbroken customer keep your glass clean, and your mate will see the real you.
7. Will the bulletin be repeated at 1045 or 1145?
8. I saw Pauline's new computer it's a beauty.
9. The cheesecakes you ordered are these mocha, strawberry, and lemon.
10. Name the time name the place, and I'll be there.

EXERCISE • 22

Follow the instructions for Exercise 21.

1. Did you read Act I ii of *A Raisin in the Sun* yet?
2. The rescue attempt was made more difficult by these factors rain, fog, and cold.
3. Peter is a proud father in addition, he is a very proud grandfather.
4. *The Blood People A Division of the Blackfoot Confederacy* is one of several books by Adolf Hungry Wolf.
5. This is too long shorten it by at least ten pages.
6. You can't go wrong if you choose orange, cola or ginger ale.
7. The pizza will be here by 647 p.m. or it'll be free.
8. Of course I'm still nervous the spider is still looking at me.
9. I could visit Disney World anytime unfortunately I'd have to walk there.
10. Try the bratwurst you won't be disappointed.

EXERCISE • 23

Follow the instructions for Exercise 22.

1. Have you read these short stories "The Coronet at Night" by Sinclair Ross, "The Loons" by Margaret Laurence, and "The Snob" by Morley Callaghan?
2. Arnold had two physical ailments about which he never complained an ulcer and flat feet.
3. Yolanda visited her mother in Poland the weather was bad.
4. Do you know the meaning of these vocabulary words *complaisant*, *adroit*, *demeanour*, and *stupor*?
5. At 405 a.m., Tulla was wakened by a strange sound coming from her basement fortunately, it was only her furnace.

6. Parmajit's favourite soups are minestrone, mushroom, and vegetable.
7. What a day George had in one day two great events took place his divorce became official, and he got his long-awaited promotion at work.
8. Are these citrus fruits the same a mandarin orange, a tangerine, and a tangelo?
9. Esmine went to see *Les Misérables*, *Miss Saigon*, and *The Phantom of the Opera* last month she really enjoyed them.
10. Michael was confused consequently, he did not do well on the test.

EXERCISE • 24

Follow the instructions for Exercise 23.

1. Ken rubbed the lamp and asked for three wishes unfortunately, it was a desk lamp, and he burned his hand badly.
2. Jackie likes the following water sports best swimming, waterskiing, and scuba diving.
3. The instructor had only two comments about the test it was going to be hard, but it was going to be fair.
4. The reindeer are restless it is almost time for Santa Claus to fly.
5. Breakfast was rough the prune juice worked faster than I did.
6. What are you going to do with these items whipped cream, chocolate sauce, and a hammer?
7. Your wallet must be defective it can't hold any money.
8. John should sing Betty should dance, but you should watch.
9. This coffee is awful it tastes like swamp water.
10. My favourite flavours of sherbet are grape, orange, and lemon.

EXERCISE • 25

Write original sentences using commas, colons, semicolons, and capital letters as required.

EXAMPLE:

colon to introduce list

I have visited the following cities in Canada: Prince Rupert, British Columbia; Rosthern, Saskatchewan; and White River, Ontario.

1. semicolon

____

2. colon followed by explanatory clause

____

3. colon to introduce list

____

4. semicolon and conjunctive adverb

____

5. colon with hour and minute

____

6. semicolon with conjunctive adverb

____

7. colon to denote separation

____

8. semicolon with transitional phrase

____

9. semicolon

____

10. colon followed by explanatory clause

____

Item VI: Quotation Marks

Quotation marks are a little more challenging because they are always used with capital letters and with other punctuation marks such as commas, periods, and exclamation marks. Don't be discouraged; instead study the rules for quotation-mark usage, and look at the examples for the proper placement of accompanying punctuation and capital letters.

Use **quotation marks (" ")** in pairs for the following purposes:

1. To indicate the exact words (direct speech) of a speaker
2. To indicate words used in a special sense
3. To indicate the titles of articles, poems, short stories, and songs

1. Direct Speech

Use quotation marks to indicate a person's exact words. Follow these steps: Find the "speaking" word (*asked, inquired, shouted, said, remarked,* etc.), find the speaker, and then ask yourself, "What did the speaker say?" The answer to this question will always tell you where to place your quotation marks which must be around the speaker's statement.

Examine the following additional rules for the use of quotation marks.

a. When the quotation is a statement, place the end punctuation *within* the quotation marks.

EXAMPLES:

Sung Ha remarked, "I'm enjoying this English class."
"The full moon is so beautiful," commented Jan.

b. When direct speech is broken into several parts, place *each part* within its own set of quotation marks. When the parts of the direct speech are complete sentences, place a period after the speaking word.

EXAMPLES:

"Mocha ice cream," said Nenita, "is my favourite."
"Oh no!" shouted Hector, "I forgot to pick up the dry cleaning."
"This movie is starting to depress me," stated Kich. "I'm going to change stations."

c. When the quotation is a question, place the question mark *inside* the quotation marks.

EXAMPLES:

Jasmine inquired, "Is this the passport office?"
"How long have you been taking piano lessons?" asked the dentist.

d. When the sentence poses a question but the quotation itself is a statement, place the question mark at the end of the sentence and outside the quotation marks.

EXAMPLES:

Did you say, "I really enjoyed her sermon"?
Did Ralph remark, "This is not a good day"?

e. When both the sentence and the quotation are questions, place the question mark *within* the quotation marks.

EXAMPLES:

Did Amanda ask, "Where is the nearest phone booth?"
Did he really ask, "Why are you asking me?"

f. To indicate a quotation within another quotation, use **single quotation marks (' ')**.

EXAMPLES:

"At the meeting, Fred shouted, 'I resign!'" said Ken.

"After the farewell party, there were tears in Jim's eyes," said Brenda. "He said, 'I'll miss you all.'"

g. In **direct speech** you are quoting someone word for word. In **indirect speech**, you are reporting that someone said something but in your own words. Do *not* place quotation marks around indirect speech.

EXAMPLES:

The teacher said that she was returning the test papers on Monday.

Brian told everybody that I split my pants dancing last night.

Note that if a "speaking" word is followed by the word *that*, indirect speech is indicated.

EXERCISE ◆ 26

Place quotation marks, commas, capital letters, and closing punctuation where required in the following sentences.

EXAMPLE:

Tia said call me tomorrow.

Tia said*, "Call me tomorrow."*

1. This is my last cigarette promised Inge
2. The salesperson said this sweater has been reduced in price 50%.
3. You know I never say no to helping someone said Sunita
4. Are you barbecuing steaks tonight asked Francine
5. Did you say that you weren't going asked Zofia
6. I can't believe my eyes remarked Joy I've passed the test
7. Wow exclaimed Don that's the biggest blimp I've ever seen
8. Are you the new teacher remarked Glenda
9. The wine remarked Henri that I like best is organic
10. I read the novel before I saw the movie said Fritz

EXERCISE ◆ 27

Follow the instructions for Exercise 26.

1. David said sympathetically I know how you feel
2. Did Edna really say I made a mistake

3. They shouted together look out the bear is right behind you
4. This bump on my head said Ralph looks like a doorknob
5. Did you ask are the buns really warm
6. Can you imagine what it would be like to be a spider asked Devon
7. Lin said that she was wearing her black dress to the party.
8. I remarked Rose can't live without my morning coffee
9. Sing this song for me requested Daniel you have such a beautiful voice
10. Isaac asked where are all the guests

EXERCISE • 28

Follow the instructions for Exercise 27.

1. Trinh said the strawberries are ripe
2. What could be more important asked the bishop
3. Your eyes remarked Hilde are so bloodshot
4. How old is this roast beef coughed the choking customer
5. Take a break Maureen; you deserve it.
6. Did Glenda ask how long does it usually take
7. Did Alex say your cheeks are really red
8. The movie was really great said Alice
9. Ed shouted I can't stand this music anymore said Cynthia
10. Who asked you your age asked Margaret

EXERCISE • 29

Follow the instructions for Exercise 28.

1. Isn't the wind bitter remarked Indira
2. Ted said that he would bring the potato salad.
3. Green remarked Angela is not my favourite nail polish colour
4. I love to run through the autumn leaves said Brittany
5. Did Cosmo ask how hard can this nut be to crack
6. Help me she screamed said Walter
7. I can barely keep my eyes open whispered Annie
8. I know now commented Jose why their compact disc was on sale
9. Did Vera ask did I make the right decision to go back to school
10. You've won 4 kg of mince announced the butcher at his shop

EXERCISE • 30

Follow the instructions for Exercise 29.

1. Listen Ida whispered to the rain on the roof
2. What are the qualities of a good mate asked Sam
3. After that last remark shouted Burgess I know that you are an idiot
4. Did you order this jacket from the catalogue inquired Cassie
5. Do you know said Francine that gerbils are monogamous
6. The dates and numbers that you want are on your desk said Eugenie
7. Lin Ling said that she wasn't feeling well today.
8. The bill is for six hundred dollars said the smiling dentist
9. What remarked the boss would I do without you
10. Did Kay ask weren't you wrong last time too

2. Words Used in a Special Sense

Use quotation marks to enclose words used in an ironic, literary, or technical way.

EXAMPLES:

Have you studied "signed numbers" yet?

The teacher keeps saying that "alliteration" is a common figure of speech.

3. Titles of Articles, Poems, Songs, and Stories

Use quotation marks to enclose the titles of articles from magazines or newspapers, poems, songs, short stories, and other artistic creations such as radio and television shows.

Always italicize (in print) or underline (in type or handwritten script) titles of books, newspapers, journals, plays, and films.

EXAMPLES:

In *PC World* magazine, I enjoyed reading "Fastest CD ROM Drives in Town."

"Sonnet 43" by Elizabeth Barrett Browning is probably her most famous poem.

When Paul McCartney sings "Yesterday," Dianne's heart melts.

Is "As a Wife Has a Cow" by Gertrude Stein really a love story?

Note that if titles enclosed by quotation marks come at the end of a sentence, the end punctuation mark is also enclosed as in the first example. Question marks, however, that are not part of a title remain outside.

Try the following exercises. They will include all the rules for quotation marks you have learned in Unit 4.

EXERCISE • 31

Place quotation marks, commas, capital letters, and closing punctuation where required in the following sentences.

EXAMPLE:

Why said Gwen would I buy used cottage cheese

"Why," said Gwen, "would I buy used cottage cheese?"

1. How can I find an example of onomatopoeia in this poem when I don't even know what the word means
2. Don't say it said Barry
3. You mean that film has been in the camera since 1972 asked David
4. Certainly said Carolyn I'll be happy to give you my autograph
5. Javinder said I read the essay Three Days to See by Helen Keller when I was in high school
6. What is a stereogram
7. Don't you think that the poem The Eve of St. Agnes is a little too long remarked Sam
8. If you're going to the store said Irena get me a copy of Shape magazine
9. Greg always says it's always darkest before it turns completely black
10. Do you send Easter cards asked Ms. Prince

EXERCISE • 32

Follow the instructions for Exercise 31.

1. Have you ever tried dry column chromatography
2. I'm sure said Violet that that bird was an evening grosbeak
3. What is the article Welcome to the Shoe Store about in this issue of the English Journal
4. Did you check the expiry date on the wool socks asked Arthur
5. Your Halloween mask is scary stated Jean but not as scary as you without it
6. Hernando asked if smoking was permitted in the theatre lobby.

7. Take your time said the patient to the doctor I'm not going anywhere in this hospital gown
8. Did Neil ask has the repair person arrived yet
9. *Mapping Ourselves* is an autobiography of Canadian women
10. I think I'm doomed remarked Doris

EXERCISE ♦ 33

Follow the instructions for Exercise 32.

1. Why did Keith say this is my doughnut
2. Tomorrow's lesson is on hydrodesulfurization
3. I'll go said Sharon it's near my house
4. Do you know the song In the Shape of a Heart by Jackson Browne asked Rhonda
5. What could be more beautiful sighed Juan than the sunset reflected in your eyes
6. Ben asked for money again said Jasmine
7. Doug read every article in this month's *Start Your Own Business* magazine said Jerusha
8. Edgar Allan Poe said I make Beauty the province of the poem
9. Shut the light said Bernie I'm trying to sleep
10. Amanda said I read Do You Call Yourself a Poet in *Writer's Digest* magazine

EXERCISE ♦ 34

Complete the following phrases and clauses to include quotation marks as required.

EXAMPLE:

Elsa said

Elsa said, "I studied until midnight."

1. Did Brendan ask

   ____

2. Why is the refrigerator open

   ____

3. Stopping by Woods on a Snowy Evening is a poem by Robert Frost that

   ____

4. Did Lena explain what the term desiccator means to

   ____

5. Don't touch it shouted Russell it's

____

6. Layla is Julie's favourite Eric Clapton song

____

7. Ramona said

____

8. The paint is still wet

____

9. Lena can translate that for you

____

10. Did Jerry tell you

____

EXERCISE • 35

Write original sentences using quotation marks, commas, and capital letters as required.

EXAMPLE:

quotation is a statement
<u>Ernie said, "You're my best friend."</u>

1. quotation is a question

____

2. quotation is split in a simple sentence

____

3. quotation is a question; sentence is a question

____

4. title of a short story

____

5. quotation is a statement; sentence is a question

____

6. quotation is split in a compound sentence

____

7. quotation is a question; sentence is a statement

____

8. quotation is a statement; sentence is a question

____

9. title of a magazine article

____

10. word used in a special sense

____

UNIT • 4 • POST-TEST

If you have completed Unit 4 satisfactorily, then you are ready for the Post-Test. The answers immediately follow the test.

Place colons, semicolons, quotation marks, commas, capitals, and closing punctuation where required in the following sentences.

1. Dr Jan Smith will see you now

2. Of course I am familiar with Bliss Carman's poem The Christmas Song

3. I really enjoyed the music replied Magda

4. It's never too late I'll drive you there right now

5. In Eugene O'Neill's play *Ah, Wilderness!* what does Mrs Miller do in Act IV iii asked Yvonne

6. Tomorrow is supposed to be hot said Greg it'll be perfect for a day at the beach

7. In the play *Juno and the Paycock* by Sean O'Casey what is a paycock

8. Naturally we were stuffed after our huge dinner but we still had room for dessert commented Andy

9. Carolyn said I never heard of the song Midnight in December

10. I'm not familiar with the term cyme

11. To tell the joke properly you need a cake an apple and a doughnut

12. Don't worry remarked Mavis I saw what happened

13. When were the following devices invented the bifocal lens the hydrometer and the microphone

14. The clouds were churning quickly in fact rain had already begun to fall recalled Fiona

15. Is Jack London who wrote the short story To Build a Fire Canadian or American wondered Peter

ANSWERS • TO • UNIT • 4 • POST-TEST

Place colons, semicolons, quotation marks, commas, capitals, and closing punctuation where required in the following sentences.

1. Dr. Jan Smith will see you now.

2. Of course(,) I am familiar with Bliss Carman's poem "The Christmas Song."

3. "I really enjoyed the music," replied Magda.
4. It's never too late; I'll drive you there right now.
5. "In Eugene O'Neill's play *Ah, Wilderness!*, what does Mrs. Miller do in Act IV:iii?" asked Yvonne.
6. "Tomorrow is supposed to be hot," said Greg. "It'll be perfect for a day at the beach."
7. In the play *Juno and the Paycock* by Sean O'Casey, what is a "paycock"?
8. "Naturally, we were stuffed after our huge dinner, but we still had room for dessert," commented Andy.
9. Carolyn said, "I never heard of the song 'Midnight in December.'"
10. I'm not familiar with the term "cyme."
11. To tell the joke properly, you need a cake, an apple(,) and a doughnut.
12. "Don't worry," remarked Mavis. "I saw what happened."
13. When were the following devices invented: the bifocal lens, the hydrometer(,) and the microphone?
14. "The clouds were churning quickly; in fact, rain had already begun to fall," recalled Fiona.
15. "Is Jack London, who wrote the short story 'To Build a Fire,' Canadian or American?" wondered Peter.

U·N·I·T 5

THE WRITING PROCESS

Writing is tough. Few writers have sat down and effortlessly produced a coherent, grammatical, and stylistically sound product. Good writing is the end result of a process that requires the organization of ideas to convey the meaning of a specific subject-matter. Although writers' opinions about the writing process may vary, most writers agree in the need for painstaking writing and rewriting.

Read the following comments on the writing process by two famous Canadian authors. You'll discover that when you write, you share in the joys and frustrations of all writers, professional or amateur.

> Writers often write novels — and plays and stories and poems — which are never published. Failures, in other words. I suppose that's the way you learn to write.
>
> A writer [doesn't sit] down and turn out exactly what he wants to turn out — this time a good novel, this time just fair, this time a masterpiece. There may be some who can do it, control the quality and reach of their work, but most, I'm sure, are poor struggling, stumbling mortals who do what they can. Sometimes they're in top form, sometimes not. They make mistakes, attempt themes not suited to them, they get out of their depth — a hundred things.
>
> — Sinclair Ross

> When I've distanced myself from the whole thing much more than I am able to do when first writing it. The first time through, one is inside, seeing it from the inside. In rewriting, one is seeing it more as a whole, and not from that deeply inside viewpoint any more. The first time through, you feel

your way. The second or third times, you can think about it ... Sometimes, with everything I've written- whole pages will come easily and will hardly have a line changed. ... But more often it is a case of going over the thing and altering the parts which (when seen at a greater distance than is possible the first time) do not seem to come across well. The best times, of course, are when everything comes spontaneously, by itself, the characters finding words which express themselves. It would be good if this happened all the time, but it doesn't. And it can't be forced. I guess any writer can only hope for it to happen this way.

— Margaret Laurence

Item I: Before You Start

By now you have mastered writing the four sentence types — simple, compound, complex, and compound-complex. Organizing them in a variety of ways to convey meaning to the reader becomes the next task of the writing process.

However, this process is often hampered by the use of poor diction. Unnecessary clichés and wordiness and redundancy reduce the effectiveness of your writing and diminish its focus.

1. Clichés

Clichés are long-standing expressions that have been over used in the English language. They give quick expression to ideas but lack originality and freshness. A writer who uses clichés deadens the writing process. Avoid them in your writing and your speaking.

Here are some commonly used clichés.

add insult to injury	bite the bullet
after all is said and done	blind as a bat
all things being equal	burn the midnight oil
a last resort	bury the hatchet
as the crow flies	busy as a beaver
a real pill	clear as mud
at a loss for words	cool as a cucumber
at the crack of dawn	crazy like a fox
bark up the wrong tree	cry wolf
better late than never	cut the mustard

dead meat
dog-tired
doomed to failure
don't look a gift horse in the mouth
easier said than done
face the music
fall off the wagon
faster than greased lightning
few and far between
fly off the handle
gentle as a lamb
get cold feet
get a haircut
get the sack
get up on the wrong side of bed
give up the ghost
goes without saying
good as gold
grist for the mill
handwriting on the wall
hit the nail on the head
hold the phone
hold your horses
I'm toast
in hot water
in the doghouse
kick the bucket
knock on wood
in the long run
in the nick of time
it goes without saying
keep the ball rolling
keeping up with the Joneses
knuckle under
last but not least
manna from heaven
month of Sundays
needle in a haystack
not a happy camper
on the nose
on the right track
once in a blue moon
one and the same
out on a limb
par for the course
piece of my mind
pipe dream
pull some strings
raining cats and dogs
rotten to the core
scot-free
run hog-wild
see the light
seeing is believing
sharp as a tack
skin of one's teeth
smoke and mirrors
spill the beans
string along
strong as an ox
talk a blue streak
take a hike
touch base
upset the cart
when all is said and done
wolf in sheep's clothing

EXERCISE • 1

Improve the following sentences with clear, original expressions.

EXAMPLE:

I passed the test by the *skin of my teeth.* (cliché)
I *barely* passed the test. (improved)

Note: The following sentences have been written to give some suggestion as to the meaning of the cliché. If any are unfamiliar to you, ask your teacher for an explanation.

1. I was joking; don't fly off the handle.
2. You're off the beaten track in this neighbourhood.
3. Getting an A in this course is easier said than done.
4. After winning the lottery, George was on easy street.
5. This is quite a storm; it's raining cats and dogs.
6. My brother is strong as an ox.
7. I was dog-tired after the workout.
8. Maureen wasn't nervous; she was cool as a cucumber.
9. Take the bull by the horns, and ask your brother for a raise.
10. Ryan is a huge man, but he's gentle as a lamb.

EXERCISE • 2

Follow the instructions for Exercise 1.

1. The park is only 4 km from here as the crow flies.
2. Women like Zhen are few and far between.
3. It's par for the course to find only one blueberry in a jumbo blueberry muffin.
4. Getting William to do any housework is like beating a dead horse.
5. Gladys, you're a sight for sore eyes.
6. Aldo knows all the math answers; he's sharp as a tack.
7. Keep the news about Mensha a secret; I don't want you to spill the beans.
8. We'd better tighten our belts; there's going to be another tax hike.
9. Doreen must have got up on the wrong side of the bed this morning.
10. Everything is as clear as mud; explain it again.

EXERCISE • 3

Follow the instructions for Exercise 2.

1. I bought the business lock, stock, and barrel.
2. After inadvertently embarrassing the boss's husband, Gwen knew she was toast.
3. Use these transitional words, and you will be on the right track.
4. The children are growing by leaps and bounds.
5. Bruce left me holding the bag when he didn't pay his half of the rent.
6. When I go in to see the boss, it's like talking to a brick wall.
7. Martin looks as busy as a bee, but I wonder if it's all smoke and mirrors.
8. "Seeing is believing," said the magician.
9. Don't get cold feet.
10. I was so angry that I gave her a piece of my mind.

EXERCISE • 4

Follow the instructions for Exercise 3.

1. The streets should be safer at night in this day and age.
2. Wendell works so hard without complaining; he must be an eager beaver.
3. We were in the boat at the crack of dawn.
4. The baby was as good as gold; she never cried once.
5. It goes without saying that public speaking can be stressful.
6. Roberto Alomar of the Blue Jays was dead meat at first base in last night's game.
7. Antonio hit the nail on the head with his remarks last night.
8. Drinking to forget that you're depressed can be a vicious circle.
9. I heard that Warren got the sack.
10. Now that the baby is here we'll go out once in a blue moon.

EXERCISE • 5

Follow the instructions for Exercise 4.

1. Andrew doesn't like to play second fiddle to anyone.
2. Ed will stand by you through thick and thin.
3. We'll be there in two shakes of a lamb's tail.

4. Julia is in hot water again at work because she didn't finish the financial report.
5. Emma's new diaper dress takes the cake.
6. Since he joined Gluttons Anonymous, Bill has not fallen off the wagon.
7. Why is Adele always trying to upset the cart?
8. I need a summer job; can you pull some strings for me?
9. Hold your horses; we're not leaving for another twenty minutes.
10. Why is Stan in the doghouse this time?

2. Wordiness

Wordiness results from using too many words to express a simple idea. These excess words overburden your sentences and prevent your writing from being direct.

Here are some examples of wordy expressions.

absolutely nothing
at the present time
at this point in time
by means of
come to the conclusion
due to the fact
for the purpose of
in all likelihood
in all probably
inasmuch as
in colour
in height
in length
in shape
in size
in the near future
in the neighbourhood of
on the occasion of
on the whole
owing to the fact that
prior to
take it upon oneself
the month of
unless otherwise stated
until such time as
with regard to
with the exception of
without further delay

3. Redundancy

Redundancy is a form of wordiness in which too many words in a group express the same idea. The simplest method of remedying this problem is to remove the excess words.

Here are some commonly used redundant expressions.

above and beyond
actual fact
advance planning
adequate enough

character trait
climb up
collect together
close scrutiny
close up
concluding result
connect together
continue on
depressed and sad
disappear from view
divide in two
end result
enter into
erode away
exact replica
first and foremost
free gift
general consensus
honest truth
mental attitude
personal opinion
necessary prerequisite
other alternatives
repeat again
refer back
unexpected surprise
visible to the naked eye

EXERCISE • 6

Improve the following sentences which contain wordy and redundant expressions.

EXAMPLE:

At this point in time we can't be sure. (wordiness)
At this time we can't be sure. (improved)
At this point we can't be sure. (improved)

1. Your approach to this problem is very unique.
2. Dawn's hair is auburn in colour.
3. The bakery is opening here in the near future.
4. I read the true facts in the newspaper.
5. In all probability we will be going to Quebec this summer.
6. How much did you pay for those real genuine leather shoes?
7. At this point in time there are no job openings.
8. Boris apologized in view of the fact that he had hurt Jana's feelings.
9. When did you come to realize that the earth was round?
10. Nicholas is small in size and nervous in spirit.

EXERCISE • 7

Follow the instructions for Exercise 6.

1. Up until now I was conceited, but now I'm perfect.
2. The concluding result was that she had forgot to pay for the skirt.

3. With the exception of Milton, who threw up, we all enjoyed the ride.
4. I think that Joe was born in the month of October.
5. In my personal opinion, he should not wear a hairpiece.
6. What other alternatives are there?
7. I'd hate to enter into an argument with Fritz.
8. The message seemed plain and clear to me.
9. Climb up the ladder carefully.
10. Michael was depressed and sad for some reason.

EXERCISE • 8

Follow the instructions for Exercise 7.

1. The colour in these blue jeans fades away quickly.
2. William was almost on the verge of losing his temper.
3. The explosion caused a disastrous catastrophe.
4. You can see the city better up at the top.
5. We are not taking a vacation in the foreseeable future.
6. Due to the fact that she never studied, Irene dropped out of college.
7. Will George be able to put in an appearance at the party?
8. Peter has survived life without working by virtue of his charm.
9. They honoured Len on the occasion of his fortieth birthday.
10. The argument started for no apparent reason.

EXERCISE • 9

Follow the instructions for Exercise 8.

1. The earthquake caused a devastating tragedy.
2. This problem is clearly obvious.
3. The proposal gave advance notice that funds were going to be cut.
4. Celine is very tall in height.
5. Absolutely nothing will persuade me to eat worms.
6. The magician made the ball float in the air by means of an invisible thread.
7. Not a single solitary soul offered the beggar any money.
8. The honest truth is that I love you.
9. The UFO disappeared from view in a matter of seconds.
10. Every other day Helen alternates between driving and walking to work.

EXERCISE ♦ 10

Follow the instructions for Exercise 9.

1. The movie last night was incredibly unbelievable.
2. Will this room be adequate enough for you tonight?
3. I think that Diane's hair is purple in colour.
4. Your generosity is above and beyond what I had expected.
5. The red wine will be more preferable for supper.
6. In all likelihood Martin will become a dentist.
7. Do we have to go out into the freezing cold?
8. From time to time Jab smokes a big cigar.
9. Phil seldom ever complains about his situation.
10. Should these wires be connected together?

Item II: How Do I Start?

How many times have you sat in front of a blank piece of paper and asked yourself: "How do I start?" It may therefore surprise you that many people find that shaping the final product is the most difficult part of the writing process, and starting is the easiest part. Brainstorming and freewriting are two methods for expressing your ideas on paper as quickly as possible.

1. Brainstorming

In **brainstorming**, you write every idea that enters your mind on a certain subject. It is good to write your ideas in point form so that you don't become bogged down with the mechanics of writing. At this stage, it is important not to reject any ideas.

When you have exhausted your topic, assess your ideas and choose the most important ones to form a second list. Then examine the second list, and delete unrelated ideas or brainstorm further to add more-specific ideas.

Let's look at an example of brainstorming by a student on the topic of buying a new car. Here is his brainstorming list. What ideas would you delete or combine? How would you number them in order of importance?

Saving money	Automatic/standard
Having money	Time of year

- Best interest rate
- Best deal
- Best dealer
- Car type
- Features: colour, tape/CD, ABS, air bags, etc.
- Best price
- Haggling
- New/used
- Dealer

EXERCISE • 11

Choose one of the following topics or one you have agreed upon with your teacher, and brainstorm until you have completed a list. When your list is complete, number your ideas in order of importance.

1. borrowing money
2. a visit to the dentist
3. your favourite city
4. something that upset you
5. failing a test
6. a surprise visitor
7. buying new shoes
8. spiders
9. starting a diet
10. speaking in front of a group

EXERCISE • 12

Follow the instructions for Exercise 11.

1. an embarrassing moment
2. sleeping in
3. preparing for a job interview
4. proposing marriage
5. your only vice
6. a speeding ticket
7. a little phobia
8. New Year's Eve party
9. quitting smoking
10. a bad haircut

2. Freewriting

Like brainstorming, **freewriting** allows you to express your ideas on paper as quickly as possible. With freewriting, however, you should write for ten or fifteen minutes on anything that comes to mind. You can write sentences, phrases, or words — just keep writing no matter how silly or unconnected your ideas may seem. Chances are you will subconsciously write ideas that are related, but this is not important with freewriting. Instead, use freewriting as an exercise to "prime your writing pump."

Here is an example of a student's freewriting.

> I was so tired looking out the window at the snow falling I would be happy but I was too tired. The hockey game was on I think the Leafs were winning too. My sister came into my room to borrow a book tomorrow I'm going to Niagara Falls with my parents to see the lights I hope it's all right. Maybe I'll put on a CD and listen to it while I finish my assignment. I'll take a shower too. Anyway I'm going to stop writing what comes into my head and take five. I'm running out of things to write about.

Note that freewriting, as its name implies, has a quality of freedom in content and form.

Another kind of freewriting is *focussed freewriting* in which you write freely on a specific subject. This activity will help you to focus your thoughts in order to develop an idea.

Look at this example of focussed freewriting.

> A driver was so rude to me I could have screamed. I was just stepping to the curb to cross the street at the light and the stupid idiot pulled closer to me so that he could drive through a huge puddle. I was soaked my new fall jacket was a mess my face and hair was a muddy mess. I said some things out loud and worse in my mind that can't be repeated I sure wish he could know what it feels like to be treated so inconsiderately. I'm sure he did it out of spite and that really hurt me and ruined my day.

EXERCISE • 13

Practise focussed freewriting by choosing one of the following topics and writing about it for ten minutes.

1. stuck in traffic
2. a toothache
3. spilling something on your clothes
4. dark basements

5. a boring teacher
6. a troublesome duty
7. snow
8. a miserable vacation
9. missing a pet
10. the flu

EXERCISE • 14

Follow the instructions for Exercise 13.

1. lunch
2. the boss
3. being lost
4. a broken promise
5. lightning
6. hunting for a birthday card
7. growing your own vegetables
8. unwanted piece of furniture
9. being caught in the rain
10. really bad breath

Item III: The Topic Sentence

a. The ideas that you express through brainstorming or freewriting need to be organized around a main idea regarding your subject or topic. Always state your main idea in the topic sentence of your paragraph.

A good **topic sentence** clearly states the main idea and is supported and developed by the other sentences in the paragraph. In addition, try to express your main idea in an interesting topic sentence containing key words that compel your reader to discover what the supporting sentences will reveal. This is best achieved when the topic sentence is focussed rather than general.

Compare the following general and focussed topic sentences.

EXAMPLES:

Cheese from Canada is tasty. (general)
Cheddar cheese from Canada is tasty. (specific)

The concert was excellent. (general)
The children's Christmas concert was excellent. (specific)

Note that the addition of the key descriptive information words *Cheddar, children's,* and *Christmas* focus the subject-matter of the topic sentences.

EXERCISE • 15

Use the following ideas to form focussed topic sentences.

1. This movie is sad.
2. The park is beautiful.
3. This is the best ice cream.
4. Collecting stamps is fun.
5. We bought a puppy.
6. Choosing computer requires advice.
7. The zoo is large.
8. I hate the dark.
9. A breakdown on the road is no fun.
10. Happiness is. …

EXERCISE • 16

Follow the instructions for Exercise 15.

1. cutting the grass
2. the problem with tests
3. the joy of music
4. living at home
5. a new teacher
6. the newspaper
7. being alone
8. my first date
9. making supper
10. wallpapering

b. Here are some examples of paragraphs from short stories by Canadian authors. Note that the topic sentence (underlined) in each paragraph presents details that persuade you to continue to read.

He stepped on the gas when he reached the edge of town. The big car took hold of the pavement and began to eat up the miles on the straight, almost level, highway. With his elbow stuck through the open window he stared ahead at the shimmering greyness of road. He felt heavy and pleasantly satiated after his good small-town breakfast, and he shifted his bulk in the seat, at the same time brushing some cigar ash from the front of his salient vest. In another four hours he would be home — a day ahead of himself this trip, but with plenty to show the office for last week's work. *He unconsciously patted the wallet resting in the inside pocket of his jacket as he thought of the orders he had taken.*

— Hugh Garner, "The Yellow Sweater"

At the end of Bell Street, McKay Street, Mayo Street, there was a flood. It was the Wawanash River, which every spring overflowed its banks. Some springs, say one in every five, it covered the roads on that side of town and washed over fields, creating a shallow choppy lake. Light reflected off the water made everything bright and cold, as it is in a lakeside town, and woke or revived in people certain vague hopes of disaster. Mostly during the late afternoon and early evening, there were people straggling out to look at it, and discuss whether it was rising,and whether this time it might invade the town. *In general, those under fifteen and over sixty-five were most certain that it would.*

— Alice Munro, "The Found Boat"

My aunt Theresina Veilleux was born in our cold province of Manitoba, and to her it was a misfortune. She suffered from asthma, and the wind that blows in our parts was one of the most malign for her; the very air harmed her...except when it was gentle and scented by the wild rose, as happens in the month of June. *Then my aunt could breathe without too much fear.*

— Gabrielle Roy, "My Aunt Theresina Veilleux"

c. The **concluding sentence** in your paragraph brings a sense of completion to the reader; it should restate the premise of the topic sentence by making reference to the supporting sentences of the paragraph body. In some instances, the concluding sentence offers more than a simple summation of the principal ideas.

Depending on the type of paragraph you are writing, the concluding sentence may offer an opinion, confirm the result of a process, state the outcome of an event, or challenge the reader to respond.

Examine the concluding sentences (italicized) in the three paragraphs in the preceding section. What do these sentences accomplish?

EXERCISE • 17

For each of the following topics, write an effective topic sentence. Then write suitable concluding sentences for a paragraph that might contain the topic sentence.

1. the best French fries
2. the first day on campus
3. my favourite magazine
4. talk radio
5. cafeteria food
6. being a single parent
7. a visit to the zoo
8. the joy of horror films
9. your father
10. a day everything went wrong

EXERCISE • 18

Follow the instructions for Exercise 17.

1. people who ride escalators
2. your first airplane flight
3. your mate
4. spitting on the street
5. playing a musical instrument
6. the importance of money
7. dating after separation/divorce
8. buying a CD player
9. traveling by train
10. reducing stress at work/school

Item IV: Organizing Your Ideas

As you have already learned, brainstorming and freewriting are effective ways to generate ideas on a specific topic. Once you have completed one of these processes, you need to organize your ideas. This is the first step toward giving your paragraph unity and coherence.

1. Unity

Unity is achieved when all parts of the paragraph (the topic sentence, the body, and the concluding sentence) relate to the main idea.

2. Coherence

Coherence refers to the sequence of sentences and how they are connected in a paragraph. We have already seen how unity can be achieved.

An effective method of creating coherence in your paragraph is to organize it according to a pattern based on *time*, *space*, or *order of importance*. Each of these ordering devices will help you develop a particular type of paragraph, such as descriptive, process (explanatory and how-to), persuasive, narrative, and comparison and/or contrast.

a. Time Order

In a paragraph *organized according to time* — events, stories, and instructions follow a time sequence in which they occur. Narrative, how-to, and explanatory paragraphs are often organized according to time. Read the following examples.

At what was in 1819 a remote curve in the old government road (now County Road 4) between Perth and Richmond, west of present-day Highway 15 north of Smith Falls, Archibald Gillies opened a licensed hotel. This popular stopping place became known as Gillies Corners. For 20 years Gillies' hotel catered continuously to thirsty and weary travellers before finally closing its doors in the 1850's. Over that time a small village had developed and included a church, a school, and a number of private dwellings.

— Ron Browne, "Gillies Corners," *Ghost Towns of Ontario*

The first step in spotting with dyes is to mix the colours of the different dyes in the proportion recommended for the type of paper to be spotted. Place the brush into the concentrated mixture and transfer it to the artist's palette. This will give the darkest colour. Without rinsing the brush, place it into a container of water and transfer it to a second area of the palette. This will produce a much lighter tone than the first and is suitable for midtone areas.

— John Friar and Birthney Ardoin, *Effective Photography*

EXERCISE • 19

Write a paragraph organized by time on one of the following topics. Be sure to make a list of details or events first; then arrange them in order of occurrence and importance.

1. how to apologize graciously
2. your only blind date
3. decorating the family room
4. how to relieve stress

5. Niagara Falls
6. being caught in a summer storm
7. organizing your bedroom closet
8. waiting at the dentist's office
9. visiting your hometown
10. returning a purchase without the bill

EXERCISE • 20

Follow the instructions for Exercise 19.

1. dressing for a job interview
2. how to use an index
3. driving on icy road
4. your wedding day
5. how you met your best friend
6. making a cosy evening
7. how to make the perfect cup of coffee
8. learning to ice-skate
9. the best pizza toppings
10. winning an award

b. Space Order

In a paragraph *organized according to space*, use a predetermined pattern to arrange details that describe a person, place, or thing. For instance, arrange details from left to right, front to back, or top to bottom.

Read the following examples of paragraphs organized by space.

She was beautiful but dangerous. She had thrown one man and killed him, thrown another and broken his collar bone, and my parents, as if they knew what the sight of her idle in her stall was doing to me, never let a day go by without giving lurid details, everything from splints and stitches to the undertaker, of the painful and untimely end in store for me should I ever take it into my fool young head to try to ride her.

— Sinclair Ross,"The Outlaw"

Although she was nearly twenty-one, Alma still had the long thin shape characteristic of eleven- and twelve-year-old girls. She had small hips and a small bust, so that she gave the impression of being fragile and light. Her bones were so delicately made that they might have been fashioned from hollow glass. The two prettiest things about her were her eyes and her hair. Her eyes were a deep brown and exceptionally large, so that they dominated her face. Her hair had the luminous sheen that hazelnut shells retain for only the briefest time just after the green hull has been removed.

— W. D. Valgardson, "Skald"

EXERCISE • 21

Write a paragraph organized by space on one of the following topics.

1. a bus station washroom
2. the comfort of flannel sheets
3. a skating ring at night
4. a favourite teacher
5. the fingers on someone's (your) hands
6. a favourite painting or photo
7. the air in spring
8. the eyes of a loved one
9. a favourite relative
10. the scene in the following photo

EXERCISE • 22

Follow the instructions for Exercise 21.

1. a favourite childhood toy
2. saying goodbye at an airport, train station, etc.
3. New Year's Eve celebrations
4. a day of misfortunes
5. being lonely
6. an instance you laughed so hard
7. a slippery drive to school/work
8. a child's sleeping face
9. a disappointing evening
10. the person in the following photo

c. Order of Importance

In a paragraph *organized according to order of importance,* begin with the least important detail or event and build to the most important. This creates a sense of building to a climax.

Read the following examples of paragraphs organized by importance.

Gold was first discovered in Ontario in 1866 on the farm of John Richardson near the village of Madoc in Hastings County. A gold rush developed, and subsequently gold was found in a number of places in a belt 70 miles long extending from Belmont Township in Peterborough County, across the counties of Hastings, Frontenac, and Lennox and Addington, into Lanark County. Gold was mined in eastern Ontario from more than a dozen mines from the early 1890's until about 1917, with a total production of about $750,000. The principal mines were at Cordova and Deloro.

— D. F. Hewitt and E. B. Freeman, *Rocks and Minerals of Ontario*

George Brown was a tall, intense, red-headed Scot. The sweeping influence of his paper, the Toronto *Globe,* made him the most noted newspaper man in Canada in the mid-nineteenth century. He entered Parliament, took hold of a shattered Liberal party and built it into a massive force. Then, as part chieftain and *Globe* editor, he pushed vigorously to add the vast, empty northwest beyond the Great Lakes to the existing Canadian union. He strove equally hard to remake that union, and played a vital role in bringing about Confederation in 1867. His drive, his decisions, helped mould modern Canada.

— J.M.S. Careless, *The Canadians: George Brown*

EXERCISE • 23

Write a paragraph organized by order of importance on one of the following topics.

1. a popular singer
2. washing the kitchen floor
3. shopping for new shoes
4. setting off fireworks
5. the ideal mate
6. organizing a family reunion
7. your first teddy bear
8. the importance of good hygiene

9. buying a used car
10. the need for gun control

EXERCISE • 24

Follow the instructions for Exercise 23.

1. the features of the perfect kitchen
2. washing the car
3. your least favourite food
4. painting a ceiling
5. the best bakery
6. your favourite movie
7. making perfect tacos
8. the best way to read
9. judging yourself
10. a flat tire

Item V: The Descriptive Paragraph

A **descriptive paragraph** recreates a visual scene through the use of accurate details that appeal to the readers' senses. By using concrete nouns and effective adjectives and verbs, you develop and enhance atmosphere and emotion and enable the reader to see what you are describing.

Examine the following descriptive paragraph from a short story.

> <u>It was a town of unpaved, wide sandy streets and bare yards.</u> Only the hardy things like red and yellow nasturtiums, or a lilac bush with brown curled leaves, grew out of the cracked earth. The houses were set wide apart, with their own pumps and sheds and privies out behind; most of them were built of wood and painted green or grey or yellow. The trees that grew there were big willows or poplars, their fine leaves greyed with dust. There were no trees along the main street, but spaces of tall grass and dandelions and blowing thistles — open country between the store buildings. The town hall was surprisingly large, with a great bell in a tower, the red brick rather glaring in the midst of the town's walls of faded, pale-painted wood. The sign beside the door said that it was a memorial to the soldiers who had died in the First World War. We had a drink out of the fountain in front.
>
> — Alice Munro, "Thanks For the Ride"

Note that in her topic sentence, Munro introduces her subject (the town). The sentences that follow support and expand on the topic sentence with additional descriptive details.

EXERCISE • 25

Examine Munro's paragraph again. Note how many words Munro uses to create a picture. List as many of these words as you can.

________	________	________
________	________	________
________	________	________

Here is another paragraph from a short story. How vivid are the author's descriptions for you?

> He's like a photograph in my mind, one of those brown-tinted old-fashioned ones, and I see him standing in the open doorway of an old farmhouse in Sicily. He's still wearing his brown uniform but it's faded and floppy now and he's bareheaded. Instead of a rifle he holds a shovel and beside him is a heavy woman, her arms folded and her head turned toward the brightness in the picture that's probably the sun. Also there are two small children playing at my father's feet and their faces too are turned toward the sun. Only my father's face stares out beyond the black marks that are his eyes.
>
> — Don Bailey,"The Walrus and the Carpenter"

The picture Bailey creates of his father is made from images of an old wedding picture and stories about him told by his mother. It is a childhood image turned into words. The topic sentence states the purpose of the paragraph by focussing on the subject (a mental photograph) and the setting (place and time).

EXERCISE • 26

Find an old photograph of your mother or father (or other relative). Write down as many details and descriptions as you can. Don't forget to include any emotion the picture may evoke. Be sure to narrow the focus of your topic sentence so that it includes details of a specific scene.

1. Getting Organized

Organize the details in a descriptive paragraph according to space. The pattern may be back to front, side to side, or top to bottom. (See Unit 5, Item IV.) Also use transitional words to arrange your details. Here is a list of transitional words to help you organize a descriptive paragraph.

above	beyond	near
at the same time	centre	next to

away	far	on top
at	farther away	over
before	fron	subsequently
behind	there	then
below	in the distance	there
beneath	later	toward
beside	left	
between	middle	

2. Descriptive Paragraph Review

Have you succeeded in making your readers perceive the actions and emotions you are describing?

- Brainstorm all your ideas on the topic.
- Place them in order of importance.
- Eliminate similar or duplicate ideas.
- Use concrete nouns.
- Use effective adjectives and verbs.
- Use space order to move through your description from side to side, top to bottom, or inside to outside.
- Put all ideas into sentence form.
- Write a focussed topic sentence.
- Write supporting sentences to convey idea introduced in topic sentence.
- Write a concluding sentence that tells the reader you have expressed the idea introduced in the topic sentence.
- Write a rough draft.
- Make corrections to spelling, grammar, usage, and punctuation.
- Rewrite for your good copy.

EXERCISE • 27

Examine the two photographs. Follow the guidelines in the paragraph review for a descriptive paragraph, and write a paragraph describing each photo.

EXERCISE ♦ 28

Select a topic from the following list, and write a descriptive paragraph. Follow any instructions your teacher may have for writing on these topics.

1. your favourite bookstore
2. your favourite department store
3. a frustrating experience
4. the main street of your hometown
5. a souvenir shop
6. a bad sunburn
7. a house decorated for Halloween
9. your favourite singer
10. your best friend's only vice

EXERCISE ♦ 29

Follow the instructions for Exercise 28.

1. your boss
2. a vacation that was a disaster
3. your favourite restaurant
4. your favourite special moment
5. a lightning storm
6. a run-down neighbourhood
7. an enjoyable night class
8. the personality of a friend
9. your honeymoon
10. the worst cafeteria experience

Item VI: The Process Paragraph

Explanatory and how-to paragraphs are **process paragraphs**.

An **explanatory paragraph** presents and explains information so that the reader can understand how something has happened, how something can be accomplished, or how something works.

In a **how-to paragraph**, information is presented through details in chronological order so that the reader can understand and accomplish a task.

Examine the following explanatory paragraph, and note how the author supports her topic sentence with facts.

> Lightning is the most awesome of nature's weather phenomena — a single stroke of lightning produces more electricity than the combined output of all electrical power plants in the United States. The average cloud-to-ground lightning bolt averages only six inches in diameter, but attains a core temperature of about 50,000 degrees Fahrenheit — five times the temperature at the surface of the sun.
>
> — Janice McEwen, "Thunderstrokes and Firebolts"

EXERCISE ◆ 30

Read the explanatory paragraph on lightning again. Count how many points are made, and list them.

____

____

____

____

____

Examine the following how-to paragraph.

> Combine water and 1 tsp. sugar and stir until sugar dissolves. Sprinkle yeast over and let stand 10 minutes. Stir well. Scald milk and pour into mixing bowl. Stir in shortening, 1 tbsp. sugar and salt and cool to lukewarm. Add yeast mixture, eggs and flour and beat well. Cover with a damp cloth and let rise in a warm place until double, about 1 hour. Stir well. Grease sixteen 2 1/2 inch muffin pans. Half fill pans with batter. Heat oven to 375 degrees. Bake buns about 20 minutes or until golden. Roll hot buns quickly in melted butter, then in a mixture of 3/4 cup sugar, coffee and cinnamon. Serve warm. (Makes 16)
>
> — Margo Oliver, *Margo Oliver's Cookbook*

1. Getting Organized

Arrange ideas in explanatory and how-to paragraphs chronologically. Remember that your topic sentence should indicate the result of the process you are describing. The following transitional words can assist you in organizing your ideas in a process paragraph.

as	first	now
as soon as	finally	second
at first	initially	then
at last	lastly	therefore
before	later	third
begin	meanwhile	when
during	next	while

EXERCISE • 31

Examine the following explanatory paragraph. List the points made and suggest an appropriate title for this paragraph.

> Credit cards can be wonderful things, but if you don't choose the right cards, or if you use the ones you have improperly, they can become a tremendous headache — especially if you lose them. Always keep several lists of your cards, their numbers, the number to call to cancel them, and the proper mailing address of the credit company. If you don't notify the companies that your cards have been lost or stolen, you won't be able to use them and you may end up paying for a portion of somebody else's good times with your plastic. A tip about credit cards: the companies which issue these cards want to make money by advancing you a line of credit. What's more, because approximately one half of all credit card users are smart enough to pay their balances off before any interest starts to accrue, these companies charge a high interest rate on those outstanding balances. The fact that many consumers pay their debts off on time is being used as an excuse by these institutions to tack on their new user fees, and to keep their interest rates on these cards so high.
>
> — Brian Costello, *Your Money and How to Keep It*

2. Process Paragraph Review

Do your readers understand clearly how a process works or how something can be accomplished?

- Write down all details of a process.
- Place them in chronological order.
- Eliminate similar or duplicate ideas.

- Use concrete nouns and clear verbs.
- Use effective adjectives and verbs.
- Put all ideas into sentence form.
- Write a focussed topic sentence stating the process you will be explaining.
- Write supporting sentences to convey ideas introduced in the topic sentence.
- Use a variety of transitional words that will allow you to move from one step to the next.
- Write a concluding sentence that states the outcome of the process introduced in the topic sentence.
- Write a rough draft.
- Make corrections to spelling, grammar, usage, and punctuation.
- Rewrite for your good copy.

EXERCISE ◆ 32

Select topics from the following list, and write an explanatory or how-to paragraph. Follow any additional instructions your teacher may have for writing these topics.

1. the best way to prepare for an exam
2. how to select a lawyer
3. a recipe for inner peace
4. how to manage your free time
5. how to roast a chicken
6. the functions of your nose
7. how to buy a camera
8. how a spider makes its web
9. how to get rid of a nervous habit
10. how to floss your teeth

EXERCISE ◆ 33

Follow the instructions for Exercise 32.

1. methods for effective listening
2. how to write a résumé

3. how to repair a leaky faucet
4. how to ask for a first date
5. how potato chips are made
6. how to tell a friend about bad breath
7. recipe for the best (blueberry, pecan, etc.) muffins
8. how to act during a job interview
9. how to apologize
10. how to write a process paragraph

Item VII: The Persuasion Paragraph

The **persuasion** or **opinion paragraph** attempts to convince the reader to accept the point of view held by the writer. A good opinion paragraph presents carefully organized ideas that are designed to win the reader over by using factual and logical details. Usually the most compelling reason is presented at the end.

Examine the following persuasive paragraph, and consider the order in which the ideas are presented.

> In the past few years, educational institutions have been under severe attack. As the volume of criticism has mounted, a feeling has grown that schools and universities are not achieving that which they were intended to: namely, the enrichment of the individual's life by giving him the tools of self-improvement and the cultivated mind to use them. Naturally the bulk of this criticism has fallen upon the teacher, that poor cultural maid-of-all-work in our society, and the nearest, or at any rate, the most tangible object to seize upon in a fit of anger. Of course the fault does not lie there, or not mainly. Often it lies with unprogressive or penny-pinching school boards who engage teachers whose unsuitability is fully known to them in advance. And behind the incompetent teacher and the conservative school board stands a society which has no comprehensive vision of what education is or the aims that it ought to pursue. If we're going to start blaming, let's call the shots right.
>
> — Irving Layton,"The Role of the Teacher"

Note how Layton states his argument in his topic sentence and then presents his opinions that support his topic sentence. His conclusion adds unity to the body of the paragraph by presenting the strongest argument.

1. Getting Organized

Arrange the ideas in a persuasive paragraph in order of importance. Remember that your topic sentence must clearly state the position you are going to examine. Then write down as many supporting ideas as you can. Some of your ideas will be your personal opinion; others will refer to examples or comments by authoritative individuals or groups. Be sure to arrange your ideas in order of importance and to elaborate on them using factual details and authoritative sources.

A good persuasive paragraph uses a variety of transitional expressions to organize ideas. Here are some transitional words that will help you.

although	especially
another	for
because	in fact
consequently	lastly
mainly	of course
more importantly	primarily
moreover	since
nevertheless	therefore
thus	

2. Persuasion Paragraph Review

Have you changed the reader's point of view on your topic?

- Brainstorm all your ideas.
- Use an authoritative opinion.
- Use commanding verbs in the topic sentence to direct the point of view you will be supporting in the following sentences.
- Present the ideas in order, but save the most definitive argument for last.
- Use effective adjectives and verbs.
- Do not threaten the reader with your point of view; admit there are other points of view.
- Write a concluding sentence that states the result of your persuasive argument.
- Write a rough draft.
- Make corrections to spelling, grammar, usage, and punctuation.
- Rewrite for your good copy.

EXERCISE ◆ 34

Examine the following sentences from the concluding paragraph from "The Role of the Teacher" by Irving Layton. The sentences are not in the order in which they were written. Identify the topic sentence, and place the supporting sentences in order of importance.

_____ "Furthermore the knowledge which he acquires in his free time and which he shares with others eventually trickles into the remotest corners of the community he lives in and helps to enlarge the area of good sense up on which the preservation of civilized values ultimately depends."

_____ "This kind of teacher is always an inspiration to his pupils."

_____ "Only by pursuing knowledge, that is, by constantly enlarging his own intellectual horizons, can the teacher retain his original freshness and enthusiasm."

_____ "In the successfully creative teacher, knowledge spills over like water from a seemingly inexhaustible fountain."

EXERCISE ◆ 35

Select a topic from the following list and write a persuasive paragraph. Follow any instructions your teacher may have.

1. government should/should not dictate "proper language usage"
2. gun control is a waste of time
3. say yes/no to euthanasia
4. dieting organizations do/do not work
5. every home needs a computer
6. violence is a fact of life
7. chicken soup cures everything
8. power is usually self-destructive
9. acts of kindness are no longer fashionable
10. dental care should be subsidized by the government

EXERCISE ◆ 36

Follow the instructions for Exercise 35.

1. discrimination in Canada thrives
2. the benefits of extended warranty
3. the right amount of sleep

4. UFO's exist
5. political correctness — "Merry Christmas" vs. "Happy Holidays"
6. the educational system passes weak students
7. the eyes are windows to the soul
8. photo radar is not a deterrent to speeders
9. safe sex is only in history books
10. selling cigarettes is a financial not a health issue

Item VIII: The Narrative Paragraph

A **narrative paragraph** tells a story. It does this by presenting events in a chronological order until the story is told. A narrative paragraph differs from a descriptive paragraph in that it concentrates on the facts of the event rather than the sensory details of the event.

Read the following example of a narrative paragraph.

> We always had the ceremony of the two Christmas trees. One was in the late afternoon of Christmas Day, and was at the home of my grandparents, my mother's people, at the big brick house. There would be a whole congregation of aunts and uncles and cousins there on that day, and we would have the tree (that is how we said it) before dinner. One of my aunts was head of the nursing division in Saskatchewan's public health department, and was a distinguished professional woman. I didn't know about that then. What I knew was that each Christmas she came back home with an astounding assortment of rare and wonderful things from what I felt must be the centre of the great wide world, namely Regina. She used to bring us those packages of Swiss cheese, each tiny piece wrapped in silver paper, and decorations for the table (a Santa with reindeer and sleigh, pine-cone men painted iridescent white with red felt caps), and chocolate Santas in red and gold paper, and chocolate coins contained in heavy gold foil so that they looked like my idea of Spanish doubloons and pieces of eight, as in *Treasure Island*.
>
> — Margaret Laurence,"Upon a Midnight Clear"

In this narrative paragraph, note that Laurence introduces in her topic sentence the event that is to be discussed. The sentences that support the topic sentence present the events that make up the ceremony of the "two Christmases."

EXERCISE • 37

Read the narrative paragraph by Margaret Laurence again. List the events that occur in it.

____

____

____

____

____

1. Getting Organized

Arrange ideas in a narrative paragraph chronologically in order to outline a sequence of events. Be sure to highlight these events with descriptive details, and remember that your topic sentence must introduce your subject. Using some of the following transitional words will help you organize your ideas.

after a while	first	soon
at last	gradually	suddenly
during	meanwhile	then
eventually	next	
finally	now	

2. Narrative Paragraph Review

Have you succeeded in relating a story to your readers outlining the main ideas in chronological order?

- Brainstorm the events of your topic.
- Concentrate on events rather than descriptions.
- Place the ideas in the natural order of the events.
- Write supporting sentences in sequential order.
- Use transitional words that connect ideas step by step.
- Write a rough draft.
- Make corrections to spelling, grammar, usage, and punctuation.
- Rewrite for your good copy.

EXERCISE • 38

Select a topic from the following list and write a narrative paragraph. Follow any instructions your teacher may have.

1. a frightening experience
2. staying up late to finish a paper
3. realizing your wallet is missing after the waiter has brought the bill
4. being late on the first day of class/work
5. having a tooth extracted
6. a bad fishing trip
7. watching an achievement of your children
8. a walk in the country in autumn
9. a day in which everything went perfectly
10. being lost as a child

EXERCISE • 39

Follow the instructions for Exercise 38.

1. a practical joke played on you
2. the day you saw a ghost
3. an encounter with something you dislike (a dentist, a spider, etc.)
4. your greatest accomplishment
5. the day you arrived in Canada
6. your most embarrassing moment
7. the time you locked your keys in the car
8. your first horseback riding experience
9. the day you forgot an important anniversary/birthday
10. answering an advertisement for companionship

Item IX: The Comparison and Contrast Paragraph

Comparison and **contrast paragraphs** present similarities and differences between persons, things, or ideas. When you analyze the similarities, you are making a comparison. When you examine the differences, you are making a contrast.

Good comparison and contrast paragraphs always examine subject-matter in the same category. Comparison and contrast writing is an effective form of explanatory writing.

Read the following example in which the differences between two brothers are presented.

> You'd never know we were brothers. You could tell exactly how he was going to look as a man, and I looked like a child that couldn't make up his mind *what* shape his face would take on later. He could lift me and my load (though he'd never once glance my way if I tackled anything beyond my strength — trying to lead a steer that was tough in the neck, or putting a cordwood butt on top of the pile, or anything). But I always seemed the older, somehow. He always seemed to — well, look up to me or something, it didn't matter how often I was mean to him.
>
> — Ernest Buckler, "The Wild Goose"

In a contrast paragraph differences are emphasized. Note how Buckler establishes the fact that he will be contrasting the brothers in the topic sentence. The sentences which follow are arranged in parallel blocks of information; that is, a detail is given about one brother and is immediately followed by a detail concerning the other.

EXERCISE • 40

In the paragraph by Buckler, identify what is being contrasted and make two columns in which you list the parallel information concerning each brother.

____________________	____________________
____________________	____________________
____________________	____________________
____________________	____________________

Now examine the following comparison paragraph, which details the *similarities* between two brothers.

> Between Brian and his younger brother existed a casual relationship to which the older boy contributed a careless patronage, and Bobbie for the most part, an easy going fondness relieved now and then by sudden and deeper flashes of feeling. Brian felt them too. The brothers were utterly loyal to each other, but no more than to their other companions. The years of childhood are long; the space between the two brothers was two years wide. Both placed equally high value upon their father's attention and vied for it; for the mother there was respect, a recognition of the vein of iron in her will, and from time to time a warmer emotion which she looked for often but would not demand.
>
> — W. O. Mitchell, *Who Has Seen the Wind*

In the above comparison paragraph Mitchell presents parallel information about the brothers in order to emphasize their similarities.

EXERCISE • 41

Reread the paragraph by Mitchell, and make two columns in which you list what is being compared in each brother.

____________________	____________________
____________________	____________________
____________________	____________________
____________________	____________________

1. Getting Organized

Remember that in a comparison or contrast paragraph your topic sentence should state what you intend to compare or contrast. Then list as many similarities or differences as you can; review your list, and select your main points. In making your list, numbering your information will help you organize your material.

In the examples you have examined, comparisons and contrasts have been made by alternating the information about the brothers within the same sentence or between sentences. Another effective method is to present the information about one person, place, or thing in one block of sentences (or paragraphs if it is an essay) and then all the information about the second person, place, or thing.

Using effective transitional words will help you to organize your comparisons and contrasts. Here is a list of suitable expressions for comparing and contrasting.

comparison

again	each	in the same way
also	equally	like
as well as	in addition	likewise
both	in other words	similarly

contrast

although	even though	on the contrary
but	however	on the other hand
conversely	in contrast	otherwise
despite	nevertheless	yet

2. Comparison and Contrast Paragraph Review

Have you succeeded in making the readers understand that you are comparing or contrasting items on a particular subject?

- Make two separate lists (contrast or comparison).
- Organize points for the alternating method or for the block method.
- State in the topic sentence the subjects being compared or contrasted.
- Use transitional words appropriate to comparison or contrast.
- Be certain that the balance is correct for the alternate method or the block method.
- Write a concluding sentence that offers an opinion about both subjects compared or contrasted.
- Write a rough draft.
- Make corrections to spelling, grammar, usage, and punctuation.
- Rewrite for your good copy.

EXERCISE • 42

Examine the following photographs; then make a list of similarities for a paragraph of comparison.

EXERCISE • 43

Examine the following photographs; then make a list of differences for a paragraph of contrast.

EXERCISE • 44

Select a topic from the following list to write comparison and contrast paragraphs. Follow any instructions your teacher may have.

1. two religious customs
2. when you were in school/your parents were in school
3. being single/being with someone
4. a good vacation/a bad vacation
5. two children
6. the expectation/the reality of a night class
7. having an apartment/having a house
8. air travel now and forty years ago
9. public television/commercial television
10. the microwave oven/the convection oven

EXERCISE • 45

Follow the instructions for Exercise 44.

1. a cafeteria and a dining room
2. two small towns
3. two tourist attractions
4. two pets you have had
5. Canadian produce/imported produce
6. your hometown then and now
7. Chinese food and Italian food
9. living in the city/in the suburbs
10. a mother/daughter; a father/son

ADDENDUM

THE PARTS OF SPEECH

A

In Addendum A you will refresh your memory about the **parts of speech**, and you will gain practice in using them. Knowing the function of the different parts of speech will improve your writing skills.

"Dad, did they have parts of speech when you were a kid?"

PRE-TEST

Complete this Pre-Test to measure your existing knowledge of the material covered in Addendum A. The answers immediately follow the test.

Identify the underlined words as nouns, pronouns, verbs, adjectives, adverbs, prepositions, conjunctions, or interjections.

1. That is not the cheese that you smell. ____________
2. That expression is overused. ____________
3. You were nearly hit by that ball. ____________
4. Ouch! I hurt my arm on the door. ____________
5. Don't be late. ____________
6. Please come in. ____________
7. What is in the box? ____________
8. She is the best player on the team. ____________
9. That car will be mine one day. ____________
10. I'll wait another ten minutes. ____________
11. When you are ready, we'll go. ____________
12. Sorial and his wife are on vacation. ____________
13. Everyone can dance except me. ____________
14. I don't like to eat alone. ____________
15. It's always easier to judge someone else. ____________

ANSWERS • TO • PRE-TEST

1. pronoun, verb
2. adjective, adjective
3. adverb, preposition
4. interjection, verb
5. adverb, adjective
6. verb, adverb
7. preposition, noun
8. pronoun, adjective
9. verb, adjective
10. verb, noun

11. conjunction, adjective
12. conjunction, pronoun
13. verb, preposition
14. pronoun, adverb
15. adverb, adjective

Item I: Nouns

A **noun** is a part of speech that identifies a person, place, thing, or idea. Nouns are words that identify what you are talking about.

1. Nouns for Persons

All words that stand for persons (*lawyer, janitor, nurse*) are nouns. As well, all **proper names** (*Patricia, Andrew, Aladdin*) are always nouns and are always capitalized.

EXAMPLES:
Maritza is a *dentist.*
The *skiers* are enjoying themselves.

2. Nouns for Places

All words that identify places (*Ottawa, fairgrounds, kitchen*) are nouns.

EXAMPLES:
Edberg, Alberta is a small *town.*
Where is the *washroom* in this *restaurant*?

3. Nouns for Things

All words that indicate things, whether living or non-living (*flower, bear, money*), are nouns.

EXAMPLES:
The *snake's skin* is rough.
The *grass* needs *water.*

Note that words with apostrophes can be nouns too.

4. Nouns for Ideas

Words that identify ideas (*peace, fear, worry*) or qualities (*beauty, endurance, courage*) are called **abstract nouns**. You cannot touch them with your hands, but you can understand them with your mind.

EXAMPLES:

He really has *fortitude*.
Love can be *happiness* and *sorrow*.

EXERCISE • 1

Underline the nouns in the following sentences.

EXAMPLE:

This cheese is from Canada.

1. The clarinet has a wonderful sound.
2. Harold is sitting on the fence.
3. Maureen needs new glasses.
4. The bed is made of pine.
5. Cows are interesting animals.
6. The college is closed this Friday.
7. Last year there was a snowstorm on this day.
8. The rose is from my garden.
9. Eat all your spinach and broccoli or no dessert.
10. There is a leak in your pipe.

EXERCISE • 2

Follow the instructions for Exercise 1.

1. Beauty can be found in many things.
2. John moved to Sudbury, Ontario last week.
3. Claire can't drink warm milk.
4. The committee is not meeting this Thursday.
5. David likes chicken better than beef.
6. Order the pizza for lunch.
7. The tree on our front lawn is a maple.
8. Your teeth need a dentist.

9. Calgary is the capital of Alberta.
10. Your imagination can get you into trouble.

EXERCISE • 3

Follow the instructions for Exercise 2.

1. Listen to this poem by Thomas Hardy.
2. What colour is the paint?
3. The boy's leg is bruised.
4. The new bookcase is hungry for books.
5. How did the rabbit lose the race to the turtle?
6. Maxine bumped her elbow on the back of the chair.
7. Give Alex a tissue for his nose.
8. What part of the chicken did this piece come from?
9. The mood of the teacher was not good.
10. The gloves are drying on the radiator.

EXERCISE • 4

Follow the instructions for Exercise 3.

1. Health is more important than wealth.
2. The cellist has beautiful hands.
3. Your smile is food for my heart.
4. The pigeon dropped a message on my sleeve.
5. Terry could not see the boat at the dock because of the fog.
6. Antarctica has no snakes.
7. The kind of food that Benny likes comes from Korea.
8. Which wine are you serving with the fish for dinner.
9. The hygienist looked at my teeth and shook her head.
10. This mask of a vampire frightens the children.

EXERCISE • 5

Follow the instructions for Exercise 4.

1. Are diamonds really a person's best friend?
2. Fear of the unknown is a common phobia.

3. At what time will the bus arrive?
4. Read this novel by Margaret Atwood by Tuesday.
5. The smell from your locker is lethal.
6. Wish me luck on the test.
7. The relatives have arrived for dinner.
8. The expression on his face was incredible.
9. The plumber will stay at the house until tomorrow.
10. Jerry opened the wrong end of the box.

EXERCISE ◆ 6

Write ten original sentences in which you use at least two nouns. Underline the nouns.

EXAMPLE:

The muffins are still in the oven.

EXERCISE ◆ 7

Follow the instructions for Exercise 6.

Item II: Pronouns

A **pronoun** is a part of speech that takes the place of a noun. Using pronouns avoids repetition and allows more variety in your writing. There are several types of pronouns but the most commonly used is the personal pronoun.

1. Personal Pronouns

Personal pronouns have several forms which are determined by how they are used in a sentence. Familiarize yourself with the following forms of the personal pronoun. (See Unit 3, Items II, III, and IV.)

subject form	*object form*	*possessive form*
I	me	my, mine
we	us	our, ours
you	you	your, yours
he	him	his

she	her	her, hers
it	it	its
they	them	their, theirs

The following examples show how pronouns take the place of nouns.

EXAMPLES:

Alison cooked the *turkey*. (nouns)
She cooked *it*. (pronouns)

Fritz and *Olga* saw the *accident*. (nouns)
They saw *it*. (pronouns)

2. Demonstrative Pronouns

Demonstrative pronouns take the place of nouns, but they also point out or "demonstrate" particular persons or things. There are only four demonstrative pronouns.

singular	*plural*
this	these
that	those

EXAMPLES:

This has been a nice day.
That is the truth.
Are you familiar with *these*?
Some of *these* belong to Jana.

3. Indefinite Pronouns

Indefinite pronouns take the place of nouns but refer to no particular person or thing. Indefinite pronouns have singular and plural forms, and some forms of the indefinite pronoun may be singular or plural.

	singular	
another	everybody	nothing
anybody	everyone	someday
anyone	everything	someone
anything	neither	something
each	nobody	
either	no one	

plural

both	others
few	several
many	some

singular or plural

all	most
any	none
more	some

EXAMPLES:

Everybody is eligible to enter the contest. (singular)
Several of the ornaments are from Austria. (plural)

None of the money is missing. (singular)
None of the television shows are worth watching. (plural)

4. Relative Pronouns

Relative pronouns refer to the nouns they replace. A relative pronoun indicates the relationships between different parts of a sentence and is always preceded by the noun or pronoun it relates to in the sentence.

who, whose, whom	-	refer to persons
which	-	refers to animals and things
that	-	refers to people, animals, and things

EXAMPLES:

The sweatshirt *that* you like is on sale at The Bay.
The car *which* was stolen was found abandoned at the school.
Khang, *who* is our karate teacher, is a gentle man.

EXERCISE • 8

Underline the personal, demonstrative, indefinite, and relative pronouns in the following sentences.

EXAMPLES:

<u>That</u> is the right <u>one</u>.

1. The money that you lost has been found.
2. Most of his ideas were rejected.
3. This is the person who can help you.
4. He realized his mistake too late.
5. Everybody should be like her.
6. She was confused by his attitude.
7. One of them is yours.
8. This is the restaurant I like best.
9. Any of these will be suitable.
10. They knew it was impossible.

EXERCISE ♦ 9

Follow the instructions for Exercise 8.

1. This is my favourite cheesecake.
2. Send it to them by tomorrow.
3. Whom did you see at the circus?
4. Anyone can make a mistake.
5. The books are mine and hers, not theirs.
6. Can anyone help me?
7. You need to see it in the light.
8. These are fresher than those.
9. The cat hurt its paw.
10. The flowers that Helen sent are beautiful.

EXERCISE ♦ 10

Follow the instructions for Exercise 9.

1. A few of these are old.
2. The gum has lost its flavour.
3. One of you is responsible for the accident.
4. To whom did you send an invitation?
5. I would like a car like that.
6. Mine is wider than yours.
7. All of it is for you.
8. The crowd that went to the concert last night was boisterous.

9. I think it is they who called on you last night.
10. Several of the them are nervous.

EXERCISE • 11

Write sentences using the pronouns indicated. Underline the pronouns you have used.

EXAMPLE:

all

Give <u>all</u> of the money before <u>you</u> go.

1. them
2. ours
3. those
4. anyone
5. which
6. it
7. that
8. most
9. mine
10. these

EXERCISE • 12

Follow the instructions for Exercise 11.

1. who
2. both
3. them
4. nothing
5. we
6. yours
7. anything
8. this
9. some
10. few

EXERCISE • 13

Underline all nouns once and all pronouns twice in the following sentences.

EXAMPLE:

The elephant hurt its trunk.

1. I want some of the doughnuts.
2. The strong beer that you gave me tastes skunky.
3. Can you open the door for the children?
4. The movie about bats was scary.
5. Neither of the sisters wanted any of the candy.
6. Give me your answer in the morning.
7. Marty forgot to buy the newspaper.
8. These are my two children.
9. I needed more time to write the test.
10. This is the house that Jack built.

EXERCISE • 14

Follow the instructions for Exercise 12.

1. These are the mushrooms for the soup.
2. The mouse ran up the clock.
3. A few of them have left their mother.
4. He is pursuing the truth.
5. She is the one who deserves all the credit.
6. Everything will be all right after the test.
7. Do you remember how to communicate with fish?
8. Drop them a line.
9. The day that you chose for the picnic is perfect.
10. This is not clear to me.

Item III: Verbs

A **verb** is the part of speech that identifies an action, condition, or state of being. A verb states what a thing or person is doing or in what condition it exists.

The following examples show how verbs express action, condition, and state of being.

EXAMPLES:

Cecily ate the spinach. (action)
Hank seems depressed. (condition)
Cliff is a mountain climber. (state of being)

Most verbs fall into one of two groups: action and non-action. Action verbs express activity or movement; non-action verbs express a condition, a state of being, or a general truth.

1. Action Verbs

Action verbs can express either physical or mental action.

EXAMPLES:

Sandy painted the basement floor. (physical)
Marie understands the problem now. (mental)

Note that sometimes finding the verb can be tricky for several reasons as follows.

a. The verb is made up of more than one word (four is maximum).

EXAMPLES:

The doctor could have been delayed.
We are going out for lunch today.

b. The verb is in an interrogative sentence. (See Unit 2, Item II.)

EXAMPLES:

Do you know the answer?
Has he delivered the parcel yet?

c. The verb begins the sentence as a command. (See Unit 2, Item II.)

EXAMPLES:

Get a haircut!
Bring it to me now.

d. The verb is used with adverbs such as *not*, *even*, and *ever*. Do not include the adverb with the verb. (See Item V in this Addendum.)

EXAMPLES:

Margot often lifts weights.
They shouldn't have left so soon.

e. The verb is used with a gerund in the sentence. A gerund is not considered a verb. Verb forms ending in *-ing* that are not preceded by a "helping verb" such as *is, was, will be* are not verbs.

EXAMPLES:

Sally and Bill enjoy hiking.
You should consider working for Iain.

f. The verb is used with an infinitive in the sentence. An infinitive is not considered a verb. Infinitives are always made up of the word *to* plus the present tense of a verb.

EXAMPLES:

Josh likes to read.
Esther swims to keep in shape.

EXERCISE • 15

Underline the complete action verb twice in the following sentences.

EXAMPLE:

The doctor told us the joke about the monkey.

1. The children read all the stories.
2. How much does that ring cost?
3. The wind is still blowing hard.
4. Keep reminding me.
5. Melissa enjoys singing in the choir.

6. Frank has already paid me.
7. Are you getting a cold?
8. I don't like to speak in public.
9. They hung the picture in the dining room.
10. Quit smoking today.

EXERCISE • 16

Follow the instructions for Exercise 15.

1. Sharon has cut the grass.
2. How long did you sleep last night?
3. I was hoping for better weather.
4. Did you mistake Dave for Santa Claus?
5. Take the shortcut.
6. Thad should never have complained to his coach.
7. Are you going to join the club?
8. The sun hasn't set yet.
9. Erwin keeps wishing away his life.
10. Tell him, not me.

EXERCISE • 17

Follow the instructions for Exercise 16.

1. The tomatoes were grown in Ontario.
2. The clown is not wearing a happy face.
3. How long have you been watching?
4. No one likes washing dishes.
5. He couldn't speak Spanish very well.
6. The bee stung Greg in the leg.
7. Do you drool in your sleep?
8. I will deliver the goods tomorrow.
9. Denny finally understood the lesson about verbs.
10. He could have apologized sooner.

EXERCISE • 18

Follow the instructions for Exercise 16.

1. Put these books in order.
2. How did you tear your sleeve?

3. They wanted more ice cream.
4. The air conditioning unit wasn't working very well.
5. Bob went fishing near Vancouver Island.
6. Judith must have forgotten the letter at home.
7. Did the bus leave already?
8. Sign your name on the bottom line.
9. Were you going to sit there?
10. The electrician shocked me with the bill.

EXERCISE • 19

Follow the instructions for Exercise 18.

1. Your anger is showing.
2. The chipmunks scampered up the tree.
3. Did you take the last cookie?
4. Try again with the screwdriver.
5. Why was everyone laughing so hard?
6. The ice on the driveway is finally melting.
7. Have you made the beds yet?
8. You baked the pie perfectly.
9. What are you doing tomorrow?
10. The last performance ends at 11:30 p.m.

2. Non-action Verbs

Non-action verbs express a condition, state of being, or general truth. When a non-action verb is followed by an adjective, it usually expresses a condition. When a non-action verb is followed by a noun, the verb denotes a state of being. Non-action verbs are expressed by some form of the verb *to be*, or sometimes by a "verb of the senses."

a. The Verb *To Be*

All forms of the verb *to be* (*is, are, was, will be*) are non-action. (See all forms of the verb *to be* in the section on tenses in this Item.)

EXAMPLES:

Carol is an opera singer. (state of being)
Mark will be tired after the workout. (condition)
They are always late for class. (general truth)

b. Verbs of the Senses

In addition to the verb *to be,* the verbs of the senses sometimes function as non-action verbs. This occurs when the verb of the senses expresses the condition of the subject. When this happens, the verb of the senses is always followed by an adjective.

Here is a list of some common verbs of the senses.

appear	look	smell	taste
feel	seem	sound	touch

EXAMPLES:

The teacher sounds hoarse. (non-action — expresses condition of the teacher)

The teacher sounds the fire alarm. (action — expresses action teacher performs)

In addition to these verbs, *become, get, grow, remain,* and *stay* usually function as non-action verbs.

EXERCISE • 20

Underline twice the complete non-action verbs in the following sentences.

EXAMPLE:

You will not be late.

1. She is our new neighbour.
2. He is being stubborn again.
3. That couldn't be true.
4. Sigfried should be on his way.
5. Violet looks pale.
6. These chicken livers are not fresh.
7. Just stay calm.
8. Are you feeling better?
9. I should have been a doctor.
10. I am sure about everything.

EXERCISE • 21

Follow the instructions for Exercise 20.

1. You have been on my mind all day.
2. This song sounds like a Christmas melody.

3. I was in Ottawa last week.
4. The next lottery winner could be you.
5. Weren't they in the principal's office yesterday?
6. Yok Shion seems upset today.
7. The muffins should be ready in ten minutes.
8. Where were you last night?
9. These cheese balls smell like old socks.
10. I feel bad about my test result.

EXERCISE ♦ 22

Underline twice the complete verbs in the following sentences. Indicate if they are action or non-action.

EXAMPLE:

I feel better today. non-action

1. Who is ringing his bell? ______
2. The bell sounds nice. ______
3. Elizabeth is still growing tomatoes. ______
4. Chad is growing tired of hearing about it. ______
5. Are you trying to confuse me? ______
6. If you were nicer, I could be happier. ______
7. Remain still. ______
8. The game isn't over yet. ______
9. Emma feels so tired. ______
10. Feel the soft leather. ______

EXERCISE ♦ 23

Follow the instructions for Exercise 22.

1. Your complaints are becoming tiresome. ______
2. Al will always be a good father. ______
3. Please be more careful. ______
4. That cologne smells good. ______
5. May I have the next dance? ______
6. Get the dishes out of the cupboard. ______
7. What are you thinking? ______

8. This chili is potent. ____________
9. Marion checked it twice. ____________
10. Drink this slowly. ____________

EXERCISE • 24

Follow the instructions for Exercise 23.

1. This chocolate cake tastes rich. ____________
2. Stir the stew again. ____________
3. Are you still showering? ____________
4. Hanna really enjoys your pasta. ____________
5. Stop making those noises with your nose. ____________
6. You would be upset too. ____________
7. This dress looks great on you. ____________
8. Why couldn't you be a teacher? ____________
9. Your idea seems good to me. ____________
10. Sarah is getting a new jacket. ____________

3. Troublesome Verbs

Lie, lay; rise, raise; and *sit, set* are three pairs of verbs which are troublesome because their form and meaning are similar. Speakers and writers often mix them up.

Let's examine the four principal parts of these troublesome verbs.

present	*past*	*past participle* (*with* has, have, *or* had)	*present participle*
lie	lay	lain	lying
lay	laid	laid	laying
rise	rose	risen	rising
raise	raised	raised	raising
sit	sat	sat	sitting
set	set	set	setting

A common method of avoiding confusion is to understand which verb in the pair is *transitive* and which *intransitive*. When you look up a verb in the dictionary, you will notice that the abbreviations *v.t.*, *v.i.*, or both often appear with the verb. These abbreviations stand for "verb transitive" and "verb intransitive."

a. Transitive

A **transitive verb** is an action verb that transfers the action of the subject to some noun or pronoun in the sentence.

EXAMPLES:

Yvonne kissed Sid.

Didi hammered the nail.

b. Intransitive

An **intransitive verb** does not transfer the action of the subject to any noun or pronoun in the sentence. Instead, the action refers to the subject.

EXAMPLES:

The train arrived on time.

Peter left early last night.

Sometimes, however, the same verb can be used either transitively or intransitively.

EXAMPLES:

I drove the car to White River. (transitive)

I drove all night. (intransitive)

c. Lie/Lay

Lie means to recline or rest. It is an intransitive verb.

EXAMPLES:

They have lain on the beach since noon.

Russell lay down for a short nap.

Lay means to place or put. It is a transitive verb.

EXAMPLES:

She laid the tiles on the floor.

Did you lay the money aside?

d. Rise/Raise

Rise means to come, go, or extend upwards. It is intransitive.

EXAMPLES:

Jim is slowly rising out of bed.

The birds have already risen.

Raise means to bring to a higher upright position. It is a transitive verb.

EXAMPLES:

John and Margot are raising chickens on their farm.

The professor raised her eyebrows at the question.

e. Sit/Set

Sit means to rest on the buttocks. It is an intransitive verb.

EXAMPLES:

Claudine always sits in the same chair.

We have been sitting here for two hours.

Set means to put, place, or stand a thing in position. It is a transitive verb.

EXAMPLES:

(You) Please set the flowers on the table.

They have set aside their differences.

EXERCISE ♦ 25

Underline the correct verb form in the parentheses.

EXAMPLE:

Do you (lie, lay) in the sun very often?

1. Does Toronto (lie, lay) south of Chicago?
2. Maurice (has lain, has laid) aside some money for new skis.
3. What time do you (rise, raise) in the morning?
4. He (set, sit) the china on the table.
5. Joan (has sit, has set) the alarm already.
6. This fossil (has been lying, has been laying) here for thousands of years.
7. The broken cup (is sitting, is setting) on the kitchen floor.
8. Betty (has been rising, has been raising) at the same time every morning for months.
9. The miners (sit, set) the explosive charges.
10. She (was lying, was laying) on the beach near the water.

EXERCISE ♦ 26

Follow the instructions for Exercise 25.

1. You (must lay, must lie) still a moment longer.
2. The stock prices (have risen, have raised) very quickly.
3. The workers (lay, laid) the carpet down in the family room.

4. Are the interest rates (rising, raising) again?
5. Fortunately, her temperature is not (rising, raising).
6. The radio (is sitting, is setting) on the kitchen counter.
7. Matt (is sitting, is setting) up the old tent.
8. You (should rise, should raise) above the problem.
9. The chicken (is sitting, is setting) on her eggs.
10. Her speech (rose, raised) serious concerns.

EXERCISE ♦ 27

Follow the instructions for Exercise 26.

1. I (will rise, will raise) before dawn tomorrow.
2. The children could not (sit, set) still during dinner.
3. The painting (has risen, has raised) in value in the last few years.
4. The father gently (lay, laid) the baby in the crib.
5. Eight guests (will be sitting, will be setting) for supper.
6. We (lay, laid) by the fire for hours.
7. Are you (sitting, setting) a good example?
8. Emma (has risen, has raised) five children by herself.
9. The puppy (rose, raised) its head in anticipation of dinner.
10. The abandoned mica mine (lies, lays) next to the corn field.

4. Tenses

As you already know, verbs express action or condition. Actions though, can occur in different times (for example, in the past or in the future). When a verb form changes to express a different time, it changes **tense**.

EXAMPLES:

My neighbour's dog barks all the time. (present tense)
Jessie cracked his knuckles. (past tense)
The next concert will be tomorrow. (future tense)

There are six tenses in English: three *simple* tenses (present, past, and future) and three *perfect* tenses (present, past, and future). In addition, each of the six tenses has a *progressive* form.

The **perfect tenses** allow you to speak more specifically about the time of actions and about actions that will be completed before or after another action takes place.

The **progressive tenses**, as the name suggests, allow you to emphasize the progression or continuation of an action over a long period of time.

a. The Simple Present Tense

The **simple present tense** has several uses.

Use it to express an action or condition that is occurring now.

EXAMPLES:

Patrick enjoys Disney movies.
The road is long.

Use the simple present tense to express a general truth.

EXAMPLES:

Christmas comes once a year.
The zebra is not a common pet.

Use the simple present tense to express habitual or repeated action.

EXAMPLES:

Dina walks to work every day.
Madeleine always sits at the front.

Use the simple present tense to express the notion of near-future time.

EXAMPLES:

Summer vacation begins on Friday.
The grocery store strike ends tomorrow.

b. The Simple Past

Use the **simple past tense** to express an action or condition that both began and ended in the past.

EXAMPLES:

You broke my heart.
The movie was sad.

Also use the simple past tense to express a repeated action or condition that began and ended in the past.

EXAMPLES:

He rarely took my advice.
My neighbour never shovelled his walk after a snowfall.

c. The Simple Future

Use the **simple future tense** to express determination with *will* or *shall* or to express uncertainty with *should, could,* or *might*.

EXAMPLES:

I will meet you in the cafeteria. (simple forecast)
He will write the cheque now. (promise)
Tony will save the money for college. (determination)
You could drive more carefully. (suggestion of uncertainty)

Note that generally *shall* is used with the first person singular and plural. Use *will* with all other persons. Also note that *would* and *should* form the past tense of *will* and *shall* and must be used in a sentence if a previous verb is in the past tense.

EXAMPLES:

I knew that I should have been more considerate.
Martin always believed that his grades would improve.

d. The Present Perfect Tense

Use the **present perfect tense** to express an action or condition that began in the past but continues to affect the present time. *Has* or *have* (present tense of *to have*) is the helping verb used with this form.

EXAMPLES:

Gwen has always enjoyed her summers at the cottage.
They have ordered their firewood from the same farm for the past ten years.

e. The Past Perfect Tense

Use the **past perfect tense** to express an action that began and was completed in the past before another past action. *Had* (past tense of *to have*) is the helping verb used with this form.

EXAMPLES:

Tom said that they had taken the turkey out of the oven.

Golda wrote the chemistry test even though she had broken her wrist.

f. The Future Perfect Tense

Use the **future perfect tense** to express an action or condition that will have occurred before some other action or before a definite time in the future. *Will/shall have* is the helping verb used with this form.

EXAMPLES:

You will have improved your English by the time you finish this book.

After this purchase, I shall have accumulated over 200 antique glass bottles.

The following list displays the verb *to be* in all persons (singular and plural) and in all forms of the simple and perfect tenses.

present	*first person*	*singular*	I am
		plural	we are
	second person	*singular*	you are
		plural	you are
	third person	*singular*	he, she, it
		plural	they are
past	*first person*	*singular*	I was
		plural	we were
	second person	*singular*	you were
		plural	you were
	third person	*singular*	he, she, it was
		plural	they were
future	*first person*	*singular*	I shall
		plural	we shall
	second person	*singular*	you will
		plural	you will
	third person	*singular*	he, she, it will
		plural	they will

present perfect	*first person*	*singular*	I have been
		plural	we have been
	second person	*singular*	you have been
		plural	you have been
	third person	*singular*	he, she, it has been
		plural	they have been
past perfect	*first person*	*singular*	I had been
		plural	we had been
	second person	*singular*	you had been
		plural	you had been
	third person	*singular*	he, she, had been
		plural	they had been
future perfect	*first person*	*singular*	I shall have been
		plural	we shall have been
	second person	*singular*	you will have been
		plural	you will have been
	third person	*singular*	he, she, it will have been
		plural	they will have been

EXERCISE • 28

Write sentences using the correct verb tense indicated.

EXAMPLE:

send   future

I shall send the cheque tomorrow.

1. know — past
2. buy — future
3. throb — present
4. visit — present perfect
5. organize — future
6. cook — past perfect
7. save — future perfect
8. order — past
9. walk — present perfect
10. build — future

EXERCISE • 29

Follow the instructions for Exercise 28.

1.	forget	past
2.	average	present perfect
3.	deliver	past perfect
4.	research	future
5.	dance	present
6.	tell	present perfect
7.	study	past
8.	walk	future
9.	dream	present
10.	break	past perfect

EXERCISE • 30

Follow the instructions for Exercise 29.

1.	gather	future
2.	eat	future perfect
3.	be	past
4.	see	present perfect
5.	plant	future
6.	wash	past perfect
7.	pour	present
8.	leak	past
9.	rise	future perfect
10.	bake	present perfect

EXERCISE • 31

Follow the instructions for Exercise 30.

1.	advise	present
2.	exercise	present perfect
3.	realize	past perfect
4.	fall	past
5.	succeed	future

6. save — future perfect
7. receive — present perfect
8. fix — future
9. believe — past
10. speak — past perfect

EXERCISE • 32

Follow the instructions for Exercise 31.

1. sew — present perfect
2. catch — present
3. make — future perfect
4. freeze — past perfect
5. enjoy — future
6. mow — past
7. spread — present
8. fish — present perfect
9. go — past perfect
10. hug — past

g. The Present Progressive Tense

Use the **present progressive tense** to express an action or condition that is taking place or existing now and may continue to occur or exist for a while longer. The present progressive tense emphasizes the ongoing activity. *Am, are,* and *is* are the helping verbs used with this form.

EXAMPLES:

John is meeting me here today.
They are still complaining about the service.

The present progressive form, like the simple present tense, can also express a notion of future time.

EXAMPLES:

Celine is writing the test tomorrow.
Robert is leaving for Vancouver this evening.

h. The Past Progressive Tense

Use the **past progressive tense** to emphasize action that was continuing in the past. *Was* and *were* are the helping verbs used with this form.

EXAMPLES:
She was building her own bookcase in the basement.
They were skiing down the large slope this morning.

i. The Future Progressive Tense

Use the **future progressive tense** to express continuing action in the future. Also use the future progressive tense to express an action or event that will occur at some specific time in the future, especially important events.

EXAMPLES:
Tomorrow I will be meeting Sam at the office.
They will be singing in the auditorium this afternoon.

j. The Present Perfect Progressive Tense

Use the **present perfect progressive tense** to express an action that began in the past and has continued to the present time.

EXAMPLES:
Morley has been fishing in the same lake for years.
They have been working on that project for months.

k. The Past Perfect Progressive Tense

Use the **past perfect progressive tense** to emphasize an action that continued in the past until another action in the past interrupted it.

EXAMPLES:
Chris had been eating in the restaurant only a few hours before it caught fire.
They had been driving for an hour when the snowstorm arrived.

1. The Future Perfect Progressive Tense

Use the **future perfect progressive tense** to indicate an action that will have continued for some time in the future before another action or before a specific time in the future arrives. Note that this tense is rarely used.

EXAMPLES:

When Ron is 55, he will have been teaching for 35 years.

By the time you reach the finish line, you will have been walking for more than 7 hours.

The following chart displays the verb *to be* in all persons (singular and plural) and in all forms of the simple and perfect progressive tenses)

present progressive	*first person*	*singular*	I am being
		plural	we are being
	second person	*singular*	you are being
		plural	they are being
	third person	*singular*	he, she, it is being
		plural	they are being
past progressive	*first person*	*singular*	I was being
		plural	we were being
	second person	*singular*	you were being
		plural	you were being
	third person	*singular*	he, she, it was being
		plural	they were being
future progressive	*first person*	*singular*	I shall be being
		plural	we shall be being
	second person	*singular*	you will be being
		plural	you will be being
	third person	*singular*	he, she, it will be being
		plural	they will be being

present perfect progressive	*first person*	*singular*	I have been being
		plural	we have been being
	second person	*singular*	you have been being
		plural	you have been being
	third person	*singular*	he, she, it has been being
		plural	they have been being
past perfect progressive	*first person*	*singular*	I had been being
		plural	we had been being
	second person	*singular*	you had been being
		plural	you had been being
	third person	*singular*	he, she, it had been being
		plural	they had been being
future perfect progressive	*first person*	*singular*	I shall have been being
		plural	we shall have been being
	second person	*singular*	you will have been being
		plural	you will have been being
	third person	*singular*	he, she, it will have been being
		plural	they will have been being

EXERCISE • 33

Write sentences using the correct verb tense indicated.

EXAMPLE:

think present perfect progressive

I <u>have been thinking</u> about you.

1. study future perfect progressive
2. watch past perfect progressive
3. take future progressive
4. steal present perfect progressive
5. dream past progressive
6. carry past perfect progressive
7. bring present progressive

8.	drive	future progressive
9.	show	present perfect progressive
10.	dance	past perfect progressive

EXERCISE • 34

Follow the instructions for Exercise 33.

1.	lose	past progressive
2.	deliver	present perfect progressive
3.	mail	future progressive
4.	wish	past perfect progressive
5.	drink	present progressive
6.	pay	future progressive
7.	draw	past perfect progressive
8.	cook	future perfect progressive
9.	be	present perfect progressive
10.	sell	past progressive

EXERCISE • 35

Follow the instructions for Exercise 34.

1.	manage	present perfect progressive
2.	slice	past perfect progressive
3.	tell	past progressive
4.	give	present perfect progressive
5.	take	future progressive
6.	wonder	past perfect progressive
7.	hang	present progressive
8.	design	future progressive
9.	go	past perfect progressive
10.	collect	future perfect progressive

EXERCISE • 36

Follow the instructions for Exercise 35.

1.	care	present perfect progressive
2.	play	future progressive

3. fold	present progressive
4. jog	past perfect progressive
5. whistle	past progressive
6. plant	present perfect progressive
7. scrape	future perfect progressive
8. lend	present progressive
9. fly	future progressive
10. rise	past perfect progressive

EXERCISE ♦ 37

Follow the instructions for Exercise 36.

1. cry	past perfect progressive
2. arrange	past progressive
3. clean	present perfect progressive
4. pay	future perfect progressive
5. use	present progressive
6. visit	future progressive
7. establish	past perfect progressive
8. read	future perfect progressive
9. count	present perfect progressive
10. smile	past progressive

5. Active and Passive Voice

If a verb is used to make a statement of the pattern "John *broke* it," it is said to be **in the active voice**. If it is used to direct the action back to the subject in a statement of the pattern "It *was broken*," it is said to be **in the passive voice**. In the second case, it is often combined with a prepositional phrase (see Item VI in this Addendum) as in "It was broken *by John*."

a. The passive voice of a given verb is formed by *to be* plus the past participle of the given verb.

Note: In most cases, you should use the active voice; the passive voice tends to weaken your writing because it lacks focus and directness.

EXAMPLES:

Marta *locked* the car door. (active voice)
The car door *was locked* by Marta. (passive voice)

Ravi *dated* Irena before. (active voice)
Irena *has been dated* by Ravi before. (passive voice)

Sue *is baking* a cake. (active voice)
The cake *is being baked* by Sue. (passive voice)

Note that while the passive voice is not recommended, there are occasions when using it can make your writing effective.

b. Use the passive voice when the doer of the action is unknown.

EXAMPLES:

The liquor store was robbed last night. (who robbed the liquor store is unknown)
The blouse was made in China. (who made the blouse is unknown)

c. Use the passive voice to emphasize and set apart the doer of the action from what is stated in the sentence.

EXAMPLES:

The food drive was made a success by the participating grade schools. (information about food drive emphasized)
The roads were flooded by the heavy rains. (information about roads emphasized)

EXERCISE • 38

Identify the verbs in the following sentences as being in the in the active or passive voice.

EXAMPLE:

This wall hanging was made by my sister. passive

1. The dentist will see you now. ____________
2. Your goose was cooked this morning. ____________
3. This essay was written by Eve. ____________
4. Joanie will not be going with Carolyn. ____________
5. Most of the snow was shoveled by John and me. ____________
6. The basement was cleaned on the weekend by us. ____________
7. We jogged for an hour this morning. ____________
8. When are you taking your vacation? ____________

9. The bill was paid by Olive. ____________
10. Betty wants a few more napkins. ____________

EXERCISE • 39

Follow the instructions for Exercise 38.

1. I was embarrassed by my brother. ____________
2. How many empty bottles did you collect? ____________
3. Claire was bedridden with a bad cold. ____________
4. Daria and Syed are leaving for Nova Scotia. ____________
5. It was written into the marriage contract. ____________
6. This dress was hand-sewn in Vietnam. ____________
7. The sun is setting already. ____________
8. The carrots were planted by the children. ____________
9. This new board game was developed by me. ____________
10. Yeah! I was paid on time. ____________

EXERCISE • 40

Change the voice of the verbs from active to passive or passive to active in the following sentences.

EXAMPLES:

The coffee was made by Joe.
<u>Joe made the coffee.</u>

They sanded the floors.
<u>The floors were sanded by them.</u>

1. George and Shanta visited her parents.
2. The move was organized by Ethel.
3. The cookie jar was knocked over by the cat.
4. Joanne sewed the blouse and skirt.
5. The grass was cut by our neighbour.
6. Kelly has caught a huge salmon.
7. The package was delivered by the post office.
8. She told the truth.
9. The kitten was drinking the milk.
10. Jay is painting the garage door.

EXERCISE • 41

Follow the instructions for Exercise 40.

1. The award was presented by the vice president.
2. The UFO was seen by hundreds of people.
3. They visited Gloria last summer.
4. The couch was donated to the charity drive by Ina.
5. Matt had a fit at the lawyer's office.
6. The taxes were raised by City Hall.
7. Oops! I burned the toast.
8. My leg was bitten by a mosquito.
9. Danny was told to get a haircut by his friends.
10. They delivered the newspaper before dawn.

EXERCISE • 42

Write sentences using the active and passive voice with the verbs indicated.

EXAMPLE:

Maria emptied the garbage. (active)
The garbage was emptied by Maria. (passive)

1. wash
2. break
3. visit
4. scratch
5. heat
6. see
7. move
8. love
9. complete
10. sign

Item IV: Adjectives

An **adjective** is the part of speech that describes a noun or pronoun. An adjective answers the questions "What kind of?" and "How many?"

1. Adjectives Describe Nouns

An adjective describes a noun; sometimes more than one adjective describes the same noun.

EXAMPLES:

This is a *sad* movie.

John has been married for *three* years.

Your *blue ski* hat is in the closet.

The *tall, dark, rich* man is my husband.

Sometimes adjectives are separated from the noun they describe by the non-action verb *to be* or by a verb of the senses when it is used as a non-action verb.

EXAMPLES:

Liyi was *sleepy* after the test.

The lettuce tastes *bitter.*

2. Adjectives Describe Pronouns

In most cases adjectives describe pronouns when they follow the non-action verb *to be* or a verb of the senses.

EXAMPLES:

No one was *upset.*

He feels *energetic.*

EXERCISE • 43

Underline the adjectives in the following sentences, and draw an arrow to the noun or pronoun each adjective describes.

EXAMPLE:

The mystery story is a famous one.

1. The fresh chicken is in the refrigerator.
2. Anthony was lonely but happy.
3. The smelly cheese tastes good.
4. I am certain that the answer is wrong.
5. The heavy fog covered the winding road.
6. Sue is kind and considerate.
7. Are you able to repair the old deck?
8. He whispered silly things to me.
9. The soup is cold and tasteless.
10. Ivan likes horror movies.

EXERCISE • 44

Follow the instructions for Exercise 43.

1. Your lawn is green and healthy.
2. Give me the blue scarf not the yellow one.
3. The old graveyard is full.
4. I like steamed rice.
5. Are these fresh cabbages?
6. Dorota has thick wavy hair.
7. What is the difference between salted and unsalted butter?
8. Jill's virus is contagious.
9. The large pillow is for your enormous ego.
10. The pink flowers smell good.

EXERCISE • 45

Follow the instructions for Exercise 43.

1. The dental appointment is in two days.
2. Mel was envious of everyone.

3. The flat tire was bad luck for us.
4. The last movie starts in five minutes.
5. Did the new commercial make a false promise?
6. There is more soup in the large pot.
7. The tow truck is waiting.
8. Your feet are cold.
9. I need two more days to decide.
10. Do you want a peaceful holiday?

EXERCISE • 46

Follow the instructions for Exercise 45.

1. Martha makes delicious baked potatoes.
2. The robin was hungry and weary after its long flight.
3. Your grey sweater is my favourite.
4. The cottage is on a secluded road.
5. The hot sun burned Clara's sensitive skin.
6. Michael displayed poor behaviour at the party last night.
7. A few of the students are ill.
8. The apple pie is home-made.
9. The slippery sidewalk is dangerous.
10. Frozen yogurt can be expensive.

EXERCISE • 47

Write ten sentences in which you use at least two adjectives. Underline the adjectives, and draw arrows to the words the adjectives describe.

3. Nouns as Adjectives

Sometimes nouns function as adjectives. When a noun is used to describe another noun it becomes an adjective.

EXAMPLES:

The *apartment* building was built in 1901.

The *banana* bread is on the counter.

4. Pronouns as Adjectives

When a pronoun is used to describe another noun, the pronoun functions as an adjective. Demonstrative and indefinite pronouns commonly function as adjectives.

a. The demonstrative pronouns *this, that, these,* and *those* become adjectives when they describe a noun.

EXAMPLES:

How much does *this* car cost?

That man is my father.

Do you know *these* people?

Those clothes are for the Goodwill Society.

b. Indefinite pronouns such as *another, each, either, neither, one, both, few, many, other, several, more, all, anymore,* and *some* become adjectives when they describe a noun.

EXAMPLES:

Both couples won prizes.

All chocolate does not taste the same.

EXERCISE • 48

In the space provided, indicate whether the italicized word is a noun or an adjective.

EXAMPLE:

Angie likes *this* music. adjective

1. The *grocery* store is open until midnight. ____________
2. Eva is *someone* special. ____________
3. *Someone* of your academic status will be successful. ____________
4. *These* boots are useless in the slush. ____________
5. *This* is not what I expected. ____________
6. A lot of *those* games are becoming popular. ____________

7. *Many* men disagree with that opinion. ________________
8. How far is the *furniture* factory from your house? ________________
9. We would like new *furniture* for the bedroom. ________________
10. The *dog* show is in the auditorium. ________________

EXERCISE ◆ 49

Follow the instructions for Exercise 48.

1. *Many* of you are underpaid. ________________
2. *Neither* of the brothers can agree on a solution. ________________
3. *Neither* one hears what the other is saying. ________________
4. *Those* get-well cards made me laugh. ________________
5. The tree *branch* fell on my car. ________________
6. What *branch* of the provincial government is this? ________________
7. The teacher would not listen to *any* complaints. ________________
8. He said that there is a *noun* clause in this sentence. ________________
9. *Nouns* are much easier to understand. ________________
10. *Everyone* is pleased with the news. ________________

EXERCISE ◆ 50

Follow the instructions for Exercise 49.

1. I agree with *that* opinion. ________________
2. *That* is what I think too. ________________
3. I would enjoy a *meatball* sandwich right now. ________________
4. Why is this *meat* green? ________________
5. The *room* service is terrible. ________________
6. Sit beside me; there's lots of *room*. ________________
7. Your *hands* are rough and dry. ________________
8. You need some *hand* cream. ________________
9. *Either* one would be fine. ________________
10. *Either* is perfect. ________________

EXERCISE ◆ 51

Follow the instructions for Exercise 50.

1. I like *watermelon*. ________________
2. Do *watermelon* jelly beans taste like watermelon? ________________

3. It showed for *several* days. ____________
4. *Several* of the stores closed early. ____________
5. What are your *vacation* plans? ____________
6. No *vacation* is too long. ____________
7. This *photo* of you is great. ____________
8. Where is the *photo* album? ____________
9. This is my favourite *radio* station. ____________
10. The *radio* is too loud. ____________

EXERCISE • 52

Write sentences using each of the following words as both a pronoun and an adjective.

EXAMPLE:

A *few* of us were late. (pronoun)
Few lessons are easily learned. (adjective)

1. all
2. another
3. both
4. either
5. each
6. more
7. these
8. some
9. that
10. one

5. Adjectives and Comparisons

Adjectives can be used to show degrees of comparison. The three degrees of comparison are *positive, comparative,* and *superlative.* Many adjectives follow the familiar pattern of adding *-er* for the comparative and *-est* for the superlative. Other adjectives require the use of intensifiers such as *more* and *most,* or *less* and *least.*

a. The **positive degree** is the main form of the adjective and indicates the presence of the quality.

EXAMPLES:

The blue towel is *soft*.
The puzzle is *difficult*.
This stew is *spicy*.

b. The **comparative degree** indicates a comparison between two things, individuals, or groups.

EXAMPLES:

This blue towel is *softer* than the green one.
The puzzle is *more difficult* than I thought.
This stew is *less spicy* than the meat loaf.

c. The **superlative degree** indicates a comparison between one and many other persons or things.

EXAMPLES:

The blue towel is the *softest* one in the bathroom.
This is the *most difficult* puzzle I have ever tried.
This stew is the *least spicy* item on the menu.

d. Never use the intensifiers *more, most, less,* and *least* with adjectives that indicate the comparative and superlative forms with *-er* or *-est* endings.

EXAMPLES:

Fred is *more tireder*. (incorrect)
Fred is *more tired*. (correct)

This apartment is the *most nicest* one in the building. (incorrect)
This apartment is the *nicest* one in the building. (correct)

e. Some adjectives have irregular comparative and superlative forms.

positive	*comparative*	*superlative*
good	better	best
bad	worse	worst
ill	worse	worst
some	more	most
little (amount)	less	least

f. Some adjectives already express the superlative degree in their usual form. These adjectives should not be used in comparisons.

complete	equal
dead	moderate
definite	perfect
empty	unique

EXERCISE • 53

Some of the following sentences contain errors in adjective usage. Make corrections where they are needed. If the sentence is correct, write "C" beside it.

EXAMPLE:

Leanne is more shorter than Ona. (incorrect)
Leanne is shorter than Ona. (correct)

1. This coffee is the creamiest of the two.
2. Which road is easier in life?
3. This painting is more unique.
4. The picture on your television is much more better than mine.
5. Take this peach; it's the freshest one.
6. Did you try your most hardest?
7. I think that Dan is more slimmer than his brother.
8. Brenda is more clever than I.
9. In our class, Brenda is the smarter one.
10. This movie is the more boring one I have ever seen.

EXERCISE • 54

Follow the instructions for Exercise 53.

1. I am almost calmest than Al.
2. You need to develop a more thicker skin.
3. Sean is certainly the luckier one in the family.
4. What is the longest river in Canada?
5. Today is more windier than yesterday.
6. This cane is more sturdier than my last one.
7. Lisa's cold is worser today.
8. English is the harder subject of all.

9. That is the most foolish thing I have ever heard.
10. You are more weaker than I.

EXERCISE ♦ 55

Write sentences in which you use the forms of the adjectives indicated.

EXAMPLE:

tall	comparative

Jerome is *taller* than I.

1.	white	superlative
2.	low	comparative
3.	lovelier	positive
4.	rusty	superlative
5.	tidy	comparative
6.	sore	superlative
7.	healthy	superlative
8.	uncertain	comparative
9.	leanest	positive
10.	dirty	comparative

EXERCISE ♦ 56

Follow the instructions for Exercise 55.

1.	friendly	comparative
2.	clean	superlative
3.	ugly	superlative
4.	quickest	positive
5.	much	comparative
6.	good	superlative
7.	smelly	superlative
8.	rocky	comparative
9.	older	positive
10.	shiny	comparative

EXERCISE ♦ 57

Follow the instructions for Exercise 56.

1.	bold	comparative
2.	silly	superlative

3.	lively	superlative
4.	wealthiest	positive
5.	clear	superlative
6.	lonely	comparative
7.	smokey	superlative
8.	bad	comparative
9.	more honest	positive
10.	hard	comparative

Item V: Adverbs

Adverbs describe verbs, adjectives, and other adverbs. Adverbs answer the questions "How?" "When?" "Where?" "How much?" "To what extent?" "Under what condition?"

1. Adverbs Describe Verbs

EXAMPLES:

He answered the phone *quickly*.

Sally ran *downstairs*.

When adverbs describe verbs, the adverbs sometimes separate the helping verbs from the main verbs.

Here is a list of adverbs that often appear to be part of the verb but are not.

actually	generally	probably
already	immediately	really
also	just	suddenly
always	never	supposedly
ever	not	only

EXAMPLES:

She could*n't* have done it.

He was *always* daydreaming in class.

Gord has *already* paid me.

2. Adverbs Describe Adjectives

EXAMPLES:

Edna is *completely* exhausted.

This puppy is *probably* lost.

3. Adverbs Describe Adverbs

EXAMPLES:

Simon works *very effectively* with people.

You drive *too fast*.

EXERCISE • 58

Underline the adverbs in the following sentences. Draw an arrow to the verbs, adjectives, or adverbs the adverbs describe.

EXAMPLE:

Walter is <u>very</u> confused.

1. Greg waited patiently in the doctor's office.
2. Are you quite sure about this information?
3. The road was completely blocked by the overturned truck.
4. You study too hard.
5. This mosquito-bite ointment is very soothing.
6. Lower your voice; you are speaking too loudly.
7. Give up; the police have arrived.
8. Cynthia is truly happy.
9. Why does Eugene chew so loudly?
10. The car runs much better today.

EXERCISE • 59

Follow the instructions for Exercise 58.

1. The teacher speaks too slowly.
2. Do you always wash your feet after lunch?

3. They finally ended their relationship.
4. I really didn't need that advice.
5. Mohammed nervously stepped into the doctor's office.
6. That car is following too closely.
7. Why are you being so silly?
8. Alban frequently visits the race track.
9. You shouldn't use your deodorant before you shower.
10. We just ordered the espresso machine.

EXERCISE ◆ 60

Follow the instructions for Exercise 59.

1. Always cover your mouth when you cough.
2. The pizza will arrive momentarily.
3. Is Ken a highly skilled auto mechanic?
4. I was completely confused by the test.
5. Speak clearly and slowly.
6. The basement is partially finished.
7. You are really good for my heart.
8. I can't work very well after a big lunch.
9. Steve actually remembered his anniversary.
10. Move your arm slowly; there's a huge spider on it.

EXERCISE ◆ 61

Write sentences using the adverbs indicated.

EXAMPLE:

slowly
The traffic is moving slowly.

1. definitely
2. courageously
3. carefully
4. loosely
5. identically
6. longingly
7. wildly
8. favourably
9. uncontrollably
10. simply

EXERCISE • 62

Follow the instructions for Exercise 61.

1. only
2. ever
3. not
4. effectively
5. neatly
6. just
7. purposely
8. knowingly
9. locally
10. faithfully

4. Adverbs of Condition, Place, Quantity, and Time

Sometimes it is difficult to determine if an adverb is describing a verb, adjective, or adverb. When this occurs, the adverb is usually expressing condition, place, quantity, or time.

Here is a partial list of these adverbs. Note that they do not have comparative or superlative forms.

condition	*place*	*quantity*	*time*
alone	ahead	almost	always
indeed	back	quite	before
no	below	so	ever
thus	down	very	hour
together	here	too	next
yes	in		now
	inside		often
	out		once
	there		past
	up		still
			sometimes
			then
			today
			tomorrow
			yesterday
			yet

EXAMPLES:

Once upon a time a nice teacher taught in a distant kingdom. (time)
Get *back* to the house quickly! (place)

EXERCISE • 63

Underline the adverbs of condition, place, quantity, and time in the following sentences.

EXAMPLE:

Are you going <u>back</u> <u>alone</u>?

1. Let's finish the painting together.
2. Do you want the money now or tomorrow?
3. The taxi is here.
4. I almost fell down.
5. Try it once; it's delicious.
6. I don't want to climb up again.
7. Get down; they'll see you.
8. I'm still tired.
9. Angie jogged alone yesterday.
10. Go away now.

EXERCISE • 64

Follow the instructions for Exercise 63.

1. Sometimes things go too far.
2. Why is Melanie so unhappy?
3. Aleksandra wants her soup now, not later.
4. Put it on; the sweater should fit.
5. These fries are too hot.
6. Are you ever going to Newfoundland?
7. We stopped there earlier today.
8. How often do you floss?
9. Bring the towels in; it's raining out.
10. I'll be here if you need me.

EXERCISE ♦ 65

Write sentences using the adverbs of condition, place, quantity, and time indicated.

EXAMPLE:

together Let's go together.

1. out ____________________
2. not ____________________
3. before ____________________
4. never ____________________
5. up ____________________
6. there ____________________
7. below ____________________
8. sometimes ____________________
9. alone ____________________
10. next ____________________

5. Adverbs and Comparisons

Adverbs have the same three degrees of comparison as adjectives — *positive*, *comparative*, and *superlative*.

a. The **positive degree** states the presence of quality.

EXAMPLES:

Harry ran *fast* in the race.
Brenda studied *hard* for the test.

b. The **comparative degree** indicates a comparison between two things, individuals, or groups.

EXAMPLES:

Harry ran *faster* than Glen.
Brenda studied *harder* than Dennis.

c. The **superlative degree** indicates a comparison between one thing or person and a number of other things or persons.

EXAMPLES:

Harry ran *fastest* of all in the race.
Brenda studied *hardest* for the test.

d. Most adverbs can be formed by adding *-ly* to the positive form of the adjective. Some adverbs, however, retain the same form of the adjective.

Here is a partial list of these.

positive	*comparative*	*superlative*
hard	harder	hardest
far	farther	farthest
fast	faster	fastest
late	later	latest
many	more	most
much	more	most
well	better	best

EXAMPLES:

Kathy enjoyed the *late* show. (adjective)

Kathy arrived *late* for work. (adverb)

e. As with adjectives, do not use the intensifiers *more, most, less, least* with adverbs that indicate the comparative and superlative forms with *-er* or *-est* endings.

EXAMPLES:

Dale ran more faster than I. (incorrect)
Dale ran faster than I. (correct)

f. Do not place the article *the* in front of *best* and *most* when they are being used as adverbs.

EXAMPLES:

I love you *the most.* (incorrect)
I love you *most.*

I love you *the best.* (incorrect)
I love you *best.* (correct)

BUT:

You are *the best.* (correct — *best* used as noun)
You are *the best* student. (correct — *best* used as an adjective)

6. Adverb/Adjective Confusion

Do not interchange adjective/adverb forms. Remember that adjectives describe nouns and pronouns, and adverbs describe verbs, adjectives, and adverbs. Study the following adverb usage problems and how to correct them.

a. *Good* and *Well*

Good and *well* are frequently used but also frequently confused.

Good is always an adjective and describes nouns and pronouns. It cannot describe a verb. (See Unit 1, Item III.)

EXAMPLES:

Carlos is a *good* dancer. (correct)
Carlos dances *good*. (incorrect)

Well is an adverb when it describes a verb, and it is an adjective when it refers to appearance or health.

EXAMPLES:

They dance *well* together. (adverb)
Erin looks *well* today. (adjective)
Carlos feels *well* after his rest. (adjective — refers to health)

b. *Bad* and *Badly*

Bad and *badly* are also often confused.

Bad is always an adjective and describes a noun or pronoun.

EXAMPLES:

You have a *bad* attitude. (correct)
Donna sings really *bad*. (incorrect — bad used as an adverb)

Badly is always an adverb and describes a verb, adjective, or another adverb.

EXAMPLES:

Sharon feels *bad* about the accident. (correct — adjective describes noun Sharon)
I felt *badly* after eating the chili. (incorrect — *badly* used as an adjective)

c. Other Troublesome Pairs

Other adjective/adverb pairs that are often confused are *real, really*; *quick, quickly*; *sure, surely*; and *thin, thinly*. The adjective forms in these pairs are often used as adverbs.

This practice is usually accepted in spoken English because it sounds better; however, in written formal English the adverb form must be used as required.

EXAMPLES:

Quick, answer the phone. (incorrect — adjective)
Quickly, answer the phone. (correct — adverb)

Sure I love you. (incorrect — adjective)
Surely I love you. (correct — adverb)

He sliced the bread *thin*. (incorrect — adjective)
He sliced the bread *thinly*. (correct — adverb)

EXERCISE • 66

Underline the correct form of the adverb in the parentheses.

EXAMPLE:

Come (closer, more closer).

1. Think (careful, carefully) before you speak.
2. This is a (real, really) nice car.
3. Can you get here any (faster, more faster)?
4. You need to get a haircut (sooner, more sooner).
5. What smells so (bad, badly) in the kitchen?
6. (Quick, Quickly), run to the store for me.
7. I should have finished (earlier, more earlier).
8. These two students are working (the best, best) in the class.
9. I wish I could dance as (good, well) as you.
10. This train arrives (later, more later) than the express.

EXERCISE • 67

Follow the instructions for Exercise 66.

1. The (sooner, more sooner) you finish the (happier, more happier) you will be.
2. Who writes (the best, best) in this class?

3. She does feel (bad, badly) about the mistake.
4. This is going to be (real, really) hard for me to do.
5. You know you do it (the best, best).
6. Why did you screw the cap on so (tight, tightly)?
7. (Sure, Surely) I will go out with you.
8. This old clock still runs (good, well).
9. Which of the two bartenders is (older, oldest)?
10. I think my shoelaces are tied too (loose, loosely).

EXERCISE • 68

Some of the following sentences contain errors in adjective and adverb usage. Make corrections where necessary. If the sentence is correct, write "C" beside it.

EXAMPLE:

Jeremy delivered his speech too slow. (incorrect)
Jeremy delivered his speech too slowly. (correct)

1. Go quiet; the children are sleeping.
2. The time went so quick!
3. You speak well, but you write poor.
4. Cindy looks good in her new skirt.
5. I don't think you copied this correct.
6. Of course, Don's car is more faster than yours.
7. Marilyn studies hardest than her sister.
8. It's snowing heavier now.
9. The ambulance arrived very quick.
10. This sentence ended well.

EXERCISE • 69

Follow the instructions for Exercise 68.

1. Is your cold more worse today?
2. Ken and Bertha work real well together.
3. The sky is bluer than yesterday.
4. Is the bread or the banana loaf cut too thin?
5. You know you acted improper last night.
6. Things don't always go smooth.

7. The onions were chopped too coarse.
8. The speaker expressed herself real clear.
9. Sophie researched this material very careful.
10. You completed this exercise good.

EXERCISE • 70

Underline the adjectives once and the adverbs twice in the following sentences.

EXAMPLE:

Nicole is a very healthy baby.

1. Where did you go last night?
2. Greg is a very gentle man.
3. Stop talking so loudly; I can hear you very clearly.
4. Have you ever seen a real dinosaur fossil?
5. You can't go home yet: it's still early.
6. The hardest beans to grow are jelly beans.
7. Wipe your big feet thoroughly; then you can come in.
8. Naturally, I was very polite to the police officer.
9. Why are you so proud of your old gym shorts?
10. Look deeply into your heart, and the correct answer will come to you soon.

EXERCISE • 71

Follow the instructions for Exercise 70.

1. This is definitely the freshest doughnut I have ever eaten.
2. Never go there when the moon is full.
3. My back tooth is very sore.
4. What's wrong with my new purse?
5. This rusty old car will never run again.
6. What is the best definition of ugly?
7. Is that a real phone or a toy phone?
8. The motor starts quickly, so hang on tightly.
9. They had a brief conversation earlier.
10. Did you wake up on the wrong side of bed again?

EXERCISE • 72

Follow the instructions for Exercise 71.

1. This rope is definitely longer than that one.
2. When will the social worker come back?

3. Ralph is a very dedicated Latin teacher.
4. Perhaps you should call later.
5. Thu reluctantly played one more game of cards.
6. Down below you will find the buried treasure.
7. You will feel better in a few days.
8. The wind is really gusty today.
9. Sincere and dedicated are the volunteers at the relief centre.
10. Please don't ever give me a perfunctory kiss.

Item VI: Prepositions, Conjunctions, and Interjections

1. Prepositions

Prepositions often express time, space, or conceptual relationships between nouns and verbs in a sentence. Prepositions never change form. Familiarize yourself with this list of common prepositions.

about	beneath	in	through
above	beside	inside	till
across	besides	into	to
after	between	near	toward
against	beyond	of	under
along	concerning	off	underneath
among	down	on	until
at	during	over	upon
before	except	regarding	with
behind	far	respecting	without
below	from	since	

Note the following prepositions which are made up of more than one word.

according to	by means of	in front of
ahead of	by way of	in place of
apart from	contrary to	in reference to
as far as	devoid of	in spite of
as for	from behind	instead of
back of	from out	on account of
because of	in addition to	with respect to

a. A Prepositional Phrase

A **prepositional phrase** is a group of related words that begins with a preposition but is not a sentence. A prepositional phrase states a fact, describes someone or something, or indicates condition, time, or place in a sentence.

A prepositional phrase begins with a preposition and ends in a noun or pronoun. It does not contain a subject and verb. The noun or pronoun that ends a prepositional phrase is called the **object of the preposition**. There can be more than one object of the preposition.

EXAMPLES:

under the bridge
over the next hill
without Mary or me

There can be more than one prepositional phrase in a sentence.

EXAMPLES:

(*After* dinner) they went (*into* the family room)(*for* dessert).
You can learn a lot (*about* prepositions) (*by* reading a good English usage book).

b. Prepositions and Infinitives

Don't confuse prepositional phrases with infinitives. Prepositional phrases that begin with *to* must be followed by a noun or pronoun. **Infinitives** always begin with *to* and must be followed by the present tense of the verb.

EXAMPLES:

Joan likes *to play* tennis in the morning. (infinitive)
When did you go (*to* the grocery store)? (prepositional phrase)

c. Prepositions at the End of a Sentence

In general, the traditional rule that a preposition should never end a sentence is true. However, on occasion, the syntax (word order) of a sentence is clearer when the preposition is left at the end of the sentence.

EXAMPLES:

Is this a project you are committed *to*? (Is this a project *to which* you are committed?)

This is the restaurant that I told you *about*. (This is the restaurant *about which* I told you.)

Be careful, however, not to confuse prepositions with adverbs at the end of a sentence.

EXAMPLES:

Which religion do you believe *in*? (preposition)
This is the pond the homes will be built *around*. (preposition)
The bats were flying all *around*. (adverb)
Please come *in*. (adverb)

EXERCISE • 73

Place parentheses around the prepositional phrases in the following sentences.

EXAMPLE:

Pull into the gas station on the corner.
Pull (into the gas station) (on the corner).

1. With you everything is possible for me.
2. About an hour from here is a beautiful old inn.
3. On Thursday he had a short nap during the English lesson.
4. Most of the heat from the fireplace must be going up the chimney.
5. Because of the snowstorm, school was canceled in the afternoon.
6. I can't see beyond the grocery store across the street.
7. This composition was handed to me by Inez.
8. Instead of complaining, do something about it.
9. I like a hot cup of coffee with a warm croissant for breakfast.
10. Within all of us is the potential for achieving success.

EXERCISE • 74

Follow the instructions for Exercise 73.

1. By the look on his face, I could see that Eugene was not happy.
2. Neither one of us wants to visit the rendering factory again.
3. The killer must be devoid of any feeling.
4. Everyone of the students went to Niagara Falls except me.
5. A snowfall in the woods can be soothing to the spirit.
6. Dino had a fistful of twenty's in his wallet.
7. Meet me by the water fountain in the park.

8. By noon Yolanta is ready for her lunch break.
9. The moral of the good seeds and the bad seeds is worth repeating.
10. I would love to walk in the moonlight with you.

EXERCISE • 75

Follow the instructions for Exercise 74.

1. These Western boots were made by Greg and Ethel at their store.
2. You can count on me for my support in the office.
3. Which one of these new dresses are you going to wear to the party?
4. Is this the club to which you belong?
5. Save a seat for me at the game.
6. On the other side of the fence only some of the grass was greener.
7. In some ways you are right about Tony and Lindsey.
8. Slipping into a warm bed with a good book on a cold night sounds good to me.
9. On the way to your cottage, I saw a deer on the side of the road.
10. Go through the parking lot to reach the back of the theatre.

EXERCISE • 76

Write sentences using the prepositions indicated. Place parentheses around your prepositional phrases.

EXAMPLE:

of

The three (of us) should visit him tomorrow.

1. underneath
2. along
3. on
4. among
5. with
6. beyond
7. because of
8. except
9. at
10. in front of

EXERCISE • 77

Follow the instructions for Exercise 76.

1. with
2. during

3. against
4. since
5. behind
6. regarding
7. near
8. under
9. by
10. instead of

2. Conjunctions

Conjunctions connect groups of words, phrases, or clauses in a sentence. There are two main types of conjunctions: *coordinating* and *subordinating*.

a. Coordinating Conjunctions

Coordinating conjunctions join words, phrases, and main clauses. Here is a list of coordinating conjunctions.

and	or
but	so
for	yet
nor	

EXAMPLES:

Julie *and* Al *and* Justine rented the jet skis for the weekend. (nouns)
You can go to the bank at the corner *or* across the street. (phrases)
Shin-Kwon bought a microwave oven, *and* she paid cash for it. (main clauses)

b. Correlative Conjunctions

Conjunctions that are used in pairs are called **correlative conjunctions**. These also join words, phrases, and clauses in a sentence. Note the following correlative conjunctions.

as … as	not only … but also
both … and	so … as
either … or	whether … or
neither … nor	

EXAMPLES:

Dominic is *not only* a talented singer *but also* a great dancer.
You're not *as* old *as* Marcel.

Note that you should use *either* only with *or* and *neither* only with *nor*.

c. Subordinating Conjunctions

Subordinating conjunctions introduce subordinate clauses and join them to main clauses. Here is a partial list of commonly used subordinating conjunctions.

after	even if	rather than	when
although	even though	since	whenever
as	how	so that	until
as if	if	supposing	where
as long as	in order that	than	whereas
as soon as	now that	that	wherever
as though	on condition that	though	whether
because	provided that	unless	while
			why

EXAMPLES:

Call us *when* the pizza arrives.
Even though Sol was rich, he was not happy.

Note that some conjunctions have the same form as prepositions — *after*, *before*, *but* (when it means *except*), *for*, and *until*. Note that conjunctions introduce whole clauses whereas prepositions are followed by nouns and pronouns.

EXAMPLES:

You've changed *since* you've gone back to school. (conjunction)
You've changed *since* yesterday. (preposition)

Jordon became a professional athlete, *for* he really enjoys sports. (conjunction)
Are these flowers *for* me? (preposition)

EXERCISE • 78

Underline the conjunctions in the following sentences.

EXAMPLE:

If you need some help, give me a call.
<u>If</u> you need some help, give me a call.

1. Because Joan was tired, she had a nap at her desk.
2. Either Tim will drive you or Barry will.
3. I know when I should leave.
4. She was offered the promotion, but Edna did not want the added stress.
5. If you hurry, you can make it to the bank before it closes.
6. When Bert walks on stage, Andy and Gerta will follow.
7. Jia had free tickets to the game, but she was too tired to go.
8. I don't like apple pie and cheddar cheese.
9. Both Susan and Barbara are going to help Anne with her homework.
10. Do you know whether Paramjit or Fred has the keys?

EXERCISE • 79

Follow the instructions for Exercise 78.

1. These muffins and doughnuts are stale, but the croissants are fresh.
2. Neither Rubina nor Chady knows what you mean.
3. Take care until we meet again.
4. Ching Ha said that it was supposed to rain today.
5. If Afren calls, tell him that I'll be back in ten minutes.
6. Whenever it rains, Gord gets a headache.
7. I can imagine how you and Mel must feel.
8. As soon as I said it, I knew that I had made a terrible mistake.
9. Could you pour the wine before you sit down?
10. Lucy is not friends with Alicia or Roland.

EXERCISE • 80

Follow the instructions for Exercise 79.

1. Although Adolfo was tired, he finished painting the kitchen before he went to bed.
2. No one knows how it happened.
3. Can you check whether Tracy is at home or still at school?
4. Because it was hot, I left my sweater at work.
5. She said that it was too early for lilac blossoms.
6. As long as you are here, help me to carry this into the basement.
7. That you were late doesn't surprise me.
8. Marian can't wait until this semester is over.

9. Julius laughed when he heard the joke about the pigeon.
10. Is this sentence as troublesome as the others?

EXERCISE • 81

Write sentences using the conjunctions indicated.

EXAMPLE:

if

I will know *if* you are lying.

1. while
2. after
3. so that
4. how
5. although
6. because
7. where
8. now that
9. even if
10. since

EXERCISE • 82

Follow the instructions for Exercise 81.

1. why
2. as
3. though
4. before
5, in order that
6. that
7. until
8. as long as
9. whether
10. provided that

3. Interjections

Interjections are used to indicate strong feelings or sudden emotion. They are not grammatically related to other words in a sentence. An interjection is separated from the rest of the sentence by a comma or by an exclamation mark if the emotion is intense.

Here is a short list of interjections.

ah	ha	ouch
bah	hey	well
gee	hmm	whew
gosh	oops	whoops
		yikes

EXAMPLES:

Hey! That's my car.
Oops, I dropped the eggs.
Whew! I am really tired.

EXERCISE • 83

Underline the conjunctions, place parentheses around the prepositional phrases, and punctuate and circle all interjections in the following sentences.

EXAMPLE:

Oh I didn't know that you were going to Florida.

(Oh,) I didn't know <u>that</u> you were going (to Florida).

1. Whoops I lost my balance on the patch of ice.
2. Meet me at the doughnut shop when you are ready to go.
3. Kyle and Roberta sold their house to my cousin from Scarborough.
4. Whew I'm glad that they've left.
5. If you don't feel better, we can go out at another time.
6. Do you want chocolate sauce on your ice cream or not?
7. Yikes the snake is near your foot.
8. Provided that I can clean the kitchen on time, I can help you with the shopping.
9. Most of the fried chicken was eaten by the children.
10. I run into Sean wherever I go.

EXERCISE • 84

Follow the instructions for Exercise 83.

1. They named the parking lot after Otto because his car was always in it.
2. Whoa slow down; you're talking too fast.
3. The alien said that his spaceship was very fuel-efficient during long flights.
4. Your socks are on the dryer in the laundry room.
5. I can't even remember what I was doing at home last night.
6. For a change, why don't you try to eat some oatmeal for breakfast.
7. Wow that is one of the largest turkeys that I have ever seen.
8. Dorian wants to know what you put in the fish soup.
9. A few of the roses were touched by frost yesterday.
10. After Diego works out, he has a huge lunch at the restaurant across the street.

EXERCISE • 85

Follow the instructions for Exercise 84.

1. Cassandra and Sik Men enjoy old black-and-white movies best of all.
2. Bah you don't know what you are doing.
3. As soon as I have enough money, I'm going on a long vacation to the West Indies.
4. Either Janica or Angela will be teaching the line-dancing class at the community centre.
5. Whenever Choi's leg itches on a Friday, it rains all weekend.
6. Phew what kind of deodorant are you wearing?
7. Terry and you are made for each other.
8. Did you finish counting all of the dimples on the golf ball yet?
9. Neither Liyi nor her mother has been to the CN Tower.
10. Neither one of these pairs of shoes suits you.

EXERCISE • 86

Follow the instructions for Exercise 85.

1. Put the salami in the refrigerator until tomorrow.
2. Before you forget, take this package with you when you go to the post office.
3. Many of us are worried about the test.
4. I wish I could buy that gold chain for you for Christmas.

5. Don't be like him and eat with your mouth open.
6. Ouch that was my finger that you hit with the shovel.
7. Whether Andrew can meet you at noon or sooner is still uncertain at this time.
8. I wanted a cake as nice as Erica's.
9. A copy of this book is available in the library.
10. These fried eggs have spots and stripes on them.

EXERCISE • 87

Follow the instructions for Exercise 86.

1. Since Betty broke her foot, she has been miserable to everybody.
2. Makeda keeps waking up in the middle of the night to go to the bathroom.
3. Egad what a miserable personality!
4. If I had known the restaurant bill was going to be so much, I would have eaten at home.
5. Before you buy a computer for the office, check with me first.
6. You could be on that plane to Hong Kong tonight.
7. This is the last of the home-made fudge that you bought for us.
8. After his checkup, Lyndon felt better about everything.
9. Gosh it's time to go home already.
10. When Sam was little, he had his baths in the kitchen sink.

POST-TEST

If you have completed Addendum A satisfactorily, you are ready for the Post-Test. The answers immediately follow the test.

I. Underline the nouns once and the pronouns twice in the following sentences.

1. This is the car of my dreams.
2. Many of the pigeons are on your roof.
3. That is a strange place for a ring.
4. The book that I am reading is about the inner self.
5. Your happiness means everything to me.

II. Underline the verbs twice in the following sentences.

1. We are getting closer.
2. Get a grip!

3. They haven't visited in over a month.
4. The doctor said that it wouldn't hurt too much.
5. When are you going fishing?

III. Underline the adjectives once and the adverbs twice in the following sentences.

1. The clown seemed so sad despite her happy face.
2. Don't go down there; the light is out.
3. Every carpet in the house is flea-ridden.
4. You definitely need to smile more often.
5. I'll meet you downtown tomorrow in front of the liquor store.

IV. Correct the errors in adjective/adverb usage in the following sentences.

1. That is a real nice drawing of your sister.

   ___

   ___

2. The more sooner you get here the better.

   ___

   ___

3. Everyone feels badly for Graham.

   ___

   ___

4. Quick, get in here before it rains.

   ___

   ___

5. Bill always acts normal in public.

   ___

   ___

V. Underline all conjuctions once, circle all interjections, and place parentheses around all prepositional phrases in the following sentences.

1. If you see Fred, let me know that you have.
2. Wanda and Emily are in the same welding class at the college.
3. Gulp! I didn't realize the mess that I made of things.
4. Are you in the mood for one more test sentence?
5. Heck, that wasn't a nice thing to say about the last question.

ANSWERS • TO • POST-TEST

I. Underline the nouns once and the pronouns twice in the following sentences.

1. This is the car of my dreams.
2. Many of the pigeons are on your roof.
3. That is a strange place for a ring.
4. The book that I am reading is about the inner self.
5. Your happiness means everything to me.

II. Underline the verbs twice in the following sentences.

1. We are getting closer.
2. Get a grip!
3. They haven't visited in over a month.
4. The doctor said that it wouldn't hurt too much.
5. When are you going fishing?

III. Underline the adjectives once and the adverbs twice in the following sentences.

1. The clown seemed so sad despite her happy face.
2. Don't go down there; the light is out.
3. Every carpet in the house is flea-ridden.
4. You definitely need to smile more often.
5. I'll meet you downtown tomorrow in front of the liquor store.

IV. Correct the errors in adjective/adverb usage in the following sentences.

1. That is a really nice drawing of your sister.
2. The sooner you get here the better.
3. Everyone feels bad for Graham.
4. Quickly, get in here before it rains.
5. Bill always acts normally in public.

V. Underline all conjunctions once, circle all interjections, and place parentheses around all prepositional phrases in the following sentences.

1. If you see Fred, let me know that you have.
2. Wanda and Emily are (in the same welding class) (at the college).

3. Gulp! I didn't realize the mess that I made (of things).
4. Are you (in the mood) (for one more test sentence)?
5. Heck, that wasn't a nice thing to say (about the last question).

ADDENDUM B

COMMON ADJECTIVE FORMS

(For further information about adjectives see Addendum A, Item IV.)

positive	*comparative*	*superlative*
able	abler	ablest
bad	worse	worst
bold	bolder	boldest
bright	brighter	brightest
calm	calmer	calmest
careful	more careful	most careful
civil	more civil	most civil
cold	colder	coldest
deep	deeper	deepest
dirty	dirtier	dirtiest
drab	drabber	drabbest
easy	easier	easiest
foggy	foggier	foggiest
foolish	more foolish	most foolish
glad	gladder	gladdest
gloomy	gloomier	gloomiest
graceful	more graceful	most graceful
happy	happier	happiest

hard	harder	hardest
high	higher	highest
ignorant	more ignorant	most ignorant
ill	worse	worst
itchy	itchier	itchiest
joyful	more joyful	most joyful
juicy	juicier	juiciest
kind	kinder	kindest
late	later (or latter)	latest (or last)
light	lighter	lightest
lively	livelier	liveliest
lofty	loftier	loftiest
lonely	lonelier	loneliest
long	longer	longest
lovely	lovelier	loveliest
lowly	lowlier	lowliest
lucky	luckier	luckiest
marshy	marshier	marshiest
merry	merrier	merriest
misty	mistier	mistiest
much	more	most
new	newer	newest
nice	nicer	nicest
nimble	nimbler	nimblest
noisy	noisier	noisiest
old	older	oldest
petty	pettier	pettiest
popular	more popular	most popular
pretty	prettier	prettiest
puny	punier	puniest
pure	purer	purest
quick	quicker	quickest
quiet	quieter	quietest
rare	rarer	rarest

ready	readier	readiest
rich	richer	richest
rocky	rockier	rockiest
scrubby	scrubbier	scrubbiest
shady	shadier	shadiest
short	shorter	shortest
sleepy	sleepier	sleepiest
slim	slimmer	slimmest
slimy	slimier	slimiest
slow	slower	slowest
sloppy	sloppier	sloppiest
smelly	smellier	smelliest
spicy	spicier	spiciest
steady	steadier	steadiest
strange	stranger	strangest
sweet	sweeter	sweetest
terrible	more terrible	most terrible
thick	thicker	thickest
tough	tougher	toughest
useful	more useful	most useful
vicious	more vicious	most vicious
vile	viler	vilest
weak	weaker	weakest
white	whiter	whitest
windy	windier	windiest
wonderful	more wonderful	most wonderful
young	younger	younger
zippy	zippier	zippiest

ADDENDUM

COMMON REGULAR AND IRREGULAR VERBS

C

(For more information about verbs see Addendum A, Item III.)

Item I: All Principal Parts Alike

present	*past*	*past participle*	*present participle*
burst	burst	burst	bursting
cast	cast	cast	casting
cost	cost	cost	costing
cut	cut	cut	cutting
hit	hit	hit	hitting
hurt	hurt	hurt	hurting
let	let	let	letting
put	put	put	putting
quit	quit	quit	quitting
read	read	read	reading
set	set	set	setting
shed	shed	shed	shedding
shut	shut	shut	shutting
slit	slit	slit	slitting
split	split	split	splitting
spread	spread	spread	spreading
thrust	thrust	thrust	thrusting

Item II: First and Second Principal Parts Alike

present	*past*	*past participle*	*present participle*
beat	beat	beaten	beating

Item III: First and Third Principal Parts Alike

present	*past*	*past participle*	*present participle*
come	came	come	coming
become	became	become	becoming
overcome	overcame	overcome	overcoming
run	ran	run	running

Item IV: Second and Third Principal Parts Alike

Note: The verbs given below are grouped into similar patterns; above each group, the most common pattern appears in parentheses.

present	*past*	*past participle*	*present participle*
(*-ang*)	(*-ung*)	(*-ung*)	(*-ing*)
cling	clung	clung	clinging
hang (objects)	hung	hung	hanging
dig	dug	dug	digging
sling	slung	slung	slinging
slink	slunk	slunk	slinking
spin	spun	spun	spinning
stick	stuck	stuck	sticking
sting	stung	stung	stinging
strike	struck	struck	striking
swing	swung	swung	swinging
wring	wrung	wrung	wringing
(*-eed*)	(*-ed*)	(*-ed*)	(*-ing*)
bleed	bled	bled	bleeding
breed	bred	bred	breeding
creep	crept	crept	creeping

dream	dreamed (dreamt)	dreamed (dreamt)	dreaming
feed	fed	fed	feeding
feel	felt	felt	feeling
flee	fled	fled	fleeing
keep	kept	kept	keeping
kneel	knelt	knelt	kneeling
lead	led	led	leading
leave	left	left	leaving
mean	meant	meant	meaning
meet	met	met	meeting
sleep	slept	slept	sleeping
speed	sped	sped	speeding
sweep	swept	swept	sweeping
weep	wept	wept	weeping
(*-ing*)	(*-ought*)	(*-ought*)	(*-ing*)
bring	brought	brought	bringing
buy	bought	bought	buying
catch	caught	caught	catching
fight	fought	fought	fighting
seek	sought	sought	seeking
teach	taught	taught	teaching
think	thought	thought	thinking
(*-ind*)	(*-ound*)	(*-ound*)	(*-ing*)
bind	bound	bound	binding
find	found	found	finding
grind	ground	ground	grinding
wind	wound	wound	winding
(*-end*)	(*-ent*)	(*-ent*)	(*-ing*)
bend	bent	bent	bending
lend	lent	lent	lending
send	sent	sent	sending
spend	spent	spent	spending

(*-ell*)	(*-old*)	(*-old*)	(*-ing*)
sell	sold	sold	selling
tell	told	told	telling
(*-ay*)	(*-aid*)	(*-aid*)	(*-ing*)
lay	laid	laid	laying
mislay	mislaid	mislaid	mislaying
pay	paid	paid	paying
say	said	said	saying

Item V: Mixed-Pattern Endings

present	*past*	*past participle*	*present participle*
forget	forgot	forgotten	forgetting
get	got	got	getting
have	had	had	having
hold	held	held	holding
light	lit (lighted)	lit (lighted)	lighting
lose	lost	lost	losing
make	made	made	making
shine	shone (shined)	shone (shined)	shining
shoot	shot	shot	shooting
sit	sat	sat	sitting
slide	slid	slid	sliding
stand	stood	stood	standing
understand	understood	understood	understanding
win	won	won	winning
withstand	withstood	withstood	withstanding

Item VI: All Three Principal Parts Alike

Note: The verbs given below are grouped into similar patterns; above each group, the most common pattern appears in parentheses.

present	*past*	*past participle*	*present participle*
(-*ing*)	(-*ang*)	(-*ung*)	(-*ing*)
ring	rang	rung	ringing
sing	sang	sung	singing
spring	sprang	sprung	springing
(-*ink*)	(-*ank*)	(-*unk*)	(-*ing*)
drink	drank	drunk	drinking
shrink	shrank	shrunk	shrinking
sink	sank	sunk	sinking
stink	stank (stunk)	stunk	stinking
	(-*e*)	(-*en*)	(-*ing*)
break	broke	broken	breaking
choose	chose	chosen	choosing
freeze	froze	frozen	freezing
speak	spoke	spoken	speaking
steal	stole	stolen	stealing
weave	wove	woven	weaving
(-*ow*)	(-*ew*)	(-*own*)	(-*ing*)
blow	blew	blown	blowing
grow	grew	grown	growing
fly	flew	flown	flying
know	knew	known	knowing
throw	threw	thrown	throwing
(-*ive*)	(-*ove*)	(-*iven*)	(-*ing*)
drive	drove	driven	driving
strive	strove	striven	striving
thrive	throve (thrived)	thriven	thriving
(-*ear*)	(-*ore*)	(-*orn*)	(-*ing*)
bear	bore	born (borne)	bearing
swear	swore	sworn	swearing
tear	tore	torn	tearing
wear	wore	worn	wearing

(-ake)	*(-ook)*	*(-aken)*	*(-ing)*
forsake	forsook	forsaken	forsaking
shake	shook	shaken	shaking
mistake	mistook	mistaken	mistaking
partake	partook	partaken	partaking
take	took	taken	taking
(-w)	*(-wed)*	*(-own)*	*(-ing)*
mow	mowed	mown	mowing
sew	sewed	sewn	sewing
show	showed	shown	showing

Item VII: Other Mixed-Pattern Endings

present	*past*	*past participle*	*present participle*
be	was	been	being
dive	dove	dived	diving
do	did	done	doing
eat	ate	eaten	eating
fall	fell	fallen	falling
lie	lay	lain	lying
see	saw	seen	seeing
slay	slew	slain	slaying
rise	rose	risen	rising

ANSWER KEY

UNIT 1: SPELLING AND USAGE IMPROVEMENT

Item I: Quick and Easy Spelling Rules

Exercise 1

1. delays
2. faxes
3. washes
4. feet
5. abilities
6. hypotheses
7. daughters-in-law
8. innuendoes
9. suffixes
10. sheaves

Exercise 2

1. swishes
2. waltzes
3. mulattoes
4. fizzes
5. theses
6. stitches
7. piccolos
8. prime ministers

9. embargoes
10. mice

Exercise 3

1. briefs
2. entities
3. babies
4. stretches
5. halos OR haloes
6. phenomena
7. lilies of the valley
8. tomatoes
9. deer
10. leaves

Exercise 4

1. halves
2. necessities
3. turkeys
4. sopranos
5. mothers-in-law
6. starches
7. wolves
8. studios
9. moose
10. classes

Exercise 5

1. thieves
2. ditches
3. torches
4. calves
5. worries
6. ladies
7. passersby
8. ferries
9. dresses
10. mosquitos OR mosquitoes

Exercise 6

1. codeine
2. sieve

3. achieve
4. forfeit
5. receive
6. veil
7. friend
8. siege
9. neither
10. relief

Exercise 7

1. seize
2. ceiling
3. believe
4. conceive
5. Fahrenheit
6. sleigh
7. conceit
8. weigh
9. heir
10. species

Exercise 8

1. beige
2. weird
3. glacier
4. pier
5. heinous
6. their
7. leisure
8. brief
9. believe
10. either

Exercise 9

1. hygiene
2. freight
3. chief
4. briefly
5. veins
6. yield
7. deceive
8. fierce

9. neigh
10. retrieve

Exercise 10

1. ancient
2. perceive
3. relieve
4. veil
5. seize
6. eight
7. caffeine
8. height
9. sleight of hand
10. conceive

Exercise 11

1. caring
2. hopeful
3. devotion
4. engagement
5. discouraging
6. keying
7. noticeable
8. budgeting
9. estimation
10. icing

Exercise 12

1. polluting
2. femininity
3. sedately
4. gluing
5. sensuously
6. perforation
7. involvement
8. reduction
9. marriageable
10. skiing

Exercise 13

1. harmonious
2. snoring

3. festival
4. manufacturing
5. evaporation
6. pressuring
7. advisable
8. hesitation
9. traceable
10. dining

Exercise 14

1. deceiving
2. astuteness
3. staring
4. retrievable
5. malicious
6. adorable
7. confusing
8. manageable
9. whining
10. embraceable

Exercise 15

1. insurable
2. virtuous
3. retirement
4. definitely
5. solvable
6. enticing
7. advantageous
8. seeing
9. disposable
10. stylize

Exercise 16

1. saltier
2. implying
3. fanciest
4. playable
5. windier
6. fortifying
7. hairier
8. drying

9. moodiness
10. employable

Exercise 17

1. creamier
2. verifying
3. angriest
4. scarier
5. noisily
6. sunnier
7. hardiness
8. qualifying
9. fanciful
10. merriment

Exercise 18

1. healthier
2. satisfying
3. livelihood
4. rustiest
5. haughtier
6. worrisome
7. sandier
8. readiness
9. friendlier
10. paunchiness

Exercise 19

1. likelihood
2. steadily
3. heaviness
4. dismaying
5. handier
6. complying
7. silliness
8. reliable
9. flashiness
10. clumsily

Exercise 20

1. occupying
2. hungrily

3. identifiable
4. dirtier
5. wavier
6. defying
7. pitiable
8. heartier
9. flurrying
10. silkiest

Exercise 21

1. wrecking
2. conferred
3. equipping
4. allowable
5. recurring
6. pitted
7. drooping
8. repaired
9. committed
10. snapping

Exercise 22

1. controllable
2. barring
3. submitted
4. ranking
5. flogged
6. accountable
7. incurred
8. booking
9. soiled
10. matted

Exercise 23

1. propelled
2. starring
3. exhausted
4. lending
5. emitting
6. presented
7. quitting
8. forgetting

9. healed
10. hottest

Exercise 24

1. strolling
2. knotted
3. cracking
4. booted
5. benefiting
6. permitted
7. gossiping
8. scooping
9. petted
10. gloating

Exercise 25

1. conforming
2. rebelling
3. transferred
4. clinking
5. hosted
6. regrettable
7. beginning
8. murmured
9. boating
10. camped

Item II: Words with Troublesome Spelling

Exercise 30

1. Take a night course; your grammar is terrible.
2. Who is saying their speech first?
3. I want a house, but I don't want a mortgage.
4. How long have you been collecting miniature cars?
5. A fear of heights is a common phobia.
6. Don't forget to mark my birthday on your calendar.
7. There is a great discrepancy between my work and my pay.
8. Is forty middle-aged or not?
9. It's a relief to see that you're all right.
10. Did you misspell *precede* again?

Exercise 31

1. Of course, this is a genuine government document.
2. Whoever started this argument should apologize.
3. Soon you will be ninety, but you still need guidance.
4. You are too aggressive.
5. There is no necessity to pay the bill yet.
6. Now he is both grumpy and irregular.
7. Your absence has made a big difference in our lives.
8. I find this theory is very unique.
9. Be careful; bad spelling is unacceptable.
10. Only you think that this exercise is humorous.

Item III: Good Word Usage

Exercise 32

1. First go to the market; (than, then) go to the post office.
2. Because of the nice weather, there were (fewer, less) students in class today.
3. Mirka always dresses so (good, well).
4. I must be gaining weight; my skirt is not as (lose, loose) as it (use to, used to) be.
5. My dream of owning a house seems to be getting (farther, further) and (farther, further) away.
6. Your friendship means (alot, a lot) to me.
7. (Whose, Who's) in the mood for pizza?
8. After dinner, the waiter brought a magnificent (desert, dessert) cart to our table.
9. Xiang Zhao (already, all ready) has a Grade 12 certificate.
10. It is a very (quiet, quite) evening.

Exercise 33

1. Marek laughed so hard watching television that he fell (off, off of) the couch.
2. This is starting to make my temperature (rise, raise).
3. Ljubo smiled for the photographer (irregardless, regardless) of the fact that he had a toothache.
4. The elevator operator is a (decent, descent) person.
5. Grazyna forgot to set her alarm and woke up two hours (later, latter) (than, then) usual.
6. The car was destroyed in the crash, but Olga and Jan are (alright, all right).
7. "(Maybe, May be) I do know how you feel," remarked Heiman.
8. The best way to (precede, proceed) is to apologize to Tomoko first.
9. Why does grandfather always (refer back, refer) to "the good old days"?
10. Try and remain (stationery, stationary) until I take all the photos.

Item IV: Articles

Exercise 37

1. This is an unusual story.
2. Dino is a capable worker.
3. The dentist needs to take an x-ray.
4. Pass the pepper.
5. Did you see the mystery movie last night?
6. Give me the pipe wrench.
7. Did you hear about the accident?
8. Take a vacation.
9. Take the vacation I told you about.
10. There is a useful exercise on this page.

Exercise 38

1. When did you see the Rockies?
2. What an idiot!
3. Did you have a hernia operation?
4. Al should get a Ph.D. for all his hard work.
5. I need an opinion from a neutral party.
6. Did you get an A or a B on your English composition?
7. I'm in the mood for a burger.
8. The restaurant around the corner has the best burgers.
9. Is this a new couch?
10. This is the same couch we've had for years.

Exercise 39

1. The car offer is a one-time opportunity.
2. Dale has an interesting occupation.
3. He is an osteopath.
4. Can you drive me to the hospital?
5. What an ugly painting!
6. The job should be completed in a day.
7. Ben has a fear of the dark.
8. Arthur Miller wrote *Death of a Salesman.*
9. The harp is not a common household musical instrument.
10. This is an unbelievable coincidence.

Exercise 40

1. How long have you been a Girl Guide leader?
2. Did you see the full moon last night?

3. That is an outrageous suggestion.
4. Neil is definitely an honest man.
5. You have chosen a unique gift for someone.
6. Did the teacher forget the *r* in *regret*?
7. I want to taste the cake you baked.
8. The way out is through the basement.
9. We all need a little appreciation.
10. Compromise is an important ingredient in a marriage.

Exercise 41

1. Are you having an x-ray today?
2. The article on the proper use of articles is confusing.
3. Did you read "Ode to the West Wind" by Percy Bysshe Shelley?
4. Are you going to the United States this summer?
5. Oh, do I ever have a bad headache!
6. Did you find an apartment yet?
7. The apartment I saw last night was too small.
8. They gave Ed a heartfelt thank-you present.
9. Steve wanted an A; anyone can get a B.
10. Did you enjoy the swim class?

Item V: The Apostrophe

Exercise 42

1. a good day's work
2. someone's books
3. Harris' OR Harris's attitude
4. a deer's antlers
5. a mother's love
6. the players' cards
7. the children's toys
8. Xiao Ping's new friends
9. the kitten's OR kittens' mother
10. the chocolate bar's flavour

Exercise 43

1. the skunk's scent
2. ladies' old shoes
3. the insurance agent's offer
4. Patrick's and Andrew's apartments
5. Ioana and Jia's apartment
6. a judge's chambers

7. the elephants' trunks
8. anybody's guess
9. the government's agenda
10. Delta's dilemma

Exercise 44

1. Fu Tian's glasses
2. Cecilia's and Nora's dentists
3. Miron's misconception
4. the student's last words
5. Ross' OR Ross's novels
6. Doreen and Stan's cottage
7. the psychiatrists' offices
8. the baby's first tooth
9. the politician's OR politicians' promises
10. Moira's new sandals

Exercise 45

1. can't
2. who's
3. hasn't
4. we'll
5. who's
6. doesn't
7. who'll
8. aren't
9. I'm
10. don't

Exercise 46

1. it's
2. she'll
3. he's
4. won't
5. we're
6. who's
7. shouldn't
8. you'll
9. they've
10. it'll

Exercise 47

1. they'll
2. we're
3. wouldn't
4. aren't
5. who'll
6. she's
7. aren't
8. won't
9. we've
10. couldn't

Exercise 48

1. Who's in charge here?
2. I wasn't there last night.
3. It was a 50's dance.
4. There was a twenty minutes' subway delay.
5. It's not what you think.
6. Hanna doesn't know what colour to choose.
7. Were there more yes's or no's in yesterday's vote?
8. Ted never crosses his *t*'s.
9. I'm not sure it's the one you want.
10. The future's always uncertain.

Exercise 49

1. The *but*'s in your brochure against smoking are misspelled.
2. You've always made time to see us.
3. These are my last two 5's.
4. The bridge repair caused an hour's delay to downtown traffic.
5. You won't believe your eyes.
6. Who said two wrongs don't make a right?
7. The motorbike's rear tire is flat.
8. I can't believe that this essay is hers.
9. Adam wanted to achieve straight A's but got three B's and two C's.
10. Giselle always ends her sentences with a couple of *right*'s when she speaks.

Exercise 50

1. Everyone's here for Lourdes' OR Lourdes's party.
2. Are there two or three *m*'s in Sammy's name?
3. We've been told that there'll be another ten minutes' delay.

4. Because the blue jay is related to the crow, it's not pleasant to listen to its call.
5. What's your prediction on tonight's game?
6. Phuong and Ken's CD player was a gift from friends of theirs.
7. After this exercise, I could use a whole day's sleep.
8. There are six *in*'s in the opening paragraph of Hemingway's *A Farewell To Arms*.
9. My four brothers-in-law's bathrooms all have bidets.
10. The coffee's aroma permeated the house.

Exercise 51

1. I'd be lying if I didn't admit that she's the one I love.
2. Their best friends Dalia and Kim always get 100's on their tests.
3. Wouldn't you like to fly to Paris for two weeks' vacation?
4. It's hard to believe that Tim's and Jay's apartments are in the same building.
5. The junkyard dog's bite is much worse than its bark.
6. The long day's wait was finally over for the new mother.
7. My sister's boyfriend's brother is seven feet tall.
8. I've been told that James' OR James's ability to pick winning lottery numbers is amazing.
9. Sonia and Mark's friendship has continued for more than twenty years.
10. My mother-in-law's chocolate cheesecake is the best I've ever tasted.

Exercise 52

1. You'll feel better in the morning if you don't look in the mirror.
2. I don't think there are any *f* s in phobia.
3. Mel didn't like the look on the bank manager's face.
4. Most of it is yours; the rest is hers.
5. Did you see Dorota's picture in Thursday's paper?
6. Because of this bill, I haven't had a good night's sleep in days.
7. It would be better if you did not use *and*'s and *but*'s to start your sentences.
8. They're predicting rain for Bess' OR Bess's wedding day.
9. Dorrel's, Jose's, and Mahnaz's cars are the same make.
10. There should be three more 0's before the decimal point on my paycheque.

Item VI: Capital Letters

Exercise 53

1. Do you want a Danish pastry or an English muffin?
2. Molly likes to shop in downtown Toronto for Christmas.
3. Did you know that Uncle is moving to Saskatoon, Saskatchewan?
4. "I'm learning to speak Cantonese," remarked Jose.
5. C
6. I know that Mars is the fourth planet from the sun.

7. Is Manitoulin Island the largest fresh-water island in the world?
8. There is a reason Lake Superior is a superior lake.
9. Will you arrive at the Georgian Court Hotel in Vancouver, British Columbia on Tuesday or Wednesday?
10. Marvin's favourite subject is Lunch 101.

Exercise 54

1. I think the Church of St. Patrick is on Highway 7.
2. Is Halloween a holiday?
3. You should get the *Concise Oxford Dictionary of Quotations*.
4. Winter hasn't started, and I'm already anxious for spring.
5. James Herbert wrote the horror novel entitled *Creed*.
6. Why does Cousin John act like such an idiot?
7. Sometimes I think the Dark Ages aren't over.
8. When my English professor said my compound sentence needed a surgeon, I called Dr. Miller right away.
9. *Words We Use* is a book published by Prentice Hall.
10. The Vietnamese long dress is made to measure only.

Exercise 55

1. The Bank of Montreal is having another mortgage sale.
2. What is the mathematics homework assigned by Ms. Brackets?
3. It's almost June; Father's Day will be here soon.
4. The Prairies in winter can appear bleak, but they are always beautiful.
5. Polish food and West Indian food and Chinese food and all ethnic foods, to tell the truth, are my favourites.
6. Do you have this month's copy of the *Journal of Commonwealth Literature*?
7. I'm sure the Salmon River runs into Lake Ontario.
8. Are you visiting or residing in Kingston Penitentiary?
9. Marjorie agrees that the freight trains along Dupont Street are noisy.
10. You should get a copy of the *Concise Oxford Dictionary of Proverbs* to find out what "Nothing succeeds like success" means.

Exercise 56

1. Barbara was surprised to learn that Otty Lake has more than 400 cottages on it.
2. When Olga retires, she's moving to the warm South.
3. Ray really enjoys his visits to Killarney Provincial Park.
4. Jayne was born in Vietnam, but I'm sure she is Chinese.
5. Do you have the current issue of the *Journal of Canadian Studies?*
6. I hope that Dr. Selwin can help me to quit smoking.
7. When did Alberta join Confederation?

8. The special thing about Yom Kippur is that is a time of deep reflection.
9. Everyone should read "Lines Composed a Few Miles Above Tintern Abbey."
10. Are you familiar with any of the teachings of Buddha?

Exercise 57

1. How far is Vancouver Island from the mainland?
2. What did Aunt ask you to buy?
3. Yanyu thought that Christmas Day had come early when she scored 100% on her English test.
4. At the St. Lawrence Market in Toronto, you can always find something good to eat.
5. Is that Judge Vidicki?
6. I would like to visit the Northwest Territories.
7. When was the Renaissance period?
8. Take History 203; the professor is great.
9. Haig said that he is ready to travel to Venus.
10. Turn east at the lights; go two blocks, and you'll reach Simmons Street.

UNIT 2: SENTENCE IMPROVEMENT

Item I: Subjects and Predicates

Exercise 1

1. Mija is visiting her aunt in Korea.
2. The French toast should be ready.
3. I need a new life.
4. The children are restless tonight.
5. They can see the full moon clearly.
6. You need a breath mint.
7. Cockroaches make me nervous.
8. Suad wished for a million dollars.
9. Mariola's stomach was grumbling in class today.
10. You worry too much about money.

Exercise 2

1. The vampire's nose is red.
2. I feel a pain in my neck.
3. The sink is full of dirty dishes again.
4. The air conditioning system only works in winter.
5. English grammar is Yen Tao's main phobia.
6. You should get a haircut soon.

7. These cookies are really hard.
8. Her kiss was soft but sad.
9. These chocolate-covered cherries were made in Switzerland.
10. Carmina was dreaming about winning the lottery.

Exercise 3

1. I know the subject in this sentence.
2. The storm clouds have appeared.
3. We heard the loon on the lake last night.
4. Lizzeth wants to visit Australia some day.
5. Your hives seem worse after an English test.
6. This timetable is terrible.
7. Everyone needs more money.
8. Piotr never goes anywhere without his good luck charm.
9. Life can be complicated.
10. John has an extensive beer can collection.

Exercise 4

1. Most Europeans have a six-week summer vacation.
2. The weather person predicted the snowstorm's arrival correctly.
3. Mirko is afraid of illness, not old age.
4. This bathroom scale must be broken.
5. Sonya misses her native country, Chile.
6. The Christmas catalogue has bathing suits in it.
7. The explosion was in Aldo's wine cellar.
8. Quebec is the largest province in Canada.
9. Gulnar saw the accident from the bus window.
10. The starlings were pecking in the snow for food.

Exercise 5

1. Blueberry pie is my favourite dessert.
2. You lick postage stamps, not rubber stamps.
3. The firewood will be delivered on Friday.
4. You need a good back massage.
5. Aminul prefers black-and-white movies.
6. Pauline sings in the church choir.
7. The dice are rolling in your favour.
8. Khanh complains about everything.
9. Angie has bought a new car.
10. The complaint department is closed.

Item II: More Subjects and Predicates

Exercise 6

1. All (of your friends) are here.
2. What is the difference (between a city and a town)?
3. The view (from Spy Rock) (in Westport, Ontario) is spectacular.
4. There are no prerequisites.
5. Who is your favourite politician?
6. (You) Start your engines!
7. Why do men hate asking (for directions)?
8. Here are your compact discs and tapes.
9. The light (at the end) (of the tunnel) is growing dimmer.
10. There is never a subject (of a verb) (in a prepositional phrase).

Exercise 7

1. (You) Count your blessings!
2. How does a bat catch mosquitoes?
3. Some (of the nuts) are hard to crack.
4. Here is the key.
5. Melissa made a wish and blew out the candles.
6. (You) Leave it (on the table).
7. Every one (of your dishes) is dirty.
8. Are you going (to Nova Scotia) this summer?
9. There were four cupcakes (on the table) (before lunch).
10. Much (of his wealth) comes (from his mother).

Exercise 8

1. The mood (of the teacher) was cool.
2. Are you dating Elwood?
3. Have Nora and you been (to the new dentist) yet?
4. (You) Don't say another word.
5. When is the baby due?
6. There are many large snakes (at the reptile exhibit).
7. (You) Tell Susan and Marie the truth.
8. You should see your face.
9. Wojciech and Anna went (to Egypt) and saw the office buildings.
10. Did you visit Eduardo and his pet monkey?

Exercise 9

1. I know more English now.
2. Did you go (to the Billy Joel concert)?

3. Have you counted and rolled all the pennies (in the jar)?
4. The value and importance (of a good friendship) should be cherished.
5. (You) Pick a card, any card.
6. Some mornings Dorin feels (like staying) home but goes (to school) anyway.
7. Why did the man throw the butter (out the window)?
8. He wanted to see butter fly.
9. (In this sentence) the subject is the fifth word.
10. (On the detour), a car and boat collided.

Exercise 10

1. Is John Mellencamp a singer or a recreation park?
2. (You) Never pick your teeth (in public).
3. One (of the hot-air balloons) was shaped (like a cola can).
4. Jean-Paul Sartre and Boris Pasternak declined the Nobel Prize (for literature).
5. Here is a sentence (with one subject and one predicate).
6. A receding hairline has nothing to do (with rabbits).
7. Maria and Carlos were chosen as the best dancers (in the "Do the Twist" competition).
8. Guy folded the sweater and put it (on the shelf) (in his closet).
9. Some (of the teachers) are more effective (than a tranquilizer).
10. Have you read or studied any (of Irving Layton's poetry)?

Item III: Clauses

Exercise 11

1. subordinate
2. main
3. subordinate
4. subordinate
5. main
6. main
7. main
8. subordinate
9. subordinate
10. main

Exercise 12

1. main
2. subordinate
3. main
4. main
5. subordinate

6. subordinate
7. subordinate
8. subordinate
9. main
10. main

Exercise 13

1. This is the tutor who is helping me with adjective clauses.
2. The antique chair that Stan ordered was delivered in a modern truck.
3. Have you ever read *College Business English* which is published by Prentice Hall?
4. Thelma, who is a surgical nurse, is always telling us funny stories from work.
5. Where is the meat in this mince pie that you ordered?
6. Buy some wine that everyone likes.
7. I would never date a man who flosses his teeth in a restaurant.
8. Where are the clothes that you wore this morning?
9. This perfume has a fragrance which is very pleasant.
10. Is this the cheese that you tried last night?

Exercise 14

1. Linguini is the pasta that Norbert likes best.
2. Unfortunately, the apartment that is infested with cockroaches is mine.
3. I can't read the writing manual that you gave me.
4. This water has a colour which cannot be defined.
5. The individual whose dentures were lost is offering a reward.
6. Is this the computer disk that has the most storage space?
7. Joseph was able to listen to a broadcast that came from Korea on his shortwave radio.
8. Did you get the parts which you needed to repair the toaster oven?
9. You are the one who has always loved me most.
10. There are so many things that I still have to learn.

Exercise 16

1. When it is two o'clock, we can leave.
2. If you pay, I will go out with you.
3. Karen washed the dishes while you were at the store.
4. How long has it been since you last looked in a mirror?
5. The supervisor treated her employees as if they were part of her own family.
6. When you finish this exercise, go to the next one.
7. Since you last visited, four homes have been sold on this street.
8. Orland acted as if he had just seen a ghost.
9. Before you start complaining, let me explain everything.
10. The students needed a break because they had been studying so hard.

Exercise 17

1. We arrived at the cabin just as the thunderstorm began.
2. Alex was running as fast as he could just to keep up with the other joggers.
3. Ramon is acting that way because he is in love.
4. If you want some dessert, you have to eat all your spinach first.
5. How much did an ice cream cone cost when you were little?
6. The government will sponsor these students provided that they attend regularly.
7. Last night it snowed so much that most schools were closed the next day.
8. I'm going to call before she asks me again.
9. You need to hang it properly so that it won't wrinkle.
10. Don't be disappointed because this is the last sentence.

Exercise 19

1. Why you feel this way is a mystery to all of us.
2. Jibril said that you knew the answer.
3. His only fault is that he has really bad breath.
4. We will buy whichever computer you recommend.
5. That he had no money was no surprise.
6. I agree with how Troung responded to him.
7. One fact to keep in mind is that you should never give up.
8. Vanessa understood why he had to leave her.
9. Did anyone ask Claire what was moving in the soup?
10. The double chocolate cheesecake is what Norman wants for his birthday.

Exercise 20

1. Don't tell me how I look.	object of verb
2. What you need to do is eat more beans.	subject
3. The new cinema is around the corner from where you live.	object of preposition
4. That she beat you at chess is a testament to her ability.	subject
5. There is a lot of sense in what Syed says.	object of preposition
6. What a person can achieve under duress is amazing.	subject
7. A new husband is what Heather really wants for Christmas.	subject complement
8. What Sean did with the whipped cream cannot be mentioned in this sentence.	subject
9. George explained to me why you suffer from extreme body odour.	object of verb
10. Don't be discouraged by what you have just read.	object of preposition

Exercise 22

1. adverb
2. noun

3. adjective
4. main
5. noun
6. adjective
7. noun
8. adverb
9. main
10. adverb

Exercise 23

1. adjective
2. adverb
3. noun
4. main
5. adverb
6. noun
7. main
8. adjective
9. main
10. adjective

Exercise 24

1. adverb
2. adjective
3. adverb
4. noun
5. adjective
6. main
7. adjective
8. main
9. adjective
10. noun

Exercise 25

1. main
2. adverb
3. main
4. noun
5. main
6. noun
7. adverb

8. adjective
9. noun
10. adverb

Exercise 26

1. main
2. main
3. noun
4. adverb
5. adjective
6. main
7. adverb
8. adverb
9. adjective
10. main

Item IV: Sentence Types

Exercise 29

1. compound
2. simple
3. compound
4. simple
5. compound
6. compound
7. compound
8. simple
9. simple
10. compound

Exercise 30

1. compound
2. simple
3. compound
4. simple
5. simple
6. compound
7. simple
8. simple
9. compound
10. compound

Exercise 31

1. compound
2. main
3. simple
4. simple
5. simple
6. compound
7. compound
8. simple
9. compound
10. compound

Exercise 32

1. compound
2. simple
3. simple
4. simple
5. compound
6. compound
7. compound
8. simple
9. compound
10. simple

Exercise 33

1. simple
2. simple
3. compound
4. simple
5. compound
6. simple
7. compound
8. simple
9. compound
10. simple

Exercise 36

1. complex
2. complex
3. complex

4. compound
5. complex
6. simple
7. compound
8. complex
9. simple
10. compound

Exercise 37

1. simple
2. compound
3. complex
4. complex
5. compound
6. complex
7. complex
8. complex
9. compound
10. simple

Exercise 38

1. complex
2. complex
3. simple
4. complex
5. complex
6. complex
7. simple
8. simple
9. compound
10. complex

Exercise 41

1. simple
2. complex
3. compound-complex
4. complex
5. compound-complex
6. compound
7. complex

8. compound
9. complex
10. complex

Exercise 42

1. complex
2. compound-complex
3. simple
4. compound
5. complex
6. compound
7. simple
8. compound
9. compound
10. compound

Exercise 43

1. compound-complex
2. complex
3. complex
4. compound
5. complex
6. simple
7. complex
8. simple
9. complex
10. compound-complex

Item V: Correcting Run-On Sentences

Exercise 46

Answers may vary.

1. Andrew and Patrick are not the same age; Patrick is almost two years older.
2. Baby toads are cute; in fact, they look like adult toads.
3. Ed never asks any questions; he just signs the cheques.
4. Line dancing is a lot of fun, but it has nothing to do with fishing.
5. C
6. The college campus is downtown; unfortunately, I live in the suburbs.
7. Some collective nouns for animals sound strange; for instance, a group of starlings is called a "murmuration."
8. C

9. Where did you buy these chocolate-coated coffee beans, and how much did they cost?
10. Every Christmas the same mysterious thing happens; we open the boxes of ornaments and find that several are broken.

Exercise 47

Answers may vary.

1. The moon doesn't always hit you in the eye like a big pizza pie when you fall in love; it just feels like it.
2. Dinosaurs are very popular; my favourite is the stegosaurus.
3. The number 13 doesn't worry Joanne; undoubtedly, she doesn't have triskaidekaphobia.
4. Invest in a food bank; the return is great.
5. We were temporarily lost in the woods; even our guide couldn't find the trail at first.
6. C
7. The good news was that I was going to win the lottery today; the bad news was that I wouldn't be able to buy a ticket.
8. Spending money is too easy, and saving it is too hard.
9. You mixed up the cans; this tuna is for cats only.
10. The Bank of China is high; after all, it has seventy-two storeys.

Exercise 48

Answers may vary.

1. Miguel doesn't understand life; to tell the truth, every time he gets some unexpected money, he also gets some unexpected bills.
2. C
3. Bourbon is a whisky, but it's also the name of our cat.
4. Pyramids began appearing around 2700 B.C.; now that's a long time ago.
5. It rains about three days a year in Málaga, Spain, but Salvatore tries not to complain.
6. Daria really enjoys horror films; however, she never watches them alone.
7. C
8. Jay wants to be a professional sprinter; to tell the truth, he's hoping to enter the Olympics.
9. MSG is a flavour enhancer for food, not a skin treatment, so don't rub it into your face any more.
10. Some people feel that Father's Day is unnecessary; it was created to benefit merchants first and fathers second.

Exercise 49

Answers may vary.

1. English is so confusing; "storm" and "worm" have very similar spelling but very different pronunciation.

2. In the light of the rising moon, Abram leaned over to kiss Adele; unfortunately, he was so nervous that his arm slipped, and he rolled down the hill and landed in the lake.
3. C
4. The last day of vacation can be depressing, and it can give you a funny feeling in the pit of your stomach.
5. Gene's sunflower plant is enormous; I'm sure that it is more than three metres high.
6. When you get to Humber College, ask for the dean, and she will answer all your questions.
7. Make the popcorn, but try not to burn it this time.
8. The parents were beaming with delight at the graduation exercises because they were so proud of their children.
9. C
10. This house is my favourite house on the street; it is my house.

Exercise 50

Answers may vary.

1. Eric Clapton is a very popular musician; on the other hand, Van Morrison is no slouch.
2. Don't give this teacher an apple, for he's so crabby he'll turn it into applesauce just by looking at it.
3. Everything happened at once; the phone rang; the doorbell sounded, and the toaster popped.
4. Casey embarrassed himself during the spelling competition; unfortunately, he spelled *embarrassed* with only one *r*.
5. The movie *Cape Fear* with Robert De Niro is good, but the original with Robert Mitchum is better.
6. Jorge eats his meals too quickly; consequently he is always complaining that his stomach hurts.
7. The thing that makes a possession so precious is simple to understand; it was touched by some person or memory that is special to you.
8. The road sign read "40 km to Timmins"; thank goodness we're almost there.
9. Gina helped me with my French homework; otherwise I wouldn't have been able to complete it.
10. Simon was exhausted from his swim across Lake Ontario, but at the same time he was exhilarated that he had completed the crossing.

Item VI: Correcting Sentence Fragments

Exercise 51

Answers vary for fragments. For corrections, consult your instructor. Complete sentences are indicated by C.

1. fragment
2. fragment
3. fragment
4. fragment
5. C
6. fragment
7. fragment
8. fragment
9. fragment
10. C

Exercise 52

Answers vary for fragments. For corrections, consult your instructor. Complete sentences are indicated by C.

1. fragment
2. fragment
3. fragment
4. C
5. fragment
6. fragment
7. fragment
8. fragment
9. fragment
10. fragment

Exercise 53

Answers vary for fragments. For corrections, consult your instructor. Complete sentences are indicated by C.

1. fragment
2. C
3. fragment
4. fragment
5. fragment
6. fragment
7. C
8. fragment
9. fragment
10. fragment

Exercise 54

Answers vary for fragments. For corrections, consult your instructor. Complete sentences are indicated by C.

1. fragment
2. fragment
3. fragment
4. fragment
5. fragment
6. C
7. fragment
8. fragment
9. fragment
10. fragment

Exercise 55

Answers vary for fragments. For corrections, consult your instructor. Complete sentences are indicated by C.

1. fragment
2. fragment
3. fragment
4. fragment
5. fragment
6. fragment
7. fragment
8. fragment
9. fragment
10. C

Exercise 56

Answers for corrections may vary.

1.	Let's wait a few minutes; it's still raining.	run-on
2.	Feeling the way you do, you should stay home today.	fragment
3.	Have you ever read *Pillars of the Earth* by Ken Follett?	correct
4.	You are right; I shouldn't have said that.	run-on
5.	Call me when you're in town again.	fragment
6.	Some people don't like cabbage; it gives them stomach gas.	correct
7.	Dale is upgrading his English skills to study sports management.	fragment
8.	The play was excellent; in fact, the cast received a standing ovation for more than five minutes.	run-on

9. Because it's three days old, I don't think we should eat it. — fragment
10. The word *typhoon* is derived from the Chinese *tai fung*, which means "big wind." — fragment

Exercise 57

Answers for corrections may vary.

1. Yolanda and Paul are dating; however, their parents are not happy about it. — run-on
2. You could go to the post office first and then meet me at the bank. — correct
3. Vyny really enjoys seafood; in fact, he has shrimp, scallops, and squid at least three times a week. — run-on
4. Realizing that life is short, Allison remarried. — fragment
5. Mija said that nothing could get her to ride in a hot-air balloon. — fragment
6. Morley Callaghan, a Canadian novelist, wrote *The Loved and the Lost*; it was published in 1951. — run-on
7. Fishing from the cottage dock is a lot of fun. — fragment
8. Many of us are developing a fear of poverty; it is called "peniaphobia." — run-on
9. After the concert in the park ended, we went to Mary Margaret's house. — fragment
10. Dari wanted to be a pediatrician; unfortunately he was not encouraged to pursue his goal. — correct

Exercise 58

Answers for corrections may vary.

1. While the moon was rising over the rippling waters of the lake, a loon cried out. — fragment
2. Confession is good for the heart. — correct
3. You ate so much cake; my stomach hurt watching you. — run-on
5. Why do you play that song? You know I hate it. — run-on
6. Take responsibility for your own actions; instead, you blame everyone but yourself. — run-on
7. The blueberry muffins that you just took out of the oven smell wonderful. — fragment
8. Andrew is grumpy when he gets out of bed. — fragment
9. This can't be a CD; it's square. — run-on
10. Knowing the ending of the movie beforehand, Jean did not enjoy it as much as her husband did. — fragment

Exercise 59

Answers for corrections may vary.

1. The wishing well must be broken; I wished for water, but there was none. — run-on
2. Determined to have the highest grade point average, Ashi even studied Friday nights. — correct
3. If you have inner peace, material possessions mean nothing. — fragment
4. This sharkfin soup is really fresh; to tell the truth, I'm sure I saw a shark swimming in it. — run-on
5. I was happy when Ying stole my heart, but I was sad when she gave it back. — run-on
6. Canadian literature professor Douglas Spettigue wrote the short story "The Haying." — fragment
7. A piece of Barb's apple pie is like a slice of heaven. — fragment
8. Don't buy the snails; instead, get some squid. — run-on
9. Verbal abuse can be very cruel; in fact, it can hurt more than physical abuse. — run-on
10. When you were busy learning about life, did you learn anything about yourself? — fragment

Exercise 60

Answers for corrections may vary.

1. Dimitri hurt his neck; in fact, he had to wear a neck collar after watching the air show. — run-on
2. No one would dance with me, so I went home early. — run-on
3. When the smoke finally cleared, we were able to enjoy our barbecue. — fragment
4. Don't sing any more; all the plants have died. — run-on
5. Quitting your job out of frustration is not a clever thing to do. — fragment
6. That was how it ended. — correct
7. Having received the notification about the accident, I rushed to the hospital. — fragment
8. What is the freshness date on the cream cheese? — correct
9. Bruce is daydreaming about the cottage vacation next summer. — fragment
10. While you were putting up another false front, someone saw your true character. — fragment

Exercise 61

Answers for corrections may vary.

Gus was very shy and soft-spoken. One day a continuing education calendar came from the local community college, and it advertised a new course entitled "Assertiveness Training — Do It for You." Gus was interested in the course because he was tired of being reticent. He decided to enroll even though he was very nervous.

There was a terrible storm the night of the first class; in fact, thunder and lightning filled the sky. The registration slip which Gus clutched in his hand was so soaked that he could not make out the room number of his class. He thought that it was Room E-366, and he knocked on the door. Within minutes, a warm glow came to Gus's cheeks. The instructor was positive, and the course was rich and invigorating.

Of course, Gus had found the wrong room; however, he was determined to finish "Wine Tasting 101" no matter how much homework he would have to do.

Item VII: Sentence Combining

Exercise 62

Answers for corrections may vary.

1. The hairstylist cut too much off the sides, and the customer was very upset.
2. Margaret Atwood is a Canadian novelist; however, Irving Layton is a Canadian poet.
3. Sam recently lost her job; as a matter a fact, she is happy about it.
4. Not only is Arron on an extended vacation, but he is also very ill.
5. House prices are very low; nevertheless, it will still require a large down payment to buy one.
6. Jenny doesn't enjoy reading murder mystery novels; fortunately, she does enjoy seeing them as films.
7. Ola's brother has an interesting hobby; to tell the truth, he repairs porcelain dolls.
8. Dan forgot to pay his traffic ticket; nevertheless, two police officers came to remind him.
9. Barbara volunteers at a literacy centre in the afternoon, and she reads to elderly patients at the hospital in the evening.
10. Harjit is fascinated by snakes, but Nora is not.

Exercise 63

Answers for corrections may vary.

1. Timo has been eager to become a Canadian citizen; moreover, his dream has come true.
2. Darren will not eat a soft-boiled egg; after all, he can't stand the soft glop in it.
3. Edna seems to be very outgoing, but she is really quite shy.

4. Memorizing a poem can be tough; nevertheless, repeating each line can help.
5. Sidney can neither dance nor carry a tune.
6. Prunes are tasty, but their side-effects are open to interpretation.
7. Helena was at the theatre last night; at the same time, someone stole her car.
8. Jay holds the door open for everyone; furthermore, he is courteous to everyone.
9. Lian took the expressway home, and she reached home in twenty minutes.
10. Either stop at the dry cleaners, or stop at the window cleaners.

Exercise 64

Answers for corrections may vary.

1. The greeting card was very touching; at the same time, it made me feel better.
2. Tequila Sunrise is a nice drink, but she prefers Margaritas.
3. Lam worked until 2 in the morning; nevertheless, he is going to class at 8 a.m.
4. I'll be back in three hours; in the meantime, finish vacuuming the hallway.
5. Lorne surprised everyone by dancing on the table; to tell the truth, he is usually quiet and reserved.
6. You pay for the tickets, and I'll pay for the dinner.
7. Mel didn't have supper again, for he doesn't get paid until Thursday.
8. The school trip to the zoo was cancelled; therefore we studied grammar.
9. The CNE is in Ontario, but the PNE is in British Columbia.
10. This bagel is great, yet some cream cheese would make it better.

Exercise 67

Answers may vary.

1. Lanark is a small town in eastern Ontario which is famous for maple syrup.
2. Miron was not allowed to leave the restaurant because he did not pay the bill.
3. Although Fred is ninety-four, he jogs 5 km every day.
4. Jill, whose father is a chef, hates to cook.
5. The two kilograms of nuts that Hanna bought are very expensive.
6. The toilet backed up again while you were at the bank.
7. In her heart, Felice repeated her proposal many times in order that it be perfect.
8. The troll, which has red hair, has brought me only bad luck.
9. After he ate six burgers, he drank four large colas.
10. We all love you even if you are a little weird.

Exercise 68

Answers may vary.

1. I like to travel where the people are friendly.
2. Stephen Leacock, who is a well-known Canadian humourist, was born in 1869, in England.

3. Read the instructions before you light the barbecue.
4. If the barometric pressure is low, I'm sure it will rain soon.
5. Herman was the centre of attention on the dance floor even though he has never had a single dance lesson.
6. Alexander Dumas, a French novelist whom I admire very much, wrote *The Count of Monte Cristo*.
7. The black mamba snake can run as fast as 33 km/h.
8. You will end it all unless you tie the bungee cord to your ankles first.
9. Whenever Gary sings at parties, everyone cries.
10. Louise inherited a great deal of money so that she never has to work again.

Exercise 69

Answers may vary.

1. The accordion band played rock and roll, and it was hot.
2. Lizzeth, who is very zealous, really enjoys life.
3. Because Vito forgot his wallet at home, he was unable to buy his lunch at work.
4. Arabic is the official language of Morocco which is located on the northwest coast of Africa.
5. Aldo wakes early in the morning even though he goes to bed late.
6. Ferehiwot agreed to marry Julius, but he had to get a job first.
7. Charles washed the car while Jenna washed the children.
8. Dim went to the movie with her brother, but she didn't want to go.
9. The H. J. Heinz Company, which makes ketchup, also makes 9Lives cat food.
10. It was October, and the weather was cool, and leaves fell from the trees.

Exercise 70

Answers may vary.

1. After Alyson poured the coffee, she sneezed suddenly, so she made fresh coffee.
2. As the spider rushed up the wall, Monica rushed out of the room.
3. After the surgery was completed, Mary Anne had a new nose that looked like her mother's nose.
4. The passport office was very busy; in fact, more than two hundred people were in the room.
5. The bus was a half-hour late because it had had a flat tire.
6. When Connie played the ring-toss game at the carnival, she spent $40 and won a large plush ostrich.
7. Patrick, who fell asleep in class, banged his head against his desk and startled himself, the other students, and the teacher.
8. The farmer began harvesting because the peaches were ripe, and some had already fallen.

9. The heron walked stealthily in the shallow water and quickly speared a small bass.
10. Perry is very ticklish; consequently, he laughs very easily.

Exercise 71

Answers may vary.

1. The grass was greener on the other side of the fence; then Wilbur climbed the fence, and the grass was the same colour.
2. Wai Lin wanted to meet her sister at the airport; as a result, she needed to leave work early.
3. The Colossus of Rhodes, a bronze statue of the sun god Helios built in the early days of 200 B.C., is one of the Seven Wonders of the World.
4. Because there were fresh bear tracks on the hiking trail, we decided to cancel our hike.
5. The cap fell off the pepper sauce bottle; as a result, the stew was extra spicy now, but we ate it anyway.
6. Joel needed to study for his math test; unfortunately, he forgot his review material at school.
7. When the roses arrived at Yvette's house, she was happy to receive them and was glad Carl remembered her birthday.
8. Gordon, who is not a plumber, fixed the shower but wrenched his elbow.
9. The first Liberal prime minister of Canada, who was the second prime minister from 1873 to 1878, was Alexander Mackenzie.
10. Trevor, who didn't have any change, decided to take a chance and park at the meter; as a result, he received a $20 parking ticket.

Exercise 72

Some answers may vary.

1. Vanessa baked almost a hundred cakes for the party.
2. At the zoo we saw a reptile that had coarse scales in a cage.
3. He cheated on tests only.
4. Jung bought a house with a large verandah in the rear through a real estate agent.
5. From my window, I could see the rain water rushing down the drain.
6. Andy often volunteers to help his friends move.
7. The instructor frequently told jokes that were really silly to his students.
8. Beven swallowed almost two golf balls when he was demonstrating that he could hold six in his mouth.
9. Myrna gave the silverware that she had just polished to the rabbi.
10. With great excitement, Joannie bought two plane tickets for France.

Exercise 73

Some answers may vary.

1. He drank nearly the whole bottle of prune juice.
2. With a bad attitude, Pam approached the office.
3. Shirin really wanted to eat a greasy burger with fried onions.
4. David visited his sister, who had a broken leg, in the hospital.
5. John doesn't even understand me.
6. Lance took the pizza, which was loaded with pepperoni, from the delivery person.
7. They picked up the birthday cake that had fudge topping and yellow flowers at the mall.
8. C
9. You need to brush your teeth often.
10. Judy bought a new cereal that was vitamin-enriched at the grocery store.

Exercise 74

1. You made me lose almost all hope.
2. A piece of dirt that came from the construction site flew into my eye.
3. We bought the tarts with the custard filling from the baker.
4. Dan gave his old suit that was striped to his brother.
5. Colin frequently liked to stay out late.
6. Men have only one bad habit.
7. They had cake that was stale in the kitchen.
8. Young Shin merely wanted to express her opinion.
9. She gave the sandwich that was loaded with chili peppers to Robert.
10. In my shorts I saw the fire in the warehouse.

Exercise 76

Corrections may vary.

Ken rarely said no to a challenge. When a friend dared him to spend an entire night in an old graveyard for English teachers, he could only say yes.

He put on his heavy jacket with a hood and stepped out into the cool night. As he reached the graveyard at the edge of town, he thought he saw something moving. He cried, "It's the ghost of my English teacher who taught me in college."

Ken almost decided to run away, but the spirit spoke to him.

"Help me! I am forced to roam the cemetery always because someone wrote my epitaph with a misplaced modifier." The spirit pointed to the gravestone that read:

Here lies Fred.
He's really dead.
Only he never thought
That he would be so lonely
In his final bed.

Exercise 77

Answers may vary.

1. After we heard the English assignment, it was hard for us to smile.
2. While Marlene was drinking the wine, the parrot started talking.
3. Having found a cockroach in my cupboard, Norma Jean became sick.
4. To be a good dancer, you should practise every day.
5. After I ate ten bags of potato chips, my stomach hurt.
6. Because we were excited about the trip, we brought out the maps.
7. While they were spitting out the watermelon seeds, several landed on the floor.
8. After Kathryn milked the cow, it mooed, "Ah, that's better."
9. C
10. To improve English grammar, you need a good usage text.

Exercise 78

Answers may vary.

1. Since I started listening to you, trouble has become my friend.
2. Overburdened with debts already, Melody received another bill.
3. While we were swimming at the lake, it began to rain.
4. After the master of ceremonies announced the winner, the prize was handed out.
5. Daydreaming in class, Nicola did not hear the question.
6. When I am dining alone, a magazine can be a good companion.
7. When George was painting the fence, the sprinkler came on.
8. While I was sneaking into the house at 2 a.m., each stair creaked more than usual.
9. While Erica was baking bread, the oven stopped working.
10. Watching the late show, we noticed that the commercials were amazing.

Exercise 79

Answers may vary.

1. While we were driving down the country road, we saw the horses.
2. Having finished dessert, they were served their coffee.
3. After Donna complained about all the rain, it snowed.
4. While I was going to the bathroom in the middle of the night, the bed creaked.
5. While she was visiting Poland, Agnes saw her second cousin for the first time.
6. C
7. While I was buttering the toast, the cat meowed loudly.
8. After Doreen considered all the options, it was still difficult for her to make a decision.
9. To find happiness, I found it necessary to look for it.
10. While Fred was looking out the window, the geese flew by.

Exercise 80

Answers may vary.

1. Rinsing with the mouthwash, I saw the spider crawl out of the drain.
   After I rinsed with the mouthwash, the spider crawled out of the drain.
2. Having loaded the trunk, we began our vacation.
   After we loaded the trunk, our vacation began.
3. Confused by the teacher, I found the lesson difficult to understand.
   After I was confused by the teacher, the lesson was difficult.
4. While visiting Fred, I saw that the dog had become sick.
   While I was visiting Fred, the dog became sick.
5. Watching the sunset, Emily saw the sky was filled with beautiful colours.
   While Emily was watching the sunset, the sky was filled with beautiful colours.
6. After buying the cream, I found it to be sour.
   After I bought the cream, it was sour.
7. Having read the book, I found that the movie was disappointing.
   After I read the book, the movie was disappointing.
8. After consolidating all the debts, I was able to make small payments.
   After Ralph consolidated all the debts, the payments were small.
9. While driving to work, I noticed that the muffler fell off the car.
   While I was driving to work, the muffler fell off the car.
10. After entering the haunted house, I saw the ghost appear.
    After I entered the haunted house, the ghost appeared.

Exercise 81

Answers may vary.

1. While dreaming about you, I felt my heart pounding.
   While I was dreaming about you, my heart pounded.
2. Having bowled all night, I needed a rest.
   After I bowled all night, a rest was needed.
3. Having set the table, she was ready to eat.
   After she set the table, it was time to eat
4. After reading this book, I changed my outlook on life completely.
   After I read this book, my outlook on life changed completely.
5. While putting peanut butter on the sandwich, I tore the bread.
   While I was putting peanut butter on the sandwich, the bread tore.
6. After finishing the report, Sam found it was necessary to get up and stretch.
   After he finished the report, it was necessary for Sam to get up and stretch.
7. Having cut the grass, I knew it was time for a cold drink.
   After I cut the grass, it was time for a cold drink.

8. While thinking about the meaning of life, she heard the baby start to cry.
   While she was thinking about the meaning of life, the baby started to cry.
9. After eating the bratwurst, I found the beer to be refreshing.
   After I ate the bratwurst, the beer was refreshing.
10. Having cleaned the garage, I now had room for the car.
    After I cleaned the garage, there was now room for the car.

Item IX: Correcting Faulty Parallel Structure

Exercise 82

Answers may vary.

1. Katrina is self-determined, well-educated, and self-centred.
2. Boris's new shoes are comfortable, soft, and expensive.
3. We ordered neither Greek food nor Chinese food.
4. Dino shouted at the football game enthusiastically and loudly.
5. We could help you decorate the room, blow up balloons, and wrap the presents.
6. Claire likes to have blueberry muffins, chocolate doughnuts, or butter tarts for breakfast.
7. The rock climbers were hungry, tired, and sore.
8. C
9. Last summer we visited Saskatchewan and saw Fort Carlton.
10. C

Exercise 83

Answers may vary.

1. Either Jerry will sell his camera through the want ads, or he will sell it privately.
2. Fortina is going to visit Spain, study Spanish, and learn the lambada.
3. By getting a good night's sleep and eating a good breakfast, Fred is ready for Monday mornings.
4. You can be sure that Waldemar's homemade sausages are fresh, spicy, and juicy.
5. Helen neither jogs nor walks to work.
6. Marco is a tireless volunteer and a generous donator.
7. Travelling to Lake Superior and touching its water was a thrill for Julie Ann.
8. C
9. Teresa is a good friend, and she listens to me.
10. To be happy, you need good health, enough money, and fresh breath.

Exercise 84

Answers may vary.

1. The rock band was raucous but entertaining.
2. Stephanie does not like going to the dentist nor to work.

3. The smell from the kitchen made our eyes burn and our throats hurt.
4. Margaret Laurence wrote many Canadian novels and portrayed complex characters in them.
5. She wired an extra electrical outlet, installed a new dishwasher, and attached an electric fan.
6. Daniella lives in London, Ontario and has become a Canadian citizen.
7. Bring the raspberries and strawberries and snow peas into the house.
8. Unfortunately, Fred was neither very handsome nor too ugly.
9. Donald was either going to quit smoking or to die trying.
10. Marcelina enjoys eating barbecued ribs, baked potatoes, and fresh vegetables.

Exercise 85

Answers may vary.

1. Laurie came back from vacation with a new attitude and eagerness to work.
2. C
3. By checking his compositions for spelling mistakes and looking out for run-on sentence errors, Bart always hands in excellent papers.
4. The doctor said Sid should either lose 20 kg, or he should buy larger clothes.
5. C
6. Bruce was convinced that Quebec is the largest province in Canada with the largest population.
7. This evening dress is elegant and alluring and expensive.
8. She wanted her children to grow up with good health, with a good education, and with inner peace.
9. C
10. Emma is always worried about what her fortuneteller is going to predict and charge.

Exercise 86

Answers may vary.

1. My boss treats his employees with attention, consideration, and patience.
2. Milk the cow, feed the chickens, and clean the barn.
3. Yvette knows neither the names nor the ages of the children.
4. Skipping stones, collecting shells, and building sand castles are fun things to do on the beach.
5. Werner baked, sliced, and buttered the bread.
6. This pasta sauce is rich, spicy, and hot.
7. C
8. These socks need washing, deodorizing, and bleaching.
9. How rich he was, how much money he made, and how old he was were what his admirers wanted to know.
10. I need to be more like Mike who is compassionate, generous, and unselfish.

Item X: Correcting Shifts in Tense

Exercise 87

Answers may vary.

1. Sara was biting into her burger when she saw one of her French fries move across the plate.
2. After Mario told the joke, no one laughed.
3. Jill turned her wheelchair around the corner and reached her class just in time.
4. The red-tailed hawk flew across the highway and rested on a hydro pole.
5. Carol studied so hard for the math test, but unfortunately she failed it badly.
6. The old cat is resting on the verandah stairs and purring.
7. Ellen read *The Cashier* by Gabrielle Roy and really enjoyed it.
8. Wendell is walking through the woods and is taking pictures.
9. She says she loves me but never shows it.
10. C

Exercise 88

Answers may vary.

1. Hector is happy when he sings in the shower; unfortunately, everyone is unhappy when he does.
2. Once Alma made up her mind, she was determined to succeed.
3. Eun and Byeong need your help, but they are too embarrassed to ask.
4. The plane lifted into the sky just as the sun set.
5. Tran met the woman of his dreams and asked her out.
6. It is hard to find a well-paying job that is suitable for someone like me.
7. I was so surprised that my brother came from Europe to visit me.
8. The smell of coffee perking makes Philip feel good, but the smell of burning milk makes him feel sick.
9. C
10. The whole class had a headache after the teacher explained "shift in tense."

Exercise 89

Answers may vary.

1. Yolanta enjoyed the smoked salmon that she bought at the market.
2. The cyclist raced down the road, ran through the red light, and bumped into a police car.
3. Idalina left the house, but she couldn't remember if she turned the stove off.
4. They checked into the Holiday Inn in Ottawa and stayed three days.
5. The snow fell very heavily and lasted until the next day.
6. Ursula is operating a small doughnut shop and is working long hours.
7. Print your first name first; then write your last name next.

8. Roland was admiring his new Porsche when a motorcycle crashed into it.
9. The music was too loud, but the food was good at Fiona's party last night.
10. C

Exercise 90

Answers may vary.

1. During his wedding ceremony, Alex was so nervous he accidentally said "I don't know" instead of "I do."
2. It was sad to see that the geese were flying south already.
3. Mark wants to apply for a teaching position in Hong Kong, but his wife doesn't want to leave Canada.
4. C
5. You need someone who is more like you.
6. We saw the diver enter the aquarium at the zoo and feed the fish.
7. The Toronto radio station CFRB 1010 states that it has news every 30 minutes.
8. David is always meeting people who are absolutely no good for him.
9. C
10. Melissa was so angry she poured the maple syrup over her boyfriend's head.

Exercise 91

Answers may vary.

1. The two gunshots that were heard turned out to be two flat tires.
2. Kim's nose became so itchy she sneezed loudly several times.
3. John shouldn't wear that shirt; it looks as if he slept in it.
4. The big bad wolf huffed and puffed, and the three little pigs shivered in fear.
5. I want to see the air show and watch the biplanes.
6. After the test was over, Francis went straight home to study some more.
7. Cynthia tasted the hot soup and burned her tongue.
8. Arnold is eating the raw meat; fortunately, he is a dog.
9. Susan embroidered the shirt and showed it to her sister.
10. Grazyna tried on the dress yesterday, and it fit perfectly.

UNIT 3: SENTENCE AGREEMENT

Item I: Subject-Verb Agreement

Exercise 1

1. is
2. are learning
3. know

4. is visiting
5. was
6. is
7. is
8. was
9. are discussing
10. costs

Exercise 2

1. are going
2. is bringing
3. is meeting
4. has
5. are printed
6. has been used
7. is
8. is
9. was
10. is starting

Exercise 3

1. plays
2. was written
3. have been entered
4. is
5. is
6. were
7. is
8. is travelling
9. is
10. don't

Exercise 4

1. has
2. knows
3. is
4. was losing
5. is
6. are
7. costs

8. appeals
9. is crossing
10. are discussing

Exercise 5

1. have completed
2. is flying
3. is
4. is
5. is
6. are complaining
7. was
8. means
9. is
10. is scheduled

Exercise 6

1. their
2. her
3. his/her
4. its
5. her/his
6. his/her
7. their
8. their
9. their
10. her/his

Exercise 7

1. their
2. their
3. her
4. its
5. their
6. their
7. his/her
8. her
9. their
10. her/his

Exercise 8

1. their
2. its
3. his
4. their
5. their
6. their
7. his
8. her/his
9. his
10. their

Exercise 9

1. her
2. its
3. their
4. their
5. her, her
6. his/her
7. their, they
8. his
9. their
10. her

Exercise 10

1. his
2. its
3. her
4. their
5. its
6. their
7. their
8. her
9. his
10. his

Exercise 11

Answers may vary.

1. No one in school can be certain that she/he/one will get a job after graduating.
2. Dominic said to his brother, "You are confused." OR Dominic said to his brother, "I am confused."

3. After two months Jack changed the cat's litter box making the air fresh again.
4. One can imagine the difficulties she/he/one might encounter if she/he/one has her/his/one's wallet stolen.
5. She said to her, "Your eyebrows are crooked." OR She said to her, "My eyebrows are crooked."
6. A student with this much determination knows that he/she will succeed.
7. After watching the Olympic track meet, Boris wanted to become a long-distance runner.
8. A person like Fred knows the answers before the questions are even asked.
9. One is often sad that he/she/one has lost his/hers/one's youth.
10. She remarked to her sister, "Your slip has slipped." OR She remarked to her sister, "My slip has slipped."

Exercise 12

Answers may vary.

1. Wanda saw the kitten at the animal shelter and wanted a kitten.
2. C
3. If they really try, they can find the error in this sentence.
4. Running out of money just before the rent is due makes me crazy.
5. Celine said to Racquel, "Your attitude has to change." OR Celine said to Racquel, "My attitude has to change."
6. If you are not sure, you should check in the dictionary.
7. After walking by the ice cream store, we wanted two ice cream cones.
8. He said to his uncle, "You are the best." OR He said to his uncle, "I am the best."
9. A person like him would always say that he/she is right.
10. I copied the notes from yesterday's class, and they are appreciated.

Exercise 13

Answers may vary.

1. Anyone can say that she/he/one saw Elvis Presley in a doughnut shop.
2. The ventriloquist said to Duncan, "You speak out of both sides of his mouth." OR The ventriloquist said to Duncan, "I speak out of both sides of my mouth."
3. She said to her mother, "You don't know whether to boil or broil the liver." OR She said to her mother, "I don't know whether to boil or broil the liver."
4. One of them said that she/he would wash the car.
5. The dog ate some mushrooms on the lawn explaining why it is not feeling well.
6. A person should follow his/her head as well as his/her heart when he/she has an important decision to make.
7. An individual can have a tremendous impact on other people if she/he gives herself/himself a chance.
8. After listening to the country CD, Kiley wanted to become a country singer.

9. Steven said to him, "You have rhinoceros breath." OR Steven said to him, "I have rhinoceros breath."
10. If persons worry too much over matters of little consequence, they could develop an ulcer.

Exercise 14

Answers may vary.

1. Joseph said to Bill, "You resemble a goose from the neck down." OR Joseph said to Bill, "I resemble a goose from the neck down."
2. They should see the manager before they lodge a complaint.
3. He will get a copy of the short story when he arrives.
4. Irwin saw the photographer working with the bride and groom at the wedding and wanted to become a wedding photographer.
5. All of the aliens in the spaceship said that they thought Earth was a nice place to visit.
6. C
7. The police officer said, "You were in the wrong place at the wrong time." OR The police officer said, "I was in the wrong place at the wrong time."
8. When Jeff saw the commercial for the burger sale, he wanted to eat a burger badly.
9. When one of the relatives said that he/she wanted hair replacement, and the other said that he/she wanted hair removal, everyone laughed.
10. C

Exercise 15

Answers may vary.

One of the food critics at a newspaper said that <u>he</u> had heard that a new Chinese restaurant had opened, and that <u>it was</u> serving great food. He <u>said to his editor, "I am going to try it."</u> As soon as he opened the door, <u>the food smelled wonderful</u>.

He was seated at a corner table, and this pleased him. He looked over the menu, but <u>he found it</u> too difficult to decide what to order. He <u>said to the waiter, "I am poor at making decisions and need a little more time."</u>

However, he eventually ordered a large, satisfying meal and told the waiter that a person knows <u>he has</u> had a great meal after eating in this restaurant.

In fact, the writer was so impressed with the food service at the restaurant that he decided to quit his job and become <u>a restaurant owner too.</u>

Item IV: Pronoun Usage Problems

Exercise 16

1. I
2. she

3. she
4. he
5. us
6. she
7. We
8. we
9. him
10. he

Exercise 17

1. her
2. them
3. she
4. he
5. him
6. them
7. us
8. he or him
9. me
10. she

Exercise 18

1. him
2. him
3. she
4. they
5. we
6. them
7. We
8. I
9. him
10. she

Exercise 19

1. they
2. us
3. him
4. I
5. he
6. he
7. her

8. he
9. they
10. her

Exercise 20

1. we
2. she
3. he
4. they
5. she, him
6. her
7. him
8. me
9. us
10. her

Exercise 21

1. her
2. them, they
3. I
4. she
5. him
6. I
7. him
8. We
9. they
10. her

Exercise 22

1. us
2. he
3. her
4. she
5. we
6. I
7. we
8. me
9. we
10. her

Exercise 23

1. us
2. her
3. I
4. him
5. she
6. us
7. him
8. I
9. he
10. us

Exercise 24

1. I
2. him
3. I
4. him
5. me, we
6. he
7. them
8. she
9. us
10. her

Exercise 25

1. them
2. them, I
3. she
4. she
5. them
6. us
7. he
8. she
9. she
10. I

UNIT 4: PUNCTUATION PERFECTION

Items I and II: The Period, the Question Mark, and the Exclamation Mark

Exercise 1

1. Say what you mean.
2. Fr. Al is still here.
3. He voted for the losing party.
4. This pasta is wonderful.
5. What will they think of next? (.)
6. When does your train arrive?
7. What's the use? (.)
8. You should have seen all the onion rings they ordered.
9. Does Dave have a B.A. or an M.A. in English literature?
10. Take a hike!

Exercise 2

1. Let's go. (!)
2. Moira enjoyed her week in Spain.
3. What can you tell me about earwigs?
4. You are strange.
5. Set the clock.
6. What a surprise this is.
7. Yikes! I forgot to turn the steaks over on the barbecue.
8. What is OXFAM?
9. *Etc.* is the abbreviation for *et cetera.*
10. Do you know what the plural of *Ms.* is?

Exercise 3

1. Don't slam the door! (.)
2. Is the whole world going crazy? (.)
3. Say it. (!)
4. Since you're so clever, what is the capital of Saskatchewan?
5. Byron wants to be an OPP officer.
6. That is good news.
7. Where did you see the UFO?
8. What a mess! (.)
9. This is extra special.
10. This is not what I expected in Ontario.

Exercise 4

1. In 1812, the United States declared war on the British.
2. Did you know that the first American invasion to Upper Canada was defeated by Indian leader Tecumseh?
3. Brenda likes all kinds of wines, e.g. Chablis and Chardonnay.
4. I think Sr. St. Joseph wanted to see you.
5. Why is George under the coffee table again?
6. Don't ask me to spell *potpourri*; I can't even pronounce it.
7. What is the good of being spiteful? (.)
8. Please, slice it thickly.
9. Gen. Smith told us about the new army manoeuvres.
10. Shoot! I forgot to pay the gas bill.

Exercise 5

1. I'm sure that Harold lives on Macklem Blvd. in Cambridge, Ontario.
2. How did you know I like pirogi?
3. I thought about what he said.
4. Did Dr. Edwards tell you to drink more water?
5. Nuts! I hate pistachios.
6. Close your eyes, and make a wish.
7. That's it; I've had enough! (.)
8. The puppy we saw at the pound became the puppy at our house.
9. I hate it when that happens.
10. Do you mind? I'm still eating.

Item III: The Comma

Exercise 6

1. Those cheese balls, onion rings(,) and potato chips are for the party.
2. No, the mouthwash doesn't work.
3. When you deliver the pizza, don't ring the doorbell; knock instead.
4. Hank, you know the rules.
5. C
6. Margaret Atwood wrote *The Robber Bride*, and Nino Ricci wrote *In a Glass House*.
7. On the desk by the phone, you will find my notes.
8. Come in for a minute, and sit down.
9. By saving some money every day, Erin was able to save up for a new wallet.
10. C

Exercise 7

1. Get a loaf of bread from the freezer, and put it on the kitchen counter.
2. Mice, rats(,) and weasels give Ida the shivers.
3. Yes, I did spill the beans.
4. Since your last visit, nothing has changed.
5. Where to stay, what to see(,) and where to eat are the items highlighted in this brochure.
6. In Iran, in China(,) and in Canada, the New Year begins on a different day.
7. When you burst out laughing, I knew that I did not translate "I love you" properly in Japanese.
8. The moon, the sun(,) and all the stars are not as bright as your eyes.
9. Instead of complaining, do something about the problem.
10. C

Exercise 8

1. Donna, when will the coffee be ready?
2. Not only does Cindy have a degree in economics, but she also runs a financial planning firm.
3. Because of the heavy rains, some of the roads were washed out.
4. C
5. The monks, nuns(,) and friars were in the habit of rising early for prayers.
6. That you can speak French, that you understand Polish(,) and that you can write Yiddish is mind-boggling.
7. Hold your breath, and then let go.
8. Matt, don't do that to the cat.
9. By drawing premature conclusions, you made a fool of yourself.
10. Why do words hurt more than sticks, bricks(,) and stones?

Exercise 9

1. Dennis was so angry with himself for being forgetful that he wanted to cry, yell(,) and scream at the same time.
2. Knowing how you feel about snails, I did not make escargots for supper.
3. C
4. Have they arrested the person who gave you that terrible haircut yet, or are they still looking for the culprit?
5. This is my college diploma, and I am very proud of it.
6. C
7. Well, what do you think of my new apartment?
8. Sid, the phone is for you.
9. The table was set, and the supper was served, but no one said thank you to the host.
10. By the time he was four, Joseph had already had the worst day of his life.

Exercise 10

1. The music, the food, the wine were not just memories.
2. Yes, a male buffalo can weigh as much as a metric ton and can grow as tall as two metres.
3. With the wind and the snow and the hail howling against him, Murray was unable to cross the street.
4. Glen, is this really your car?
5. Look in the mirror, and then tell me that you don't need a vacation.
6. While Dimitri was in the bank, it was robbed.
7. Serena sanded, stained(,) and varathaned the antique chair.
8. Read the small print, sign the document(,) and give me the money.
9. Perhaps I will attend the lecture on making positive decisions, and perhaps I won't.
10. Hey, it's only money.

Exercise 11

1. Doris, the head nurse at St. Martin's Hospital, is my cousin.
2. Fred, I might add, also collects stickers from fruit.
3. I know there is a Toronto, Ontario, but I didn't know there was an Ontario, California.
4. Henri said that he was born on March 5, 1972(,) in Hull, Quebec.
5. Doreen, without question, is the luckiest person I know.
6. Mail it to the town clerk at 45 Hillside Dr. N., Elliot Lake, Ontario.
7. C
8. The fish weighed 4 kg, 37 g.
9. In spite of a bad cold, Ms. Hill was still able to teach our class.
10. Voula, where did you learn to tap-dance so well?

Exercise 12

1. On the contrary, Ben likes milk chocolate, but he won't eat white chocolate.
2. Ms. Junn, the new science teacher, was born in Brooks, Alberta.
3. Mount Saint Vincent University, St. Francis Xavier University(,) and St. Mary's University are in Nova Scotia.
4. C
5. You, my dear friend, need more than a facelift.
6. Gil, you know, was born in 1901, five years before my grandfather.
7. Before you go out, don't forget to turn off the stove.
8. The play begins October 4, 1993(,) and should continue until 1998.
9. Bea, our accountant, thinks we should buy some mutual funds.
10. Pumpkins, squashes(,) and gourds covered the vegetable stand.

Exercise 13

1. C
2. The Great War Memorial Hospital is located at 33 Drummond St. W., Perth, Ontario.
3. No, this is not my last chance.
4. What do the words *gnaw*, *gnat*, *knead*(,) and *knout* have in common?
5. Because this is your first day on the job, someone will be here to assist you.
6. These chocolate chip cookies, I think, are made with real chocolate.
7. On July 20, 1871(,) British Columbia became Canada's sixth province.
8. Dr. Cassidy, our veterinarian, knows our pets well.
9. After eating the chili, my stomach felt strange.
10. The ceramic tile store is located on 2161 Dumont St. E., Brighton, Ontario.

Exercise 14

1. Yes, the temperature is still below zero.
2. Even though he forgot his tickets, Ivan was allowed into the theatre.
3. C
4. Peter, an avid fisher, is always looking for the best spot on the lake.
5. What is the day, month(,) and year of your birth?
6. To tell the truth, I was convinced that Cecil was wrong, but he was right.
7. The police wanted to know where she was last night, what time she left work(,) and what time she arrived home.
8. Before you say another word, read this.
9. None of these nuts, bolts(,) and washers match.
10. Cloudy, not sunny days, are best for photographing autumn colours.

Item IV: The Colon

Exercise 16

1. Meet me at 6:30 p.m., and we'll work on the newsletter.
2. There are two nice things about Jim in particular: he is determined, and he is innovative.
3. Whose photograph is taken in *The Wild Duck* I:iv?
4. C
5. Eduardo made these points clear at the staff meeting: he stated that there were longer hours, fewer benefits, and little thanks.
6. The passage John 4:34–38 is very comforting.
7. C
8. Rhonda understood his problem: he was a big spender, but he had little money.
9. I'm only up to Act II:i of *The One Day of the Year* by Alan Seymour, but I'll finish it by tomorrow.
10. You've already complained that the apartment has the following flaws: little heat, loud neighbours, and healthy mice.

Exercise 17

1. C
2. Why does the teacher use the following words when he talks about me: *lugubrious, perspicacious*, and *peccadillo*?
3. You know that Farid is interested in only two things: money and more money.
4. C
5. Before you start taking pictures, check two things: that the camera has film and that the lens cap is off.
6. C
7. In Shaw's *Heartbreak House*, Lady Utterwood says that there are only two classes in good society in England: the equestrian and the neurotic.
8. *Nova Scotia: The Lighthouse Route and the Annapolis Valley* is an exceptional picture book by Sherman Hines.
9. Ida suggested the following times for the meeting: 10:30 a.m. on Monday, 11:00 a.m. on Tuesday, or 2:30 p.m. on Thursday.
10. C

Item V: The Semicolon

Exercise 18

1. Steve finally cut the grass; it was up to his knees.
2. Warren entered the essay-writing contest; unfortunately his paper was not one of the winning entries.
3. Look in the mirror; your problem is obvious.
4. Meet me downtown; otherwise we'll never make it to the theatre on time.
5. Don't bet on that horse; it hasn't won a race in 15 years.
6. C
7. Believe me, you need an oil change; you've driven this car over 10,000 km since the last one.
8. We arrived at the county fair late; in addition, we forgot our free passes.
9. Pauline kissed her son Matthew; consequently, her daughter Melissa wanted one too.
10. This lettuce wasn't cleaned properly; it still has soil in its leaves.

Exercise 19

1. Dorothy was so excited at the hockey game; to tell the truth, she jumped up and down as she cheered her team.
2. Buy some milk tonight: otherwise we won't have any for breakfast tomorrow.
3. Ian said he had a bad headache after doing Exercise 18; however, he feels better now.
4. The pet owner taught his three parrots to sing "The Bird Dance Song" in harmony; everyone laughed when the birds sang.
5. "Alliteration" is a figure of speech in which the first sound in a group of words is repeated; an example is "lovely little lake."

6. Darian ate his pomegranate; unfortunately, no one told him to peel it first.
7. Albert always asks interesting questions; yesterday he wanted to know if sour cream ever went bad.
8. This algebra problem is impossible to solve; in fact, I think the answer in the back of the book is wrong.
9. First you didn't like my appetizer; then you complained about my main course; now you're holding your stomach after eating my dessert.
10. Doug quit smoking; to tell the truth, I didn't think he could do it.

Exercise 20

1. This is my advice: Follow your head, and follow your heart.
2. Michelle would like a pet for Christmas; for instance, she would like a hamster, a kitten, or a puppy.
3. Call me; I could use a friend.
4. Glenda has been everywhere; she has been as far as Singapore, the Philippines.
5. The dental hygienist recommended two things to keep my teeth healthy: brush after every meal, and floss before bed.
6. Are you familiar with these Patsy Cline songs: "I Fall to Pieces," "Crazy," and "Don't Ever Leave Me"?
7. Derrick agreed to the blind date; unfortunately when she opened the door, he discovered that it was his ex-girlfriend.
8. At 7:30 p.m., the drama group will be rehearsing Act III:iv of *Richard III*.
9. Tara needs a break; she's been studying more than five hours.
10. C

Exercise 21

1. There are some interesting vocabulary words in *Street Talk: The Language of Coronation Street*.
2. I hate hospitals; however, I will go with you to visit Shelly.
3. It must be a bad day; I arrived at work an hour early.
4. Can you buy me the following fishes: sole, salmon, and swordfish?
5. C
6. The bartender gave this advice to his heartbroken customer: Keep your glass clean, and your mate will see the real you.
7. Will the bulletin be repeated at 10:45 or 11:45?
8. I saw Pauline's new computer; it's a beauty.
9. The cheesecakes you ordered are these: mocha, strawberry, and lemon.
10. Name the time; name the place, and I'll be there.

Exercise 22

1. Did you read Act I:ii of *A Raisin in the Sun* yet?
2. The rescue attempt was made more difficult by these factors: rain, fog, and cold.

3. Peter is a proud father; in addition, he is a very proud grandfather.
4. *The Blood People: A Division of the Blackfoot Confederacy* is one of several books by Adolf Hungry Wolf.
5. This is too long; shorten it by at least ten pages.
6. C
7. The pizza will be here by 6:47 p.m., or it'll be free.
8. Of course I'm still nervous; the spider is still looking at me.
9. I could visit Disney World anytime; unfortunately I'd have to walk there.
10. Try the bratwurst; you won't be disappointed.

Exercise 23

1. Have you read these short stories: "The Coronet at Night" by Sinclair Ross, "The Loons" by Margaret Laurence, and "The Snob" by Morley Callaghan?
2. Arnold had two physical ailments about which he never complained: an ulcer and flat feet.
3. Yolanda visited her mother in Poland; the weather was bad.
4. Do you know the meaning of these vocabulary words: *complaisant, adroit, demeanour,* and *stupor*?
5. At 4:05 a.m., Tulla was wakened by a strange sound coming from her basement: fortunately, it was only her furnace.
6. C
7. What a day George had; in one day two great events took place: his divorce became official, and he got his long-awaited promotion at work.
8. Are these citrus fruits the same: a mandarin orange, a tangerine, and a tangelo?
9. Esmine went to see *Les Misérables, Miss Saigon,* and *The Phantom of the Opera* last month; she really enjoyed them.
10. Michael was confused; consequently, he did not do well on the test.

Exercise 24

1. Ken rubbed the lamp and asked for three wishes; unfortunately, it was a desk lamp, and he burned his hand badly.
2. Jackie likes the following water sports best: swimming, waterskiing, and scuba diving.
3. The instructor had only two comments about the test: it was going to be hard, but it was going to be fair.
4. The reindeer are restless; it is almost time for Santa Claus to fly.
5. Breakfast was rough; the prune juice worked faster than I did.
6. What are you going to do with these items: whipped cream, chocolate sauce, and a hammer?
7. Your wallet must be defective; it can't hold any money.
8. John should sing; Betty should dance, but you should watch.
9. This coffee is awful; it tastes like swamp water.
10. C

Item VI: Quotation Marks

Exercise 26

1. "This is my last cigarette," promised Inge.
2. C
3. "You know I never say no to helping someone," said Sunita.
4. "Are you barbecuing steaks tonight?" asked Francine.
5. "Did you say that you weren't going?" asked Zofia.
6. "I can't believe my eyes," remarked Joy. "I've passed the test."
7. "Wow!" exclaimed Don. "That's the biggest blimp I've ever seen."
8. "Are you the new teacher?" remarked Glenda.
9. "The wine," remarked Henri, "that I like best is organic."
10. "I read the novel before I saw the movie," said Fritz.

Exercise 27

1. David said sympathetically, "I know how you feel."
2. Did Edna really say, "I made a mistake"?
3. They shouted together, "Look out! The bear is right behind you."
4. "This bump on my head," said Ralph, "looks like a doorknob."
5. Did you ask, "Are the buns really warm?"
6. "Can you imagine what it would be like to be a spider?" asked Devon.
7. C
8. I remarked, "Rose can't live without my morning coffee."
9. "Sing this song for me," requested Daniel. "You have such a beautiful voice."
10. Isaac asked, "Where are all the guests?"

Exercise 28

1. Trinh said, "The strawberries are ripe."
2. "What could be more important?" asked the bishop.
3. "Your eyes," remarked Hilde, "are so bloodshot."
4. "How old is this roast beef?" coughed the choking customer.
5. C
6. Did Glenda ask, "How long does it usually take?"
7. Did Alex say, "Your cheeks are really red"?
8. "The movie was really great," said Alice.
9. "Ed shouted, 'I can't stand this music any more!'" said Cynthia.
10. "Who asked you your age?" asked Margaret.

Exercise 29

1. "Isn't the wind bitter? (,)" remarked Indira.
2. C

3. "Green," remarked Angela, "is not my favourite nail polish colour."
4. "I love to run through the autumn leaves," said Brittany.
5. Did Cosmo ask, "How hard can this nut be to crack?"
6. "'Help me!' she screamed," said Walter.
7. "I can barely keep my eyes open," whispered Annie.
8. "I know now," commented Jose, "why their compact disc was on sale."
9. Did Vera ask, "Did I make the right decision to go back to school?"
10. "You've won 4 kg of mince," announced the butcher at his shop.

Exercise 30

1. "Listen," Ida whispered, "to the rain on the roof."
2. "What are the qualities of a good mate?" asked Sam.
3. "After that last remark," shouted Burgess, "I know that you are an idiot!"
4. "Did you order this jacket from the catalogue?" inquired Cassie.
5. "Do you know," said Francine, "that gerbils are monogamous?"
6. "The dates and numbers that you want are on your desk," said Eugenie.
7. C
8. "The bill is for six hundred dollars," said the smiling dentist.
9. "What," remarked the boss, "would I do without you."
10. Did Kay ask, "Weren't you wrong last time too?"

Exercise 31

1. How can I find an example of "onomatopoeia" in this poem; I don't even know what it means.
2. "Don't say it, (!)" said Barry.
3. "You mean that film has been in the camera since 1972?" asked David.
4. "Certainly," said Carolyn. "I'll be happy to give you my autograph."
5. Javinder said, "I read the essay 'Three Days to See' by Helen Keller when I was in high school."
6. What is a "stereogram"?
7. "Don't you think that the poem 'The Eve of St. Agnes' is a little too long?" remarked Sam.
8. "If you're going to the store," said Irena. "Get me a copy of *Shape* magazine."
9. Greg always says, "It's always darkest before it turns completely black."
10. "Do you send Easter cards?" asked Ms. Prince.

Exercise 32

1. Have you ever tried "dry column chromatography?"
2. "I'm sure," said Violet, "that that bird was an evening grosbeak."
3. What is the article "Welcome to the Shoe Store" about in this issue of the *English Journal*?
4. "Did you check the expiry date on the wool socks?" asked Arthur.

5. "Your Halloween mask is scary," stated Jean, "but not as scary as you without it."
6. C
7. "Take your time," said the patient to the doctor. "I'm not going anywhere in this hospital gown."
8. Did Neil ask, "Has the repair person arrived yet?"
9. *Mapping Ourselves* is an autobiography of Canadian women.
10. "I think I'm doomed," remarked Doris.

Exercise 33

1. Why did Keith say, "This is my doughnut"?
2. Tomorrow's lesson is on "hydrodesulfurization."
3. "I'll go," said Sharon. "It's near my house."
4. "Do you know the song 'In the Shape of a Heart' by Jackson Browne?" asked Rhonda.
5. "What could be more beautiful," sighed Juan, "than the sunset reflected in your eyes."
6. "Ben asked for money again," said Jasmine.
7. "Doug read every article in this month's *Start Your Own Business* magazine," said Jerusha.
8. Edgar Allan Poe said, "I make Beauty the province of the poem."
9. "Shut the light," said Bernie. "I'm trying to sleep."
10. Amanda said, "I read 'Do You Call Yourself a Poet?' in *Writer's Digest* magazine."

UNIT 5: THE WRITING PROCESS

Item I: Before You Start

Exercise 1

Answers may vary.

1. I was joking; don't lose your temper.
2. You're not in a familiar neighbourhood.
3. Getting an A in this course is not easy.
4. After winning the lottery, George was rich.
5. This is quite a storm; it's pouring.
6. My brother is very strong.
7. I was exhausted after the workout.
8. Maureen wasn't nervous; she was calm.
9. Face the problem, and ask your brother for a raise.
10. Ryan is a huge man, but he is gentle.

Exercise 2

Answers may vary.

1. The park is only 4 km in a direct line from here.
2. Women like Zhen are rare.
3. It's common to find only one blueberry in a jumbo blueberry muffin.
4. Getting William to do any housework is hopeless.
5. Gladys, I'm very happy to see you.
6. Aldo knows all the math answers; he's clever.
7. Keep the news about Mensha a secret; I don't want you to tell anyone.
8. We'd better be careful with our money; there's going to be another tax hike.
9. Doreen is in a bad mood.
10. Everything is unclear; explain it again.

Exercise 3

Answers may vary.

1. I bought the entire business.
2. After inadvertently embarrassing the boss's husband, Gwen knew she was in serious trouble.
3. Use these transitional words, and you will be doing the right thing.
4. The children are growing up quickly.
5. Bruce put me in an awkward situation when he didn't pay his half of the rent.
6. When I go in to see the boss, she/he never hears what I say.
7. Martin looks busy, but I wonder if it's true.
8. "See for yourself," said the magician.
9. Don't lose courage.
10. I was so angry that I told her what I thought.

Exercise 4

Answers may vary.

1. At present, the streets should be safer at night.
2. Wendell works so hard without complaining; he must be enthusiastic.
3. We were in the boat at sunrise.
4. The baby was well-behaved; she never cried once.
5. Undoubtedly, public speaking can be stressful.
6. Roberto Alomar of the Blue Jays was out at first base in last night's game.
7. Antonio was accurate with his remarks last night.
8. Drinking to forget that you're depressed can be a hopeless cycle.
9. I heard that Warren was fired.
10. Now that the baby is here we'll rarely go out.

Exercise 5

Answers may vary.

1. Andrew doesn't like to be second to anyone.
2. Ed will always stand by you regardless of the difficulties.
3. We'll be there fast.
4. Julia is in trouble again at work because she didn't finish the financial report.
5. Emma's new diaper dress is unusual.
6. Since he joined Gluttons Anonymous, Bill has not overeaten.
7. Why is Adele always trying to change the way things are?
8. I need a summer job; can you make some arrangements for me?
9. Wait; we're not leaving for another twenty minutes.
10. Why is Stan in trouble this time?

Exercise 6

Answers may vary.

1. Your approach to this problem is unique.
2. Dawn's hair is auburn.
3. The bakery is opening here soon.
4. I read the facts in the newspaper.
5. We will probably be going to Quebec this summer.
6. How much did you pay for those genuine leather shoes?
7. At present there are no job openings.
8. Boris apologized because he had hurt Jana's feelings.
9. When did you realize that the earth was round?
10. Nicholas is small and nervous.

Exercise 7

Answers may vary.

1. I was conceited, but now I'm perfect.
2. The result was that she had forgot to pay for the skirt.
3. Excluding Milton, who threw up, we all enjoyed the ride.
4. I think that Joe was born in October.
5. In my opinion, he should not wear a hairpiece.
6. What alternatives are there?
7. I'd hate to argue with Fritz.
8. The message seemed clear to me.

9. Climb the ladder carefully.
10. Michael was depressed for some reason.

Exercise 8

Answers may vary.

1. These blue jeans fade away quickly.
2. William almost lost his temper.
3. The explosion caused a catastrophe.
4. You can see the city better at the top.
5. We are not taking a vacation for a while.
6. Because she never studied, Irene dropped out of college.
7. Will George be at the party?
8. Peter has survived life without working by his charm.
9. They honoured Len on his fortieth birthday.
10. The argument started for no reason.

Exercise 9

1. The earthquake caused a tragedy.
2. This problem is obvious.
3. The proposal gave notice that funds were going to be cut.
4. Celine is very tall.
5. Nothing will persuade me to eat worms.
6. The magician made the ball float in the air by an invisible thread.
7. Not a soul offered the beggar any money.
8. The truth is that I love you.
9. The UFO disappeared in seconds.
10. Helen alternates driving and walking to work.

Exercise 10

1. The movie last night was unbelievable.
2. Will this room be adequate for you tonight?
3. I think that Diane's hair is purple.
4. Your generosity is more than I had expected.
5. The red wine will be preferable for supper.
6. Martin will probably become a dentist.
7. Do we have to go out into the cold?
8. Periodically, Jab smokes a big cigar.

9. Phil seldom complains about his situation.
10. Should these wires be connected?

ADDENDUM A: THE PARTS OF SPEECH

Item I: Nouns

Exercise 1

1. The clarinet has a wonderful sound.
2. Harold is sitting on the fence.
3. Maureen needs new glasses.
4. The bed is made of pine.
5. Cows are interesting animals.
6. The college is closed this Friday.
7. Last year there was a snowstorm on this day.
8. The rose is from my garden.
9. Eat all your spinach and broccoli or no dessert.
10. There is a leak in your pipe.

Exercise 2

1. Beauty can be found in many things.
2. John moved to Sudbury, Ontario last week.
3. Claire can't drink warm milk.
4. The committee is not meeting this Thursday.
5. David likes chicken better than beef.
6. Order the pizza for lunch.
7. The tree on our front lawn is a maple.
8. Your teeth need a dentist.
9. Calgary is the capital of Alberta.
10. Your imagination can get you into trouble.

Exercise 3

1. Listen to this poem by Thomas Hardy.
2. What colour is the paint?
3. The boy's leg is bruised.
4. The new bookcase is hungry for books.
5. How did the rabbit lose the race to the turtle?
6. Maxine bumped her elbow on the back of the chair.
7. Give Alex a tissue for his nose.
8. What part of the chicken did this piece come from?

9. The mood of the teacher was not good.
10. The gloves are drying on the radiator.

Exercise 4

1. Health is more important than wealth.
2. The cellist has beautiful hands.
3. Your smile is food for my heart.
4. The pigeon dropped a message on my sleeve.
5. Terry could not see the boat at the dock because of the fog.
6. Antarctica has no snakes.
7. The kind of food that Benny likes comes from Korea.
8. Which wine are you serving with the fish for dinner?
9. The hygienist looked at my teeth and shook her head.
10. This mask of a vampire frightens the children.

Exercise 5

1. Are diamonds really a person's best friends?
2. Fear of the unknown is a common phobia.
3. At what time will the bus arrive?
4. Read this novel by Margaret Atwood by Tuesday.
5. The smell from your locker is lethal.
6. Wish me luck on the test.
7. The relatives have arrived for dinner.
8. The look on his face was that of surprise.
9. The plumber will stay at the house until tomorrow.
10. Jerry opened the wrong end of the box.

Item II: Pronouns

Exercise 8

1. The money that you lost has been found.
2. Most of his ideas were rejected.
3. This is the person who can help you.
4. He realized his mistake too late.
5. Everybody should be like her.
6. She was confused by his attitude.
7. One of them is yours.
8. This is the restaurant I like best.
9. Any of these will be suitable.
10. They knew it was impossible.

Exercise 9

1. This is my favourite cheesecake.
2. Send it to them by tomorrow.
3. Whom did you see at the circus?
4. Anyone can make a mistake.
5. The books are mine and hers, not theirs.
6. Can anyone help me?
7. You need to see it in the light.
8. These are fresher than those.
9. The cat hurt its paw.
10. The flowers that Helen sent are beautiful.

Exercise 10

1. A few of these are old.
2. The gum has lost its flavour.
3. One of you is responsible for the accident.
4. To whom did you send an invitation?
5. I would like a car like that.
6. Mine is wider than yours.
7. All of it is for you.
8. The crowd that went to the concert last night was boisterous.
9. I think it is they who called on you last night.
10. Several of the them are nervous.

Exercise 13

1. I want some of the doughnuts.
2. The strong beer that you gave me tastes skunky.
3. Can you open the door for the children?
4. The movie about bats was scary.
5. Neither of the sisters wanted any of the candy.
6. Give me your answer in the morning.
7. Marty forgot to buy the newspaper.
8. These are my two children.
9. I needed more time to write the test.
10. This is the house that Jack built.

Exercise 14

1. These are the mushrooms for the soup.
2. The mouse ran up the clock.
3. A few of them have left their mother.
4. He is pursuing the truth.

5. She is the one who deserves all of the credit.
6. Everything will be all right after the test.
7. Do you remember how to communicate with fish?
8. Drop them a line.
9. The day that you chose for the picnic is perfect.
10. This is not clear to me.

Item III: Verbs

Exercise 15

1. The children read all the stories.
2. How much does that ring cost?
3. The wind is still blowing hard.
4. Keep reminding me.
5. Melissa enjoys singing in the choir.
6. Frank has already paid me.
7. Are you getting a cold?
8. I don't like to speak in public.
9. They hung the picture in the dining room.
10. Quit smoking today.

Exercise 16

1. Sharon has cut the grass.
2. How long did you sleep last night?
3. I was hoping for better weather.
4. Did you mistake Dave for Santa Claus?
5. Take the shortcut.
6. Thad should never have complained to his coach.
7. Are you going to join the club?
8. The sun hasn't set yet.
9. Erwin keeps wishing away his life.
10. Tell him, not me.

Exercise 17

1. The tomatoes were grown in Ontario.
2. The clown is not wearing a happy face.
3. How long have you been watching?
4. No one likes washing dishes.
5. He couldn't speak Spanish very well.
6. The bee stung Greg in the leg.
7. Do you drool in your sleep?

8. I will deliver the goods tomorrow.
9. Denny finally understood the lesson about verbs.
10. He could have apologized sooner.

Exercise 18

1. Put these books in order.
2. How did you tear your sleeve?
3. They wanted more ice cream.
4. The air conditioning unit wasn't working very well.
5. Bob went fishing near Vancouver Island.
6. Judith must have forgotten the letter at home.
7. Did the bus leave already?
8. Sign your name on the bottom line.
9. Were you going to sit there?
10. The electrician shocked me with the bill.

Exercise 19

1. Your anger is showing.
2. The chipmunks scampered up the tree.
3. Did you take the last cookie?
4. Try again with the screwdriver.
5. Why was everyone laughing so hard?
6. The ice on the driveway is finally melting.
7. Have you made the beds yet?
8. You baked the pie perfectly.
9. What are you doing tomorrow?
10. The last performance ends at 11:30 p.m.

Exercise 20

1. She is our new neighbour.
2. He is being stubborn again.
3. That couldn't be true.
4. Sigfried should be on his way.
5. Violet looks pale.
6. These chicken livers are not fresh.
7. Just stay calm.
8. Are you feeling better?
9. I should have been a doctor.
10. I am sure about everything.

Exercise 21

1. You have been on my mind all day.
2. This song sounds like a Christmas melody.
3. I was in Ottawa last week.
4. The next lottery winner could be you.
5. Weren't they in the principal's office yesterday?
6. Yok Shion seems upset today.
7. The muffins should be ready in ten minutes.
8. Where were you last night?
9. These cheese balls smell like old socks.
10. I feel bad about my test result.

Exercise 22

1.	Who is ringing his bell?	action
2.	The bell sounds nice.	non-action
3.	Elizabeth is still growing tomatoes.	action
4.	Chad is growing tired of hearing about it.	non-action
5.	Are you trying to confuse me?	action
6.	If you were nicer, I could be happier.	non-action
7.	Remain still.	action
8.	The game isn't over yet.	non-action
9.	Emma feels so tired.	non-action
10.	Feel the soft leather.	action

Exercise 23

1.	Your complaints are becoming tiresome.	non-action
2.	Al will always be a good father.	non-action
3.	Please be more careful.	non-action
4.	That cologne smells good.	non-action
5.	May I have the next dance?	action
6.	Get the dishes out of the cupboard.	action
7.	What are you thinking?	action
8.	This chili is potent.	non-action
9.	Marion checked it twice.	action
10.	Drink this slowly.	action

Exercise 24

1.	This chocolate cake tastes rich.	non-action
2.	Stir the stew again.	action

3.	Are you still showering?	action
4.	Hanna really enjoys your pasta.	action
5.	Stop making those noises with your nose.	action
6.	You would be upset too.	non-action
7.	This dress looks great on you.	non-action
8.	Why couldn't you be a teacher?	non-action
9.	Your idea seems good to me.	non-action
10.	Sarah is getting a new jacket.	action

Exercise 25

1. lie
2. has laid
3. rise
4. set
5. has set
6. has been lying
7. is sitting
8. has been rising
9. set
10. was lying

Exercise 26

1. must lie
2. have risen
3. laid
4. rising
5. rising
6. is sitting
7. is setting
8. should rise
9. is sitting
10. raised

Exercise 27

1. will rise
2. sit
3. has risen
4. laid
5. will be sitting
6. lay

7. setting
8. has raised
9. raised
10. lies

Exercise 28

1. knew
2. will (shall) buy
3. throb(s)
4. has (have) visited
5. will (shall) organize
6. had cooked
7. will (shall) have saved
8. ordered
9. has (have) walked
10. will (shall) build

Exercise 29

1. forgot
2. has (have) averaged
3. had delivered
4. will (shall) research
5. dance(s)
6. has (have) told
7. studied
8. will (shall) walk
9. dream(s)
10. had broken

Exercise 30

1. will (shall) gather
2. will (shall) have eaten
3. was
4. has (have) seen
5. will (shall) plant
6. had washed
7. pour(s)
8. leaked
9. will (shall) have risen
10. has (have) baked

Exercise 31

1. advise(s)
2. has (have) exercised
3. had realized
4. fell
5. will (shall) succeed
6. will (shall) have saved
7. has (have) received
8. will (shall) fix
9. believed
10. had spoken

Exercise 32

1. has (have) sown
2. catch(s)
3. will (shall) have made
4. had frozen
5. will (shall) enjoy
6. mowed
7. spread(s)
8. has (have) fished
9. had gone
10. hugged

Exercise 33

1. will (shall) have been studying
2. had been watching
3. will (shall) be taking
4. has (have) been stealing
5. was (were) dreaming
6. had been carrying
7. is (are) bringing
8. will (shall) be driving
9. has (have) been showing
10. had been dancing

Exercise 34

1. was (were) losing
2. has (have) been delivering
3. will (shall) be mailing
4. had been wishing

5. is (are) drinking
6. will (shall) be paying
7. had been drawing
8. will (shall) have been cooking
9. has (have) been being
10. was (were) selling

Exercise 35

1. has (have) been managing
2. had been slicing
3. was (were) telling
4. has (have) been giving
5. will (shall) be taking
6. had been wondering
7. has is (are) hanging
8. will (shall) be designing
9. had been going
10. will (shall) have been collecting

Exercise 36

1. has (have) been caring
2. will (shall) be playing
3. is (are) folding
4. had been jogging
5. was (were) whistling
6. has (have) been planting
7. will (shall) have been scraping
8. is (are) lending
9. will (shall) be flying
10. had been rising

Exercise 37

1. had been crying
2. was (were) arranging
3. has (have) been cleaning
4. will (shall) have been paying
5. is (are) using
6. will (shall) be visiting
7. had been establishing
8. will (shall) have been reading
9. has (have) been counting
10. was (were) smiling

Exercise 38

1. active
2. passive
3. passive
4. active
5. passive
6. passive
7. active
8. active
9. passive
10. active

Exercise 39

1. passive
2. active
3. passive
4. active
5. passive
6. passive
7. active
8. passive
9. passive
10. passive

Exercise 40

1. George and Shanta were visited by her parents.
2. Ethel organized the move.
3. The cat knocked over the cookie jar.
4. The blouse and skirt were sewn by Joanne.
5. Our neighbour cut the grass.
6. A huge salmon has been caught by Kelly.
7. The post office delivered the package.
8. The truth was told by her.
9. The milk was being drunk by the kitten.
10. The garage door is being painted by Jay.

Exercise 41

1. The vice president presented the award.
2. Hundreds of people saw the UFO.
3. Gloria was visited by them last summer.
4. Ina donated the couch to the charity drive.

5. A fit was had by Matt at the lawyer's office.
6. City Hall raised the taxes.
7. Oops! The toast was burned by me.
8. A mosquito bit my leg.
9. His friends told Danny to get a haircut.
10. The newspaper was delivered before dawn.

Item IV: Adjectives

Exercise 43

1. The fresh chicken is in the refrigerator.
2. Anthony was lonely but happy.
3. The smelly cheese tastes good.
4. I am certain that the answer is wrong.
5. The heavy fog covered the winding road.
6. Sue is kind and considerate.
7. Are you able to repair the old deck?
8. He whispered silly things to me.
9. The soup is cold and tasteless.
10. Ivan likes horror movies.

Exercise 44

1. Your lawn is green and healthy.
2. Give me the blue scarf, not the yellow one.
3. The old graveyard is full.
4. I like steamed rice.
5. Are these fresh cabbages?

6. Dorota has thick, wavy hair.

7. What is the difference between salted and unsalted butter?

8. Jill's virus is contagious.

9. The large pillow is for your enormous ego.

10. The pink flowers smell good.

Exercise 45

1. The dental appointment is in two days.

2. Mel was envious of everyone.

3. The flat tire was bad luck for us.

4. The last movie starts in five minutes.

5. Did the new commercial make a false promise?

6. There is more soup in the pot.

7. The tow truck is waiting.

8. Your feet are cold.

9. I need two more days to decide.

10. Do you want a peaceful holiday?

Exercise 46

1. Martha makes delicious baked potatoes.

2. The robin was hungry and weary after its long flight.

3. Your grey sweater is my favourite one.

4. The cottage is on a secluded road.

5. The hot sun burned Clara's sensitive skin.
6. Michael displayed poor behaviour at the party last night.
7. A few of the students are ill.
8. The apple pie is home-made.
9. The slippery sidewalk is dangerous.
10. Frozen yogurt can be expensive.

Exercise 48

1. adjective
2. adjective
3. pronoun
4. adjective
5. pronoun
6. adjective
7. adjective
8. adjective
9. noun
10. adjective

Exercise 49

1. pronoun
2. pronoun
3. adjective
4. adjective
5. noun
6. noun
7. adjective
8. adjective
9. noun
10. pronoun

Exercise 50

1. adjective
2. pronoun
3. adjective

4. noun
5. adjective
6. noun
7. noun
8. adjective
9. adjective
10. pronoun

Exercise 51

1. noun
2. adjective
3. adjective
4. pronoun
5. adjective
6. noun
7. noun
8. adjective
9. adjective
10. noun

Exercise 53

1. This coffee is the creamier of the two.
2. Which road is easiest in life?
3. This painting is unique.
4. The picture on your television is much better than mine.
5. C
6. Did you try your hardest?
7. I think that Dan is slimmer than his brother.
8. C
9. In our class, Brenda is the smartest one.
10. This movie is the most boring one I have ever seen.

Exercise 54

1. I am almost calmer than Al.
2. You need to develop a thicker skin.
3. Sean is certainly the luckiest one in the family.
4. C
5. Today is windier than yesterday.
6. This cane is sturdier than my last one.
7. Lisa's cold is worse today.

8. English is the hardest subject of all.
9. C
10. You are weaker than I.

Exercise 55

1. whitest
2. lower
3. lovely
4. rustiest
5. tidier
6. sorest
7. healthiest
8. more uncertain
9. lean
10. dirtier

Exercise 56

1. friendlier
2. cleanest
3. ugliest
4. quick
5. more
6. best
7. smelliest
8. rockier
9. old
10. shinier

Exercise 57

1. bolder
2. silliest
3. liveliest
4. wealthy
5. clearest
6. lonelier
7. smokiest
8. worse
9. honest
10. harder

Item V: Adverbs

Exercise 58

1. Greg waited patiently in the doctor's office.
2. Are you quite sure about this information?
3. The road was completely blocked by the overturned truck.
4. You study too hard.
5. This mosquito-bite ointment is very soothing.
6. Lower your voice; you are speaking too loudly.
7. Give up; the police have arrived.
8. Cynthia is truly happy.
9. Why does Eugene chew so noisily?
10. The car runs much better today.

Exercise 59

1. The teacher speaks too slowly.
2. Do you always wash your feet after lunch?
3. They finally ended their relationship.
4. I really didn't need that advice.
5. Mohammed nervously stepped into the doctor's office.
6. That car is following too closely.
7. Why are you being so silly?
8. Alban frequently visits the race track.

9. You shouldn't use your deodorant before you shower.
10. We just ordered the espresso machine.

Exercise 60

1. Always cover your mouth when you cough.
2. The pizza will arrive momentarily.
3. Is Ken a highly skilled auto mechanic?
4. I was completely confused by the test.
5. Speak clearly and slowly.
6. The basement is partially finished.
7. You are really good for my heart.
8. I can't work very well after a big lunch.
9. Steve actually remembered his anniversary.
10. Move your arm slowly; there's a huge spider on it.

Exercise 63

1. Let's finish the painting together.
2. Do you want the money now or tomorrow?
3. The taxi is here.
4. I almost fell down.
5. Try it once; it's delicious.
6. I don't want to climb up again.
7. Get down; they'll see you.
8. I'm still tired.
9. Angie jogged alone yesterday.
10. Go away now.

Exercise 64

1. Sometimes things go too far.
2. Why is Melanie so unhappy?

3. Aleksandra wants her soup now, not later.
4. Put it on; the sweater should fit.
5. These fries are too hot.
6. Are you ever going to Newfoundland?
7. We stopped there earlier today.
8. How often do you floss?
9. Bring the towels in; it's raining out.
10. I'll be here if you need me.

Exercise 66

1. carefully
2. really
3. faster
4. sooner
5. bad
6. Quickly
7. earlier
8. best
9. well
10. later

Exercise 67

1. sooner, happier
2. best
3. bad
4. really
5. best
6. tightly
7. Surely
8. well
9. older
10. loosely

Exercise 68

1. Go quietly; the children are sleeping.
2. The time went so quickly!
3. You speak well, but you write poorly.
4. C
5. I don't think you copied this correctly.
6. Of course Don's car is faster than yours.

7. Marilyn studies harder than her sister.
8. It's snowing heavily now.
9. The ambulance arrived very quickly.
10. C

Exercise 69

1. Is your cold worse today?
2. Ken and Bertha work really well together.
3. C
4. Is the bread or the banana loaf cut too thinly?
5. You know you acted improperly last night.
6. Things don't always go smoothly.
7. The onions were chopped too coarsely.
8. The speaker expressed herself really clearly.
9. Sophie researched this material very carefully.
10. You completed this exercise well.

Exercise 70

1. Where did you go last night?
2. Greg is a very gentle man.
3. Stop talking so loudly; I can hear you very clearly.
4. Have you ever seen a real dinosaur fossil?
5. You can't go home yet: it's still early.
6. The hardest beans to grow are jelly beans.
7. Wipe your big feet thoroughly; then you can come in.
8. Naturally, I was very polite to the police officer.
9. Why are you so proud of your old gym shorts?
10. Look deeply into your heart, and the correct answer will come to you soon.

Exercise 71

1. This is definitely the freshest doughnut I have ever eaten.
2. Never go there when the moon is full.
3. My back tooth is very sore.
4. What's wrong with my new purse?
5. This rusty old car will never run again.
6. What is the best definition of ugly?
7. Is that a real phone or a toy phone?
8. The motor starts quickly, so hang on tightly.
9. They had a brief conversation earlier.
10. Did you wake up on the wrong side of bed again?

Exercise 72

1. This rope is definitely longer than that one.
2. When will the social worker come back?
3. Ralph is a very dedicated Latin teacher.
4. Perhaps you should call later.
5. Thu reluctantly played one more game of cards.
6. Down below you will find the buried treasure.
7. You will feel better in a few days.
8. The wind is really gusty today.
9. Sincere and dedicated are the volunteers at the relief centre.
10. Please don't ever give me a perfunctory kiss.

Item VI: Prepositions, Conjunctions, and Interjections

Exercise 73

1. (With you) everything is possible (for me).
2. (About an hour) (from here) is a beautiful old inn.
3. (On Thursday) he had a short nap (during the English lesson).
4. Most (of the heat) (from the fireplace) must be going (up the chimney).
5. (Because of the snowstorm), school was cancelled (in the afternoon).
6. I can't see (beyond the grocery store) (across the street).
7. This composition was handed (to me) (by Inez).
8. (Instead of complaining), do something (about it).
9. I like a hot cup (of coffee) (with a warm croissant) (for breakfast).
10. (Within all) (of us) is the potential (for achieving success).

Exercise 74

1. (By the look) (on his face), I could see that Eugene was not happy.
2. Neither one (of us) wants to visit the rendering factory again.
3. The killer must be devoid (of any feeling).
4. Every one (of the students) went (to Niagara Falls) (except me).
5. A snowfall (in the woods) can be soothing (to the spirit).
6. Dino had a fistful (of twenty's) (in his wallet).
7. Meet me (by the water fountain) (in the park).
8. (By noon) Yolanta is ready (for her lunch break).
9. The moral (of the good seeds and the bad seeds) is worth repeating.
10. I would love to walk (in the moonlight) (with you).

Exercise 75

1. These Western boots were made (by Greg and Ethel) (at their store).
2. You can count (on me) (for my support) (in the office).

3. Which one (of these new dresses) are you going to wear (to the party)?
4. Is this the club (to which) you belong?
5. Save a seat (for me) (at the game).
6. (On the other side) (of the fence) only some (of the grass) was greener.
7. (In some ways) you are right (about Tony and Lindsey).
8. Slipping (into a warm bed) (with a good book) (on a cold night) sounds good (to me).
9. (On the way) (to your cottage), I saw a deer (on the side) (of the road).
10. Go (through the parking lot) to reach the back (of the theatre).

Exercise 78

1. Because Joan was tired, she had a nap at her desk.
2. Either Tim will drive you or Barry will.
3. I know when I should leave.
4. She was offered the promotion, but Edna did not want the added stress.
5. If you hurry, you can make it to the bank before it closes.
6. When Bert walks on stage, Andy and Gerta will follow.
7. Jia had free tickets to the game, but she was too tired to go.
8. I don't like apple pie and cheddar cheese.
9. Both Susan and Barbara are going to help Anne with her homework.
10. Do you know whether Paramjit or Fred has the keys?

Exercise 79

1. These muffins and doughnuts are stale, but the croissants are fresh.
2. Neither Rubina nor Chady knows what you mean.
3. Take care until we meet again.
4. Ching Ha said that it was supposed to rain today.
5. If Afren calls, tell him that I'll be back in ten minutes.
6. Whenever it rains, Gord gets a headache.
7. I can imagine how you and Mel must feel.
8. As soon as I said it, I knew that I had made a terrible mistake.
9. Could you pour the wine before you sit down.
10. Lucy is not friends with Alicia or Roland.

Exercise 80

1. Although Adolfo was tired, he finished painting the kitchen before he went to bed.
2. No one knows how it happened.
3. Can you check whether Tracy is at home or still at school?
4. Because it was hot, I left my sweater at work.
5. She said that it was too early for lilac blossoms.
6. As long as you are here, help me to carry this into the basement.
7. That you were late doesn't surprise me.

8. Marian can't wait until this semester is over.
9. Julius laughed when he heard the joke about the pigeon.
10. Is this sentence as troublesome as the others?

Exercise 83

1. Whoops, I lost my balance (on the patch) (of ice).
2. Meet me (at the doughnut shop) when you are ready to go.
3. Kyle and Roberta sold their house (to my cousin) (from Scarborough).
4. Whew, I'm glad that they've left.
5. If you don't feel better, we can go out (at another time).
6. Do you want chocolate sauce (on your ice cream) or not?
7. Yikes! The snake is (near your foot).
8. Provided that I can clean the kitchen (on time), I can help you (with the shopping).
9. Most (of the fried chicken) was eaten (by the children).
10. I run (into Sean) wherever I go.

Exercise 84

1. They named the parking lot (after Otto) because his car was always (in it).
2. Whoa! Slow down; you're talking too fast.
3. The alien said that his spaceship was very fuel-efficient (during long flights).
4. Your socks are (on the dryer) (in the laundry room).
5. I can't even remember what I was doing (at home) last night.
6. (For a change) why don't you try to eat some oatmeal (for breakfast)?
7. Wow! That is one (of the largest turkeys) that I have ever seen.
8. Dorian wants to know what you put (in the fish soup).
9. A few (of the roses) were touched (by frost) yesterday.
10. After Diego works out, he has a huge lunch (at the restaurant) (across the street).

Exercise 85

1. Cassandra and Sik Men enjoy old black-and-white movies best (of all).
2. Bah! You don't know what you are doing.
3. As soon as I have enough money, I'm going (on a long vacation) (to the West Indies).
4. Either Janica or Angela will be teaching the line-dancing class (at the community centre).
5. Whenever Choi's leg itches (on a Friday), it rains all weekend.
6. Phew! What kind (of deodorant) are you wearing?
7. Terry and you are made (for each other).
8. Did you finish counting all (of the dimples) (on the golf ball) yet?
9. Neither Liyi nor her mother has been (to the CN Tower).
10. Neither one (of these pairs) (of shoes) suits you.

Exercise 86

1. Put the salami (in the refrigerator) (until tomorrow).
2. Before you forget, take this package (with you) when you go (to the post office).
3. Many (of us) are worried (about the test).
4. I wish that I could buy that gold chain (for you) (for Christmas).
5. Don't be (like him) and eat (with your mouth) open.
6. Ouch! That was my finger you hit (with the shovel).
7. Whether Andrew can meet you (at noon) or sooner is still uncertain (at this time).
8. I wanted a cake as nice as Erica's.
9. A copy (of this book) is available (in the library).
10. These fried eggs have spots and stripes (on them).

Exercise 87

1. Since Betty broke her foot, she has been miserable (to everybody).
2. Makeda keeps waking up (in the middle) (of the night) to go (to the bathroom).
3. Egad, what a miserable personality.
4. If I had known that the restaurant bill was going to be so much, I would have eaten (at home).
5. Before you buy a computer (for the office), check (with me) first.
6. You could be (on that plane) (to Hong Kong) tonight.
7. This is the last (of the home-made fudge) that you bought (for us).
8. (After his checkup), Lyndon felt better (about everything).
9. Gosh, it's time to go home already.
10. When Sam was little, he had his baths (in the kitchen sink).

LITERARY CREDITS

Page 215, From *The Lamp at Noon and Other Stories*, by Sinclair Ross. Used by permission of the Canadian Publishers, McClelland & Stewart, Toronto.

Page 216, From *Margaret Laurence* by Clara Thomas. Used by permission of the Canadian Publishers, McClelland & Stewart, Toronto.

Page 228, From "The Yellow Sweater," from *Hugh Garner's Best Stories.* Reprinted by permission of McGraw-Hill Ryerson Limited.

Page 228, From "The Found Boat" by Alice Munro in Jack David and Robert Lecker, eds., *Introduction to Fiction.* Reprinted with permission of Macmillan of Canada, a Division of Canada Publishing Corporation.

Page 228, From "My Aunt Theresina Veilleux" in *Street of Riches* by Gabrielle Roy. Used by permission of Fonds Gabrielle Roy.

Page 230, From "Gillies Corners" by Ron Brown in *Ghost Towns of Ontario.* Reprinted by permission of Cannonbooks.

Page 230, From *Effective Photography* by John Friar and Birthney Ardoin. Reprinted by permission of Prentice-Hall Inc.

Page 231, From "The Outlaw" in *The Lamp at Noon and Other Stories*, by Sinclair Ross. Used by permission of the Canadian Publishers, McClelland & Stewart, Toronto.

Page 231, From "Skald" by W.D. Valgardson in *Red Dust.* Reprinted by permission of Oberon Press.

Page 234, From *Rocks and Minerals of Ontario* by D.F. Hewitt and E. B. Freeman. Reprinted by permission of Ontario Geological Survey.

Page 234, From *George Brown* by J.M.S. Careless (The Canadian Series). Reprinted by permission of Fitzhenry & Whiteside.

Page 235, From *Dance of the Happy Shade* by Alice Munro, copyright 1973. Reprinted by permission of Macmillan of Canada, a Division of Canada Publishing Corporation.

Page 236, From "The Walrus and the Carpenter" in *If You Hum Me A Few Bars I Might Remember the Tune*, by Don Bailey. Used by permission of Oberon Press.

Page 240, "Thunderstrokes and Firebolts," by Janice McEwen, © 1978 by Camden House Publishing.

Page 240, From *Margo Oliver's Cookbook* by Margo Oliver. © Optimum Publishing International Inc. Reprinted by permission of the publisher.

Page 241, From *Your Money and How to Keep It* by Brian Costello. Reprinted by permission of Stoddart Publishing Co. Limited, 34 Lesmill Road, Don Mills, Ontario, Canada.

Page 243, From "The Role of the Teacher" in *Taking Sides: The Collected Social and Political Writings* by Irving Layton. Reprinted by permission of Mosaic Press.

Page 246, From "Upon a Midnight Clear" in *Heart of a Stranger*, by Margaret Laurence. Used by permission of the Canadian Publishers, McClelland & Stewart, Toronto.

Page 249, From "The Wild Goose" in *Rebellion of Young David* by Ernest Buckler. Reprinted by permission of Curtis Brown, Ltd. Copyright © 1975 by Ernest Buckler.

Page 249, From *Who Has Seen the Wind* by W.O. Mitchell, copyright 1947. Reprinted by permission of Macmillan of Canada, a Division of Canada Publishing Corporation.

INDEX